Contents

the natural sciences

Bill Myers

Published in 2004 by:
Nelson Thornes Ltd
Delta Place
27 Bath Road
CHELTENHAM
GL53 7TH
United Kingdom

04 05 06 07 08 / 10 9 8 7 6 5 4 3 2 1

A catalogue record for this book is available from the British Library

ISBN 0 7487 8583 3

Illustrations by Saxon Graphics Ltd, Derby
Page make-up by Saxon Graphics Ltd, Derby

Printed and bound in Great Britain by Scotprint

Acknowledgements

For Valerie. With love and respect.

The original idea for this book, and then for the Access series, came from my students at Hastings College of Arts and Technology. These texts exist largely because of the help and encouragement of the Hastings Access groups, past and present.

I must also thank Roger Horton for his invaluable advice on how best to turn my first proposals into reality.

Finally, I want to thank Keith Leech, who runs the Access programme at Hastings. Keith disproves, on a daily basis, the theory that it is impossible to be both a good teacher and a good administrator.

Chapter 1

Scientific communication and method

National unit specification.
These are the topics you will be studying for this unit:

1   What is science?
2   The branches of science
3   The theory of knowledge
4   The scientific method
5   Publication, précis and comprehension
6   Experimental design, variables and errors
7   Reporting experiments

1 What is science?

Words like 'science', 'scientist' and 'experiment' are part of everyday language and most of us use them loosely without giving too much thought to their real meanings. Modern medicine and all branches of healthcare are based almost entirely on the sciences, and evidence-based medicine is an example of a way of thinking called 'the scientific method'.

The rest of this book explains the principles of biology and chemistry and some of their most important applications. However, before we turn to the detail, it is important that you understand, in more general terms, what science is all about. In this unit, we try to answer some basic questions:

- What is science?

- How do the branches or kinds of science differ?

- How is science done?

- How does science prove things?

- How do scientists communicate amongst themselves and with wider non-specialist audiences?

An organised body of knowledge

Like many dictionary definitions, that for 'science' raises more questions than it answers. The Concise Oxford English Dictionary states:

> Science is an organised body of knowledge based on objective principles and derived from experiment and observation.

This collection of words does not look like a promising start, but a clear and useful definition emerges if we take it one step at a time.

The word 'organised' could be replaced with alternatives like 'classified' or 'categorised'. The study of anything starts with a grouping together of related things and ideas. Linguists talk about the differences between nouns, adjectives and verbs – biologists classify or organise all living things into groups or categories. More than 10 million different chemical compounds have been identified – chemistry would be impossible without first organising all these substances into groups with similar properties.

The expression 'a body of knowledge' has major implications. Scientific knowledge has accumulated over the centuries. All scientific discovery starts with what has gone before. Sometimes new work confirms earlier research; sometimes it shows **errors**. Often it provides more general explanations to link together facts and theories that were previously thought unrelated.

Many of us assume that the history of science only goes back a few hundred years – this is not so. All higher animals accumulate a body of scientific knowledge as part of learning how to survive. A sparrowhawk must 'know' something about gravity, acceleration and friction, otherwise it could not swoop and catch small birds in flight. A dog playing with a ball demonstrates a basic understanding of physics. Mankind is just another kind of animal, so we must have been accumulating scientific knowledge for at least as long as we have existed as a species.

The distinctions between men and other animals have been debated for thousands of years and the argument goes right to the centre of religious belief. We can, however, point to several differences that very few would dispute.

Man is more intelligent than other animals. We are good at solving problems, therefore we can usually adapt rapidly to changing circumstances. With increased intelligence comes increased curiosity. Science can be defined as an organised curiosity about the world we live in.

Tools and language

All animals communicate with each other but none, apart from mankind, appears to have developed a complex spoken language, writing or the use of symbols. Animals learn by example and there is evidence that some, like wolves and elephants, pass information from one generation to the next. In many animals, however, each generation has to start again from square one – without the benefit of accumulated knowledge.

Mankind is different – we can communicate across thousands of miles and thousands of years to pass on scientific knowledge to people we have never met or could not possibly meet. Pythagoras discovered a way of calculating the length of the third side of a triangle, if you know the lengths of the other two. Pythagoras wrote his theory 2500 years ago and this piece of scientific knowledge has been passed across about 100 human generations and taught to billions of people.

It was once thought that man was the only animal that used or made tools. This assumption has been disproved – chimpanzees use pointed sticks to collect insects from holes in trees and thrushes use flat stones to crush snail shells. Over thousands of years, we have invented and developed increasingly complex tools and machines. A flint axe is a tool, but so is an oil refinery, a spacecraft, a large general hospital or the Internet.

There was a huge increase in the total quantity and quality of scientific knowledge during the early 17th century. Most of this knowledge explosion was a direct result of the invention of new tools and machines. For the first time, things could be accurately weighed or measured and the scope of our senses was vastly increased. As just one example out of many thousands: the naked eye cannot see bacteria, the moons of Jupiter or X-rays, but we have invented microscopes, telescopes and X-ray photography to extend scientific knowledge.

Mankind is a long way from being the most numerous species on the planet or the one that lives in the largest colonies. Since our emergence about 150,000 years ago, around 35 billion people have been born and 6.2 billion are living today. Definitions are difficult – because arguably all humans now live in the same interconnected global village – but at the moment, the largest human colonies are Mexico City or perhaps Tokyo-Yokohama, each with populations approaching 30 million.

Human cities are different from colonies of bacteria and social insects – not because they are larger but because they are more complicated. Economists have an idea called 'division of labour'. In a colony of ants, termites, bees or wasps, there might be only a few 'jobs'. You might be a queen, a drone or a worker, for example. Each job makes a contribution to the survival and success of the colony. Humans prefer to live in large groups because, as a generalisation, it increases our chances of survival, health, prosperity and happiness. However, a city of millions only works because of microdivision of labour and a degree of cooperation that is not shown by other species. There are thousands of different jobs – this is microdivision of labour.

The words city and civilisation come from the same root – progress is far more likely if thousands or millions each contribute to the success of the human colony. Microdivision of labour greatly expands the body of human knowledge – plumbers, doctors, taxi drivers, chefs and thousands of other different kinds of worker develop specialist branches of knowledge.

Humans are not only the most cooperative species on the planet – they are also the most aggressive and the most territorial. The darker side of human nature has also greatly increased the body of human knowledge. Throughout history, the winners in war or conflict have nearly always been the ones with the greatest resources and/or the best science.

There is no way of uninventing, deleting or forgetting an advance in scientific knowledge that might be seen as inconvenient, unhelpful or dangerous in the wrong hands. Secrecy laws can slow the spread of information but they cannot offer guarantees that science will not be used to do harm.

Objective principles

The dictionary definition of science talks about a body of knowledge based on objective principles. We can use an illustration to show what this means.

Some metals are easily attacked by air and water and they rust or corrode. Iron, aluminium and zinc are the commonest examples. Other metals are less chemically active and they stay bright and lustrous for years under most conditions. These are the coinage metals or precious metals, so called because their most familiar use is as jewellery or currency.

We can compare some statements concerning four precious metals – platinum, gold, silver and copper:

> Gold is best, because platinum is too expensive, silver makes me look washed out and copper is cheap and nasty.

This statement is subjective, not objective, although it might be a completely accurate report of a conversation about earrings and bracelets. 'Gold is best' is a statement of opinion – others will have different views and an individual's opinion might change over time. If he or she could afford a platinum bracelet, would platinum then be best?

This is a subjective ranking – we do not, for example, know if gold is 10 times better than silver or 100 times. Subjective rankings are of little use in science.

Now consider a second statement:

> In today's New York market, gold closed at $378 an ounce and silver at $5.30 an ounce.

This is a kind of halfway house. It is based on objective principles because it compares market prices in units like dollars and ounces that can be precisely defined and measured. It does not, however, describe any kind of scientific truth. Over the following weeks and months, both prices will change, as will the price relationship between silver and gold. A scientist might be curious as to why people are prepared to pay 70 times more for gold than for silver. A properly conducted set of experiments would show that many factors influence the gold/silver price relationship. Some could be objectively defined; others may remain a matter of opinion. For example, the researcher might find that the world's proven reserves of silver are at least 50 times greater than the world reserves of gold. Additionally, the researcher might find that the world average cost of extracting and refining a tonne of gold is at least 20 times greater than the costs of extracting a tonne of silver. Provided the research is accurate, and terms like reserve and extraction are properly defined, these are objective statements based on sound principles. The science would partly explain the gold/silver price relationship.

Now let us look at a third statement:

> Platinum has a higher melting point than gold, silver and copper, and is also a denser metal than the others.

Table 1.1 shows the melting points and densities of the four common coinage metals and gives objective information based on scientific principles. Melting points and densities are precisely defined in internationally recognised units and any researcher could repeat the necessary experiments and get identical results. A pure sample of each metal from any and every mine in the world would also give the same values. Additionally, the density of pure copper, for example, always has been $8.92 \, g/cm^3$ and always will be.

Table 1.1   The melting points and densities of the four common coinage metals

Metal	Melting point (°C)	Density (g/cm³)
Platinum, Pt	1,772	21.45
Gold, Au	1,064	19.30
Silver, Ag	962	10.49
Copper, Cu	1,083	8.92

Experiment and observation

Science is based on experiment and observation. Later we consider experimental design in detail, but here we briefly summarise the main ideas:

- A well-designed experiment eliminates subjectivity and personal opinion.

- Experiments have to take place under standardised conditions. The most critical test of an experiment is repeatability. If you do the same thing again, you should get identical results. In the previous example, the most important standardisation would involve the purities of the metals – minor contamination could make a big difference to the melting point.

- An experiment has to be designed so that a change in some characteristic can first be observed and then precisely measured.

2 The branches of science

Earlier we talked about division of labour – as society becomes more complex and as knowledge accumulates, it is impossible for any one person to know everything. Scientists are specialists and science has fragmented into many different branches. The branches of science are sometimes called 'disciplines'. For example, chemistry and biology are different disciplines. The labels attached to each speciality can get confusing, and it helps to outline what goes where and who does what.

In medieval Europe a distinction was made between natural sciences and supernatural sciences. Natural science was concerned with the world about us; the supernatural sciences were the study of religion, philosophy and theology. Over the centuries, the word supernatural has taken on a different and narrower meaning, but we still talk about natural sciences.

Natural and social sciences

From about the beginning of the 20th century, two fundamentally different branches of science were redefined:

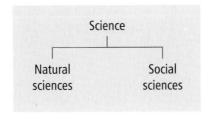

Natural science still means the study of the world and, by extension, the universe we live in. Social science concerns the way people behave as individuals, as families and in larger groups. The distinction is not clear-cut and is disputed by some.

Social science looks at characteristics like aggression, intelligence and extroversion, which cannot be directly measured. A physicist or a mathematician might therefore argue that sociology is not a real or true science.

A combination of natural and social science is often needed to explain behaviour changes. Too much alcohol, for instance, alters behaviour in most people. A chemist could measure blood alcohol content precisely, but chemistry cannot tell us why, in a sample of 100 adults, all with the same blood alcohol measurement, some want to fight, some want to be affectionate and some just want to go to sleep.

The three disciplines of the natural sciences

There is general agreement that the natural sciences divide into three main **disciplines**:

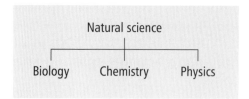

Biology is the study of living things and this again can be subdivided into many specialities. For example:

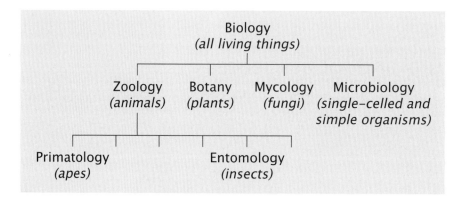

The diagram gives just a few examples. Subdivisions can be 'vertical' – an entomologist studies insects, so entomology is a specialist branch of zoology, and so on. The speciality can be 'horizontal' rather than vertical. Genetics is the study of how characteristics are inherited. A geneticist might work with many different kinds of living things – monkeys, fruit flies, oak trees, wheat or humans.

Chemistry is the study of how matter is made up, its properties and its changes. Chemistry is the central science because the rules of chemistry apply to all the material in the universe – living and non-living. An astronomer needs chemistry to understand the behaviour of a distant galaxy, but so does a microbiologist studying bacteria.

Chemistry is divided into three branches:

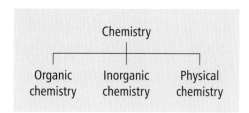

It used to be thought that there were two different kinds of chemistry, with one set of rules applying to living things or things that had once lived, like cork, wood, wool, silk, blood, bread and wine, and another set of rules applying to non-living substances such as air, water, rocks, salt and iron. We now know that this distinction is false, but we still use the word 'organic' to describe the chemistry of carbon compounds and 'inorganic' to describe all other substances.

Living things are made up mostly of carbon compounds. The word 'organic' is also used by advertisers to mean wholesome, pure or free of contaminants, but its real meaning is living or having something to do with living things.

Physical chemistry has to do with the effects of physical changes on chemical reactions. For example, the speed of a chemical reaction alters with changes in temperature and pressure, and some chemical reactions produce electricity.

Physics is not easy to define, but essentially it is the study of mass and energy, and their interrelationships. Physicists study things like speed, acceleration, friction, heat, light, magnetism and electricity. Major discoveries at the beginning of the 20th century mean that physics can also be subdivided into classical or traditional physics and modern physics. Put simply, modern physics is the branch of the subject that deals with very small particles and with objects that are moving at very high speeds.

Biochemistry underpins medicine

Healthcare and medicine are based on biology and chemistry. However, an important specialist science – biochemistry – sits halfway between the two. Living things are made from complex organic compounds. Because animals eat other animals and/or **plants** and fungi, food and living organisms have very similar compositions. The processes that maintain life are a series of chemical reactions. Biochemistry is the study of substances such as: proteins, fats, carbohydrates, **enzymes**, vitamins, minerals, DNA; functions like digestion, breathing, excretion and reproduction. Many diseases and disorders have a chemical origin – an essential reaction fails or goes wrong.

Biochemistry is the science that underpins medicine. Medicine itself is divided into hundreds of different specialist fields – Table 1.2 gives just a few examples.

There are considerable overlaps within the medical and other sciences. A radiologist will need to understand the physics of X-rays and ultrasonics; a psychiatrist will have studied the social sciences as well as medicine.

The relationship between maths and the sciences provokes endless arguments. Some think maths is a thing apart, and that knowledge can be divided into arts, science and maths. It can also be argued that all sciences are branches of maths – because science is impossible without measurement, and measurement is impossible without maths.

Table 1.2   Examples of specialist fields within medicine

Experts in particular groups	Experts in particular parts of the body	Experts in particular diseases or disorders	Other specialists
Paediatrician	Cardiologist	Oncologist	Anaesthetist
Geriatrician	Dentist	Nephrologist	Geneticist
Gynaecologist	Haematologist	Psychiatrist	Pharmacist
		Neurologist	Radiologist
		Ophthalmologist	Surgeon
			Pathologist

In the end, these debates have little practical value. All that can be said with certainty is that mathematics is an essential part of all experimentation and therefore of all sciences.

3 **The theory of knowledge**

Mathematicians, scientists and philosophers have developed a theory of knowledge.

This is a vast subject. It asks questions like 'what is absolute truth?' and 'what are the differences between knowledge and belief?'. Some students find these issues fascinating; others see the point but not the relevance of the theory to everyday life.

An Access course is not designed to turn students into professional philosophers, but a general understanding of the theory of knowledge will help enormously when you come to study the natural and social sciences.

In modern society we are surrounded by the products of science and technology, and we are constantly bombarded by scientific images and messages with a scientific content of some sort. We can all be forgiven for thinking science has all the answers and that it can solve any problem. The reality is different.

Science is a continuing process and theories or 'truths' are subject to constant revision. The greatest advances occur when a previously accepted theory is proved wrong or when it is shown only to apply in special or limited circumstances. It follows that at any one time, what you are being taught is 'that which the best informed scientists currently accept'.

Clearly, no malice or intentional deception is involved, but even a brilliant conscientious lecturer may not be passing on 'the truth, the whole truth and nothing but the truth'.

Theories can be disproved

There are countless examples from history of theories and statements that have been proved spectacularly wrong by subsequent research or discoveries.

Fire is a natural phenomenon familiar to man and most other animals, because lightning and volcanic activity start forest and bush fires. For thousands of years we have used fire to cook, process materials and as a weapon. By observation and experiment, we know that some substances like rock do not burn and others like wood and hair burn easily and quickly.

It is also clear that substances are consumed by fire. You do not need a balance or a weighing machine to show that a tree weighs more than the wood ash left behind when the tree has been burnt.

Early chemists developed the phlogiston theory to explain burning. This stated that substances which did not burn did not contain phlogiston, and that materials which burned easily contained a great deal of phlogiston. Burning was believed to release phlogiston and residues like wood ash were called dephlogisticated material. The theory also said that if you set fire to a log and extinguished the fire after, say, 10 minutes, then you would be able to set fire to it again, because some, but not all, of its phlogiston had been released. The phlogiston theory made perfect sense and it was widely accepted for many years.

We now know that this theory is completely wrong. Phlogiston has never been isolated or examined because it does not exist. The discovery of oxygen as a constituent of the atmosphere and the invention of accurate weighing machines destroyed the theory.

The following equations show the old theory and the modern one:

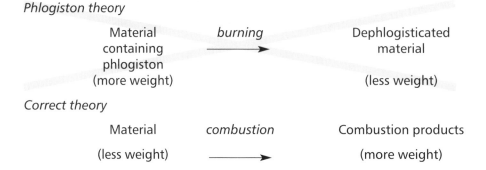

Phlogiston theory

| Material containing phlogiston (more weight) | *burning* → | Dephlogisticated material (less weight) |

Correct theory

| Material (less weight) | *combustion* → | Combustion products (more weight) |

Burning or combustion is a chemical reaction between oxygen (from the air) and the combustible material. If all the combustion products are carefully collected, they will weigh more than the combustible substance you started with. This weight gain is not immediately obvious because the combustion products are mostly gases.

The last defenders of the phlogiston theory tried to explain the experimental evidence by suggesting that phlogiston had negative weight. This extension of the theory was also wrong.

If you put one litre of petrol into a car with an empty tank and then drive until the car stops, you will obviously find that all the petrol has disappeared. A litre of petrol weighs about 700 grams – this is what actually happens:

petrol	+	oxygen	=	carbon dioxide	+	water
700 g	+	2,455 g	=	2,160 g	+	995 g

The car's engine burns a mixture of petrol and air. The combustion products leaving via the exhaust pipe are carbon dioxide and water vapour. 700 g of petrol produces a total of 3,155 g of combustion products.

A detailed experiment would show that no material has been created or destroyed by this combustion reaction. You can see that the weight of the petrol plus the oxygen exactly equals the total weight of the combustion products, carbon dioxide and water vapour.

Even the best and most prominent scientists can be overtaken by new discoveries and theories. The most famous astronomer of the 19th century, Sir William Herschel (1738–1822), said that we would never know the composition of the Sun. At the time, this was a completely reasonable assumption, because how could we possibly collect samples for analysis? Today, we know more about the materials that make up the Sun than we do about the composition of the Earth. Light and other radiation from the Sun can be analysed using spectrometers. The spectra produced give precise measures of the elements the Sun contains and their proportions.

Albert Michelson, an American physicist, was the first scientist to measure the speed of light accurately. He had a worldwide reputation as one of the most brilliant men of his generation. A quote from Michelson is often given as the biggest but most understandable mistake in modern scientific history. He said:

> The more important fundamental laws and facts of physics have all been discovered. These are now so firmly established that the possibility of their ever being supplanted by new discoveries is exceedingly remote. Our future discoveries must be looked for in the sixth place of decimals.

This quote dates to about 1908. During the following 10 years, discoveries made by Albert Einstein and Max Planck, both German physicists, totally revolutionised physics and our understanding of how the universe works.

Ironically, Einstein's work would have been impossible without the previous discoveries made by Michelson.

Michelson's reputation and credibility were not damaged by Einstein or Planck. All scientists accept that their discoveries and theories are just the latest stage in a never-ending journey.

Sample size and certainty

The natural sciences seem to offer rock solid certainties because even a very small-scale experiment involves huge numbers of atoms or **molecules**. What we actually observe is the average behaviour of enormously large samples. Looked at one at a time, atoms and the smaller particles that atoms are made from behave very oddly; modern physics shows that predicting their individual behaviour with certainty is impossible.

As sample sizes get smaller, it becomes increasingly difficult to make scientific predictions. Sample size and probability partly explain the differences between the natural and the social sciences. A very large social sciences experiment might involve observations of, say, 1000 people. The largest possible social science experiment would include everyone currently living on Earth – currently more than 6 billion people (6,000,000,000).

A sample containing 6 billion water molecules is an incredibly small volume of water, because molecules are almost unbelievably tiny. It is difficult to give comparisons because the numbers are so enormous, but this illustration might help.

If you gave everyone on earth £500 billion (£500,000,000,000) and then added up all the money that had been distributed, the answer would be 3×10^{21} pounds – that is £3,000,000,000,000,000,000,000.

There are 3×10^{21} water molecules in a single drop of water.

Common sense is unreliable

We develop a common sense view of how the world works by observation. From birth, we are constantly picking up signals through sight, hearing, touch, taste and smell. By the age of about five or six, we each have a body of knowledge that tells us how to predict future events – a ball will roll downhill tomorrow because it always has before, fire always burns, vinegar always tastes sour, and so on. However, everyday human experience is a very poor guide to the way the world and the universe really operates.

Without help from specialised tools and machines, we are deaf and blind to most of the things going on around us. We can see small insects and for distances of about 30 km on a clear day, but anything smaller or more distant is effectively invisible. We can see very large bright objects like the Sun, Moon and stars, but we have no way of working out how far they are from our eyes – without special tools and specialised science.

There are many phenomena that we cannot detect at all, such as gamma rays, X-rays, ultraviolet light, radio waves and high-frequency sound. Exposure to high-energy radiation like gamma rays, X-rays and ultraviolet can be damaging or even lethal, but our eyes and ears have not evolved to give early warning signals.

We exist on the surface of what is probably an unusual planet. Most of us spend most of our lives within a few hundred metres of sea level, and the colder polar regions are virtually uninhabited. On average, we live for about 70 years. We see our world as normal and our common sense tells us that we have experience of a very wide range of conditions and situations. This assumption is false.

We can imagine a lifetime and a span of several generations, but very short periods of time and very long ones have little meaning. The Earth is about 5 billion years old and the universe about 14 billion years old. We can appreciate that evolution takes place over millions of years, but it is difficult truly to understand an idea so different from personal experience.

Light travels at 300,000 kilometres a second, and sound at about 340 metres a second, through warm air at sea level. A world-class male sprinter can reach around 15 metres a second. The fastest land animal can accelerate briefly to a speed of 30 metres a second. Again, we can appreciate that light travels very rapidly indeed, but its real speed is beyond all human experience.

Our body of personal knowledge only covers a tiny fraction of the total possible temperature range. The average year-round temperature of the surface of the Earth is something like 15 °C; very few towns or cities are built in places where temperatures drop much below −20 °C or rise much above 40 °C. Air turns to a liquid at about −190 °C and stars have internal temperatures of millions of degrees.

Atmospheric pressure variations determine weather patterns. However, these daily and seasonal changes are minute compared with what is possible. Most of deep space is a near perfect vacuum and pressures of thousands of times normal atmospheric values are used in some chemical processes. The pressure at the centre of very large objects like stars is calculable, but for most people it is unimaginable.

We could continue with many similar illustrations, but hopefully you have read enough to be convinced that even the best intuition of the most brilliant scientists can lead to major errors. Reasonable assumptions based on sound common sense are unreliable. The more unusual the situation, the more unreliable common sense becomes.

All science uses a way of thinking called 'the scientific method'. This is based on experiment and observation instead of common sense, intuition or estimation.

4 The scientific method

The scientific method can be traced back more than 2000 years to the writings of Aristotle, the Greek philosopher. Many European academics added to the method and it was first widely used in the 16th and 17th centuries following advances in mathematics and instrument making.

It is difficult to overstate the importance of the method. It does not apply just to narrowly defined scientific problems.

Most societies begin as autocracies or absolute monarchies. Wealth and power are concentrated in the hands of one person or one family. A crime is defined as any act that displeases or is not in the interests of the ruler or ruling group. Crimes are punished ruthlessly and the concept of evidence is not involved.

The justice system in modern democracies is based on the scientific method. Procedures are followed, evidence is collected and examined. A trial is an experiment, the result is a verdict.

Randomly selected juries are asked to consider the probabilities of guilt or innocence. The appeal court is a second 'experiment' designed to check the results and conclusions of the first.

Commercial organisations start life as one or two people with a moneymaking idea. Most fail; a few grow into huge companies. At first, or sometimes for many years, all important decisions are made by the founders using their common sense or intuition. Eventually, this common sense leads to major mistakes and decisions pass to a larger group. At a third stage, the scientific method is introduced to guide decision-making or even to replace human bias altogether.

Retailers, for example, now use sophisticated mathematical models to decide when and where to open new stores and when to close or extend old ones. This system is far more reliable than the hunch or best guesses of one or two senior directors.

Medicine and the scientific method

Medicine and healthcare have been around for thousands of years. Before the scientific method, procedures were mostly based on assumption, superstition, prejudice and ignorance. Some patients were cured, but usually only by chance or accident. Medical research has constantly had to overcome or come to terms with cultural taboos. If the dissection of corpses is forbidden, then the body's structure and function can only be guessed at. If only men can become doctors, and if men are not allowed to examine women, it follows that gynaecology can be no more than belief or assumption.

An understanding of smallpox, typhoid and cholera were amongst the earliest successes of the scientific method. Infection mechanisms can only be confirmed by experiment. 'Malaria' means 'bad air': its carrier was once thought to be polluted air, not the mosquitoes that concentrate in slow moving or stagnant water.

Modern evidence-based medicine is the scientific method in action. A consultation is observation backed up by medical tests, which are experiments. A disease or disorder is diagnosed and a therapy is prescribed. Subsequent medical tests are further experiments designed to test the progress of recovery. Medicine is a body of knowledge accumulated from millions of observations and experiments.

Virtually all advances in medical science have been resisted by groups who believe that medicine interferes with the natural order. Anaesthesia was introduced against the objection of some doctors, who thought pain was natural and normal. The scientific method shows that things can be done – it does not prove that things should be done. This process continues and there are no easy answers. The current debate on the ethics of gene manipulation is just the latest example – human cloning is theoretically possible, but is it advisable? Ethical problems are not confined to cutting-edge medicine – contraception and abortion are long-established procedures.

Belief, assertion and assumption

Next we need to look at the scientific method in more detail. We should start with the meanings of some commonly used words:

- A belief or an **assertion** is a statement of personal opinion. It might be true, it might be false, or it might be impossible to tell one way or the other. An assertion can be a prediction. For example:

  Eating apple pips will give you appendicitis.
  French people are arrogant.
  Women are bad drivers.
  You will get the flu if you go out with wet hair.
  Left-handed people are good at maths.

  These statements have one thing in common – no proof is offered to support the statement or perhaps none is possible.

- An **assumption** is also a statement of opinion, but it is usually based on previous experience. This experience might or might not be relevant to the statement made. The evidence supporting the assumption, if it exists, may be substantial or trivial. Many assumptions are proved false by subsequent events. For example:

  There will never be a woman British Prime Minister (1971).
  Men have a better sense of direction than women.
  The Sun will rise next Monday morning.
  Time travel is impossible.

  It is difficult to draw a sharp dividing line between assertion and assumption.

Hypothesis and theory

The scientific method specifically excludes assertions and assumptions, but as one of its stages, it includes a statement called a 'hypothesis'.

A **hypothesis** is a basis for further investigation. The hypothesis may come from observation or from preliminary experiments.

A hypothesis might be right or wrong. The chosen experiment has to be able to tell if it is wrong, but it cannot necessarily prove that the hypothesis is correct.

This cycle of hypothesis → experiment → modified hypothesis → further experiment is usually repeated many times under a variety of conditions. At some point, a hypothesis is promoted to a **theory**. A theory is a generalised explanation of a phenomenon. The more general the theory, the greater its ability to predict future events.

A theory is no more than what we currently believe to be true, based on the best available evidence. Theories are often disproved by later hypotheses and experiments. Logically, a theory cannot be proven correct in all circumstances, because we cannot predict the future, or the results of the millionth experiment, for example.

Figure 1.1(a) shows a single experiment; Figure 1.1(b) shows a simplified version of how a theory is developed by using the conclusion of one experiment as a modified hypothesis for the next.

A hierarchy of words and ideas emerges from the scientific method. We have considered assertion, assumption, hypothesis and theory in sequence. Three more concepts are also relevant – a law, a principle and a theorem.

Figure 1.1

(a) A single experiment

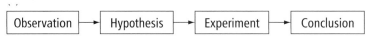

(b) How a theory might be developed

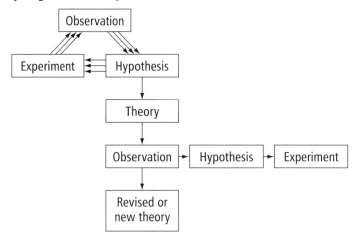

Law, principle and theorem

The commonest use of the word 'law' has nothing to do with science. By law in the UK, you may not drive at more than 30 m.p.h. in a built-up area. If you do, however, exceed the speed limit, you are not certain to have an accident, nor are you certain to be caught and fined. In this sense, a law is a set of rules or conventions.

We often use the word law in a casual way that does not involve proof or experiment. We talk about the law of the jungle – this means something like 'kill or be killed'. In scientific terms, this is an assumption.

Economists use expressions like 'the law of supply and demand'. To a scientist, this is a hypothesis.

For scientists, the word **law** means a theory that has been proved correct over a long period of time and by many different observations or experiments. Unfortunately there are no clear-cut rules and the terms are often used interchangeably – the 'law of gravity' and the 'theory of relativity', for example.

A **principle** can best be described as a mathematically provable explanation of the way the universe works. The concept is most often used in physics.

A **theorem**, as opposed to a theory, is a mathematical term. Scientific experiment cannot give absolute proof because tomorrow, or in a hundred years' time, a new experiment might show errors or basic flaws in a theory.

Mathematics is different because it is possible to show that some statements, written as mathematical formulae, are absolutely true and that no possibility of error exists.

In this way, maths is much more straightforward than science. Mathematicians recognise only three kinds of statement – those that cannot ever be true, those that are sometimes true and those that are always true. Taking a simple example:

(i) $\qquad\qquad\qquad 2 = 3$

(ii) $\qquad\qquad\qquad x = 2$

(iii) $(x + 1)(x - 1) \quad = x^2 - 1$

There has never been a time or a place when 2 equalled 3, and there never will be.

If x equals the number of your children, then there are several possibilities. At the moment, this might be a true statement, but there was certainly a time in your past when it was untrue. If you have three children, the statement is false, but will have been true at one time. If you do not have any children, it might be true at some time in the future.

The third statement is a theorem because it is always true for any value of x: at any place in the universe and at any time in the past, or, with certainty, at any time in the future.

We have explained why science cannot prove anything with certainty, or at least very little with certainty. Two obvious questions follow – "why bother?" and "how do we know that what we are being taught is true?". The answers to these questions are important.

Science cannot offer absolute proof, but it can provide very high probabilities that accepted theories are genuine descriptions of how the world really works. Current scientific theories are exceedingly useful – they will nearly always predict what will happen in new situations. Put differently, there is a huge difference between the lack of absolute proof and subjective opinion. An assumption that science is useless is far less likely to be true than an assumption that science is foolproof – this is why we bother.

Teaching and learning

The scientific method has implications for teaching and learning.

At some stage during your Access course, a lecturer will tell you that all atoms are made up of three sub-atomic particles called protons, neutrons and electrons. You will accept that this statement is true and you will probably write it down. Later you will be asked to use this information to answer questions in an exam. Your lecturer has passed on some information that every chemist and physicist in the world currently believes to be true. However, your lecturer did not design or take part in the experiments that showed that these statements are likely to be correct.

If you ask "how do we know that?" – a completely valid question based on your perfect understanding of the scientific method – your lecturer has three options:

- He or she might say: "That's just the way it is".

- Your lecturer could say: "I cannot give you a complete guarantee that protons, neutrons and electrons really exist, or that they have the properties I have just described. However, there is a very, very high probability that I am telling the truth, because no experiment yet devised has shown that protons, neutrons and electrons do not exist and do not behave in the way I have just explained".

- The third option is only possible if you, your lecturer and your college have limitless time and money. All the experiments that have led to the conclusion that protons, neutrons and electrons exist could be repeated 'before your very eyes' and you could be involved in questioning their conclusions. This would take many years and cost many millions. You might well be able to understand what an expensive procession of world-class experts tell you, but probably some of it would go 'over your head'.

Teaching in the real world always involves trust and this trust echoes back through the generations.

Your Access lecturer may have come directly from a GCSE chemistry class and may be teaching A level physics after you have left. The lecturer may have told the GCSE class that the atom is the fundamental particle, and then may go on to tell the A level students that protons, neutrons and electrons are themselves composed of smaller or elementary particles.

The lecturer is giving different stories to different groups of students. They cannot all be precisely true – and the scientific method says that all three might be nonsense.

Teaching is a progressive process – the GCSE class is not being fed lies, it is being taught a simplified version of the probable truth. This can be built upon with more detail as they progress in their learning.

5 Publication, précis and comprehension

In this topic we focus on the work scientists do in teaching and research.

Education involves increasing specialisation. At primary and secondary school, the object is to provide a broad general framework in all the important subjects and disciplines.

Most educators think specialisation is best delayed for as long as possible. Typically, specialisation begins as compulsory education ends. Your Access course is a mixture of general and specialist units. By choosing a particular pathway, you have decided on a specialist education.

A first or bachelor's degree usually takes three or four years of full-time study. First degree students are not expected to discover anything new or add to the body of knowledge.

Original research

A doctorate takes about three years of postgraduate study. A master's degree is a halfway point, usually awarded after one or two years of postgraduate study. In one major respect, postgraduate education differs from a first degree – students have to make an original contribution in their chosen field. A post-graduate student writes a thesis, a document describing and summarising his or her original research.

Scientific research is not limited to universities. Much of it takes place in commercial companies, specialised research institutes and in government-funded or supported organisations.

Scientific communication is based on three principles – publication, peer review and freedom of information.

Science is international and most non-specialists are surprised to find that information and research is freely exchanged amongst scientists and around the world. Research scientists have usually studied at two or more univer-sities, often in different countries. There is a continual exchange of staff between universities and other kinds of research institutions.

The first person to publish a piece of research is credited with its discovery. Many different groups may be working on the same problem and the 'race to publish' is a major concern. There are many historical examples of unpub-lished research pre-dating similar published work. In exceptional circum-stances, the credit can be shared between two groups. However, the 'first publication rule' is usually preserved because it encourages free interchange of information. The principles are similar to those of the patent system for new inventions.

Plagiarism is copying somebody else's research and presenting it as your own. From time to time, something might look like plagiarism but is in fact innocent coincidence, e.g. if two scientists have reached the same conclusions independently from similar experiments.

Intentional plagiarism is the worst professional offence a scientist can commit. If proven, plagiarism inevitably destroys reputation and credibility.

By publication, a scientist gives permission, amongst other things, for a process called **peer review**. Peers are equals – other scientists working in similar specialities or on similar problems. Publication is an open invitation for constructive criticism. Peer review ensures that new research is genuine, accurate and valid.

The document published may be a complete description of the work or sometimes an abstract or summary.

Publication itself can take several forms. Research is often submitted to specialist monthly magazines or journals, or it might be presented at conferences or seminars. The researchers themselves, their universities or their employers may arrange publication.

Electronic publishing and the Internet are gradually replacing traditional methods.

For this unit, you do not have to produce your own original research but the unit specification says you should be able to use and understand research published by others. The best test of understanding is the ability to put together a summary or **précis** – you will be asked to do this as a class exercise and as part of an assessment. You might have to write a précis of some written work or a science video, or both.

How to write a précis

There is a general method for preparing précis that gives good results, regardless of the subject or the complexity of the original work.

The whole point of a précis is to eliminate detail but retain the essential meaning of the original.

Précis is time-consuming. It gets easier with practice, but you should not be surprised if your first efforts take an hour or more.

Scientists use words precisely and cautiously. Definitive and absolute statements rarely feature in research. Many papers are put together by groups rather than individuals. Written style can seem odd, formal and stilted – the object of the exercise is clarity, not entertainment.

By definition, the research material will be unfamiliar and you will have little background in the subject concerned.

1. You should start by noting the subject of the paper, its title, the publication date and its authors. Your work should be headed:

A précis of............ *(title, publication date, authors)*

2. You should read through the report slowly and carefully – skimming or rapid reading is not good enough. Scientists are no different from the rest of us – some are good communicators, others are not. A well-written paper uses jargon only when necessary. However, some scientists use many complex words and expressions. The meaning is often clear from the context, but you are almost certain to come across things you do not understand. Whenever possible, you should look up the meanings of new words before you draft the précis. This may involve a trip to the library or a conversation with a lecturer.

3. Somewhere near the beginning of the report, the author will have described the hypothesis to be tested. This might be formally stated or it might be called something like the purpose or the objective of the experiment. Turn the hypothesis into your own words. Avoid jargon unless you are completely confident that you understand what it means. Try to condense the hypothesis into two or three sentences.

4. Towards the end of the report, you will always find a sub-section called conclusion, conclusions or perhaps conclusions and recommendations for further work. Again, summarise this part of the research paper in your own words. If the conclusions include numbers or a data table, it is nearly always best to include these in your précis without further modification or summary. Be extra careful not to alter the strength or the reliability of the author's conclusions. If he or she wrote that a result suggested or pointed to a particular conclusion, it is completely incorrect for your précis to say that the hypothesis has been proved.

5. You now have two reference points for your précis – the beginning and the end. All you have to do now is fill the gap in between. Most research reports are divided into separately headed sections. Even the badly written will present different ideas or different stages of the research in separate paragraphs. If possible, take a copy of the original document and use this to plan your précis. Read the report again and divide it into a number of sections or stages – draw horizontal lines to divide one section from the next. You should be able to slice the report up into more than three but fewer than, say, ten sections, but there are no hard and fast rules.

6. Unless you have very good reason to do otherwise, your précis should follow the same sequence of ideas as the original.

7. Now look at each section in turn. Reread carefully and underline or highlight what you see as the most important words or sentences. In your own style, produce a summary that includes everything you have highlighted. Only summarise diagrams, maps, charts and equations if you think you can do so without losing essential information. Data tables in the body of the report can often be reduced to headings and totals. You might find that some sections do not carry any essential information – you can exclude these from the précis.

8. The draft is unlikely to read smoothly at first. Remove any repetitions, and add linking phrases and sentences to improve flow. Create as many drafts as you need, until you have a version that you think cannot be improved.

9. You will be asked to produce a précis of a certain length. If the instruction is 'Summarise this report in no more than 400 words' this is a definite instruction – 420 words will not do, but 300 would be acceptable. 'Produce a précis of about 400 words' is a different task – between 350 and 450 words would be acceptable, but much longer or much shorter would not. Leave the word count until last. Once you have a tidy draft it is easy to add or subtract.

As a class or assessment exercise, you might be given a comprehension test based on some original research. The précis principles apply – you will not have to write a summary but you will need to be able to tell the difference between detail and the big ideas.

Communication with non-specialists

We have considered how scientists communicate amongst themselves. Finally, we need to think about how scientists communicate with wider non-specialist audiences – the general public.

As an Access student, you are receiving scientific information as part of a structured course. Most people, however, get their scientific information from three sources:

- The media – TV, radio, newspapers, magazines, the Internet.

- Commercial advertising.

- Government or other non-commercial organisations, such as the NHS and charities.

All mass market information has one thing in common – it comes to you indirectly. The original scientific work has been filtered, summarised or simplified.

The scientific method applies universally – whenever you are told something, you should ask yourself "What is the evidence for the information I have just received?". The person or organisation standing between you and the original research may have distorted it in some way – on purpose, by accident or through ignorance.

Commercial advertisers are trying to sell you something. They are not allowed to lie, but they do not have to tell the whole truth either. Judged scientifically, most advertising is no more than assertion.

The media are in business to retain or increase numbers of viewers, listeners, readers or subscribers. They do this by publishing or broadcasting stories that will capture the interest of as many people as possible. Three kinds of distortion are very common:

- Research is frequently simplified to the point where most of the original meaning is lost. Many newspaper articles are very poor précis.

- Most research reaches cautious conclusions. The mass media often mistranslate possibilities or probabilities into certainties.

- Two or more groups of scientists working on the same problem often reach different conclusions. Journalists may then conclude that both cannot be right, so both are probably wrong and therefore the whole scientific process is nonsense. All the scientists can, however, be right, but their findings might apply in different situations or conditions.

UK government-sponsored information campaigns are nearly always based on reliable evidence collected from well-designed experiments. Unfortunately, the media messages are frequently confusing and oversimplified.

Serious consequences

Sometimes a misunderstanding of scientific information can have serious consequences. The risks and benefits of immunisation are excellent examples. Many responsible, intelligent and caring parents go through a decision process something like this:

- I have read that some children are dreadfully damaged by routine immunisations.

- I know the risk is small, but the unlucky one might be my child.

- To avoid this risk I will not have my child immunised. It would be irresponsible to expose him or her to harm.

This thinking is perfectly understandable but it leads to the wrong conclusions.

The argument is wrong because it is based on two false assumptions. Common sense tells us that our present condition or situation has minimum or zero risk, and therefore doing something is more dangerous than doing nothing. The second false assumption is that the common childhood infections of our grandparents' time cannot return and in any event they are not life-threatening.

The real scientific truth is that your particular child is at far more risk without immunisation than with it. The risk to every child, yours included, increases every time a parent refuses immunisation. The point of mass immunisation is to prevent the spread of infectious disease. If 95% of children are immunised, then the infection cannot travel far before it is hemmed in by a brick wall of protected children.

Measles, for example, devastates unprotected populations. This statement is not an assertion. It is a conclusion drawn from a huge, dreadful unplanned experiment that took place in the 16th century. In 1520, the native population of what is now Mexico was 20 million. By the year 1607, a reliable census showed that this had fallen to 1.1 million. The Spanish conquerors brought measles with them. They had some natural immunity; the locals had none. Malnutrition, war and other diseases accounted for some deaths, but it is estimated that measles alone killed 15 million people.

6 Experimental design, variables and errors

As part of the assessment for this unit, you will need to plan, carry out and write a report of a practical investigation or experiment.

There are thousands to choose from – in this topic we look at the general principles and methods that apply to all experiments. Some investigations involve the measurement of human characteristics – these are a mix of social science and natural science. Others are concerned with a chemical, biological or physical change of some sort – these are natural science experiments.

All investigations have a human element and humans are fallible. We use complex instruments and equipment but, at some point, judgement is involved.

As a first example, we will plan an experiment based on a familiar idea. The hypothesis to be tested is:

Men are bigger than women.

We have considerable prior knowledge based on everyday observation. The hypothesis is likely to be true, but we do not know much about the detail. Importantly, our prior knowledge does not include numbers – how much bigger? – for example.

Science is about precision. The first hypothesis is too vague because the words 'men', 'women' and 'bigger' are not closely defined. Bigger might mean taller, heavier, with a larger waist measurement, larger shoe size, or whatever. Let us suppose we are interested in height.

A well-designed experiment gives information about the relationship between two variables, and it eliminates or controls other complicating influences.

Discrete and continuous variables

We need to define the word **variable**. Any number or quantity that can vary is called a variable, and nearly everything you observe in daily life is a variable.

Mathematicians and statisticians divide variables into two kinds – **discrete** and **continuous**. A discrete variable is something you can count and so is nearly always a positive whole number. A continuous variable is something you measure. In theory a continuous variable can have any value, provided you measure it with enough accuracy. The number of children in a class is a discrete variable; their total weight is a continuous variable.

In our experiment, we are interested in two variables and their relationship. Gender is a discrete variable because you can count the number of sexes. Height is a continuous variable because everybody in the world would have a different height if you were to measure it to enough decimal places. An experiment to investigate how height varies with weight would involve two continuous variables.

In our experiment, gender is the independent variable and height is the dependent variable – because our hypothesis says that height depends on gender.

Complicating influences are properly called extraneous variables. We know, or suspect, from previous observations that height depends on many things, not just gender. We need to eliminate, minimise or control their influence. For example:

- Height depends on age. We know that most people reach adult height in their late teens. We do not know if girls mature more rapidly than boys, or vice versa. We might suspect that older people sometimes shrink a little. We do not know if men shrink more rapidly than women.

- We know for sure that it takes many years to reach adult height. We may also think that 'people are getting taller' because of better healthcare and nutrition. Put scientifically, height might depend on absolute age, even if older people do not shrink. We cannot know precisely the height differences between generations – without another experiment – and we cannot know if men and woman are getting taller at the same rate.

- The complications do not end here. There is another variable that influences height. This is variously described as race, ethnicity or nationality. We might think it very likely that most Norwegians are taller than most Japanese. However, we know nothing precise about the relationship between nationality, gender and height.

We can now write a revised hypothesis:

Refining the hypothesis

> For those currently living in Greater London, the height of men between the ages of 25 and 40 is greater than the height of women between the ages of 25 and 40.

The new hypothesis is the basis for a reasonably reliable experiment, but it does not completely eliminate the possible effects of the identified extraneous variables. In this investigation, we have much prior knowledge – in many experiments, this luxury is not available.

Note that Greater London has definable borders and 'living in' does not mean 'born in'. Experimental design involves compromise. Any definable group could be used in place of Greater London residents.

For this unit, you do not need a detailed understanding of statistical analysis, but clearly almost all experiments have to be based on samples. About 1.5 million people between the ages of 25 and 40 live in Greater London – we know that a well chosen sample of about 200 ought to give reliable results. A representative sample would include equal numbers of men and women.

Three kinds of error

We next need to think about how we collect the gender and height information.

We might stand in Trafalgar Square, stop passers-by and ask them: "Are you a resident of Greater London? Are you between the ages of 25 and 40? And how tall are you?". To start with, assume gender is obvious, and that no one refuses our questions.

This experiment is poorly designed because it introduces **systematic error**, sometimes called 'bias'. Many people might lie about their age, so our sample of 200 would include some younger than 25 and some older than 40 – these are unlikely to balance out, as older people are perhaps more likely to lie about their age.

In a similar way, this design would not collect reliable height data. Unless they are exceedingly tall, men tend to say they are taller than they really are. Many shorter women exaggerate their height; taller women often give underestimates. We do not know if the sample will include equal numbers of height overestimates and underestimates, so this is another example of systematic error.

In a real experiment of this kind, the researcher asking the questions would get many refusals. Our design has built in the potential for additional errors:

- More women than men would refuse – probably.

- Very tall and very short people are more likely to refuse than those of near average height. Our sample would therefore underestimate the true range in heights.

- Busy people are less likely to cooperate than those who are not time-pressured.

- Some people hate research interviews; others enjoy them.

We might think that being busy or being friendly does not depend at all on a person's height. If this is true, we would define these as **random errors**, not systematic errors. Random errors are more easily understood by looking at a second design to test the same hypothesis.

We stop 200 passers-by. Each is delighted, without payment, to cooperate in our experiment. They willingly remove their shoes and stand upright, while we measure their height to the nearest centimetre. One technician does all the height measuring. We then ask all 200 people for documentary proof of their gender and date of birth. All are carrying a passport or a driving licence – nobody objects.

This second experimental design removes most of the errors of the first. However, it still cannot be perfectly reliable. Any measurement involves the potential for random errors. Some measurements will be accurate, some will be underestimates and some overestimates. Larger errors will be less common than smaller mistakes. For large samples, random errors tend to cancel each other out. Using two or more technicians would reintroduce the possibility of systematic error – their eyesight might differ, for example.

Practical considerations are important in experimental design. At 2 minutes per consultation, it would take one technician nearly 7 hours to measure 200 people. Measuring accuracy declines dramatically with tiredness and boredom. The later measurements are almost certain to include more and bigger errors than the earlier ones.

Systematic errors can be minimised by good experimental design. Similarly, random errors need not significantly reduce the reliability of an experiment's conclusions. A third kind of error is more difficult to handle – **gross error**, which is a major mistake.

In our second experiment, the technician might measure a man's height as 183 cm but enter a figure of 153 cm on the results chart. One height is about 5 feet, the other about 6 feet – both would look reasonable in a table of 200 measurements. There is no way of telling if a similar but opposite error has been or will be made. Efficient procedures, double checking and repetition reduces the scope for gross error. Some gross errors are obvious. A measured height of 152 cm recorded as 52 cm would be eliminated from the final results table – very few adults are 20 inches tall.

In this experiment, we have a preliminary idea of what is a reasonable or feasible adult height, but for some experiments or variables this is not possible.

Reliable conclusions?

The technician will measure the last person and then hand over the raw results – something like two tables, each of 100 heights. With samples of this size, it does not matter if we end up with slightly different numbers of men and women.

At this point in experiments of this kind, statistics take over. The **raw data** can be processed, to condense or summarise the information 'held inside' the 200 height values.

We would probably start by calculating the **arithmetic means** or average heights of the men and women. If these figures are 175 cm and 164 cm, for example, we can reach a conclusion:

In this sample of 100 men and 100 women, the average male height is 11 cm greater than the average female height.

Because an 11 cm difference is so much greater than the likely errors in our measurements, we can be practically certain that this conclusion is correct.

It is important to realise that further conclusions can be drawn but that none of these can be proved totally reliable. We certainly cannot conclude that all men are taller than all women. In this sample of 200, in Greater London and in most other groups, the male and female height distributions overlap. Statistical analysis can distil some more information from this experiment:

- We can draw bar charts and histograms to illustrate the extent of the overlap in male/female height distribution.

- Based on the sample results, we can calculate statistics that describe the probable variation in male and female heights across Greater London.

- Given an adult height, we could calculate the probability that someone of this height was male or female.

Experimental design in natural science

In most respects, natural science experiments are easier to design and control than investigations measuring human characteristics. The equipment and materials cannot refuse to cooperate and they do not tell lies. Nevertheless, even the simplest natural science experiments need careful design to minimise errors and produce reliable conclusions.

Experimental design in chemistry, biology and physics, for example, nearly always includes the choice of appropriate equipment and measuring instruments. Scientific advance has moved hand in hand with improvements in measurement and observation techniques. Some obvious examples are accurate thermometers in physics and chemistry, and microscopes in all branches of biology.

Modern chemistry is only possible because we have learned to isolate and purify most substances. An investigation into the reaction between two impure substances involves many extraneous variables – does the change observed result from the impurities, or from the main reaction we think we are investigating?

As a second illustration of experimental design, we will outline what seems to be a straightforward scientific experiment.

Density is a simple idea. The same volumes of different substances have different weights.

To make life easier, scientists use standardised density units – these are usually grams per cubic centimetre (cm^3). Pure water is used as a reference point – its density is $1\,g/cm^3$. Anything with a density greater than $1\,g/cm^3$ sinks in water; anything with a density less than $1\,g/cm^3$ floats.

Some substances dissolve in water; others react chemically with it. Nonetheless, we can measure the density of anything against the pure water standard. Everything weighs something so, for example, you can measure the density of air or any gas. Although 1 cm³ of air does not weigh very much, it is not weightless. In other words, its density is very low.

You could accurately weigh 1 cm³ of pure lead or 1 cm³ of solid glass. You could then repeat these experiments using lead shot and small glass marbles. Because the shot and the marbles do not fill up all the space available in a container, the weight of 1 cm³ of lead shot or 1 cm³ of small glass marbles is lower than that of the solid. The first is the absolute density. The second is the bulk density. Bulk density measurement is important in many industries – builders use sand, pebbles and aggregate as well as solid lumps of rock; most food manufacturers use particulate material like sugar, flour and salt.

Desk research

We want to design an experiment to test the following idea:

How does the relationship between absolute density and bulk density vary with the size, size variation and shape of the particles concerned?

At first glance, this looks like a simple problem. In fact it is not one problem but three or more, all of which are interrelated in a way that will be extremely difficult to investigate.

Most stages in experimental design do not need a laboratory. We need to think the problem through first. This is sometimes called 'desk research'. Let us start by looking at particle shape.

Imagine a container with internal measurements of 10 cm by 10 cm by 10 cm (Figure 1.2). A single glass particle in the shape of a perfect 10 cm³ cube would fit precisely into the container. In this case, the absolute density of glass would be identical to the bulk density of the glass particle in the container.

Figure 1.2 Container and glass particle

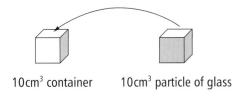

10cm³ container   10cm³ particle of glass

You could extend the idea. Eight 5 cm³ glass cubes would completely fill the container, so would 1000 1 cm³ cubes. With a bit more thought, however, these are clearly special cases of the bulk density problem. Cubes of, say, 7 cm³ could not fill the box completely and if the 5 cm³ cubes were thrown in randomly, rather than placed neatly in layers, there would be air spaces between the cubes. We have found a fourth idea – that bulk density depends on particle arrangement, not just shape, size and size variation.

Next, we could think about how bulk density varies if the particles were not cubes but, for example, spheres. It is obvious that no amount of spheres can completely fill a cubic container if all the spheres are the same size. There will always be air gaps between the spheres.

Arrangement influences bulk density regardless of shape. It also seems reasonable to conclude that irregular shapes give lower bulk densities than regular ones. We cannot, however, prove this assumption.

So far, we have only considered how the bulk density/absolute density relationship varies with the shape of particles and their size. What if the particles are the same shape but different sizes?

A mixture of larger and smaller spheres would have a higher bulk density than a container filled with identically sized spheres, because the smaller spheres can fill the air gaps between the larger ones. We can probably also conclude that the greater the size variation, the higher the bulk density – because very tiny spheres would fill the gaps between slightly bigger spheres and slightly bigger spheres might fill the gaps between the larger spheres, and so on.

Arrangement and size variation are interrelated. The air gaps can only be filled if the different sized spheres are effectively mixed.

Complex experimental design

The real relationship between bulk density and absolute density is far more complicated than it seems to be at first glance. No single experiment could give reliable conclusions, but we could design a series of investigations based on several hypotheses. For instance:

- The more orderly the arrangement of particles becomes, the more bulk density approaches the absolute density.

- The more regular a particle shape becomes, the more bulk density approaches absolute density.

- The greater the size variation of the particles concerned, the more bulk density approaches absolute density.

As an assessment or class exercise, how would you design experiments to measure the absolute and bulk densities of a sample of large pebbles, a mixture of smaller pebbles and coarse sand, and a sample of fine sand?

7 Reporting experiments

A valuable and interesting experiment can take minutes and cost virtually nothing. You learn a great deal about probability by flipping coins, throwing dice or playing cards. Flipping ten coins and observing the distribution of heads and tails is a valid, well-designed experiment. At the other end of the spectrum, the space exploration programme put together by the USA and other nations is also an experiment. This second example has extended over 50 years, involved millions of people and cost billions of dollars.

At some stage the design, procedure and results of an experiment have to be recorded and communicated to those not directly involved, or not involved at all, in its design, progress or conclusions.

There is a standard method for reporting or 'writing up' an experiment. Detail varies, but the principles are the same, regardless of the complexity, scale or cost of the experiment.

You will use this standard method when you report the results of your assessment or class exercise experiments. A checklist is provided in Figure 1.3.

Ten steps

1. An investigation report must have a title, it must list its author or authors – those who conducted the experiment – and it must be dated. The critical date is that of the completion of the experiment.

2. The report should start with an introduction that summarises the relevant theory behind the experiment and the hypothesis to be tested.

3. The next section describes the equipment used. Usually this will include a diagram or specification of the apparatus and instruments concerned.

4. This is followed by a description of procedure or method. What did you do? How did you do it? In what sequence? All experiments involve the observation and/or measurement of a change in some characteristic.

5. At this point, it is usual to include a discussion of safety precautions and procedures.

6. You need to discuss the potential for random, systematic and gross error and the precautions you took to control, minimise or eliminate them.

7. Next, you should present the results of your experiment. At this stage, it is good practice to show all the information you have collected in tabular form. As much raw data as possible should be shown.

8. Your raw data can then be summarised or processed. This could be simple averaging or totalling. It might involve statistical analysis or pictorial representation like graphs and charts.

9. Now you can present a conclusion. This might show that the hypothesis is false or likely to be correct, or that the experiment has reached no reliable conclusions. Statistical analysis will often involve probabilities. Using this, you might conclude that the hypothesis has a 95% chance of being correct, for example.

10. There is no such thing as a final or definitive experiment. All good experimental reports should include recommendations for further work.

Experiments that disprove a starting hypothesis should not be regarded as failures. Most scientific progress has been based on this kind of result.

Overclaiming is a basic error, but an easy one to make. Be especially careful not to reach a conclusion that your experimental design, procedure and results cannot justify.

To save time and money, you will probably be asked to carry out experiments in groups of two or three. Clearly, a group will have to work with the same raw data, but the reports must be individual efforts.

Figure 1.3 Checklist for an experiment report

INVESTIGATION/EXPERIMENT REPORT CHECKLIST

Always include:
- Title, date, author(s)
- Theory and hypothesis
- Apparatus and equipment
- Procedures, method, observation and measurement
- Safety precautions
- Error evaluation
- Raw data presentation
- Data analysis
- Conclusions
- Recommendations for further work

Chapter 2
Chemistry

National unit specification.
These are the topics you will be studying for
this unit:

1 Introduction and the kinetic theory
2 Elements and atoms
3 Electron arrangement
4 The periodic table
5 Compounds and mixtures
6 Ionic bonding
7 Covalent bonding
8 Equations, reactions and solutions
9 Acids, alkalis and pH
10 Organic chemistry

Additionally, you will be asked to carry out a chemistry experiment. It will help to read or reread Chapter 1, Scientific Communication and Method, before you begin to plan your laboratory work.

1 Introduction and the kinetic theory

Chemistry is the study of the properties, structure and interactions of matter.

In many ways, the word 'matter' is inadequate – it means everything there is in whatever form throughout the universe. The rules of chemistry are universal. They apply in all situations and in all locations.

Chemistry is the central science – without a basic understanding of how matter or substances interact, no other branch of science makes sense.

Originally, it was thought that matter existed in two fundamentally different forms. Inorganic material came from non-living things like rocks, air and water; organic matter derived only from living systems. Until the early 19th century, chemists said there was a 'life-force' that was essential to create organic material.

In 1828, a German chemist, Friedrich Wöhler, made urea, a simple organic compound, from inorganic starting materials – thus totally disproving the life-force theories.

The term **organic** chemistry is still used, but nowadays it describes the special chemistry of carbon compounds. The carbon atom is exceptional because it can bond with itself to form a huge variety of chains and rings. Any substance with a backbone of carbon atoms is classed as organic.

Physical chemistry is the third main branch of the science – it deals with things like the effects of heat, light, pressure and electricity on chemical reactions.

There are many specialist areas and subdivisions of chemistry, and most of modern society is based on the chemical industry. For example:

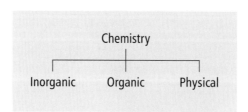

Food and drink
Brewing and distilling
Cosmetics and personal care
Pharmacy and medicine
Paints, dyes and colours
Fabrics, fibres and textiles
Packaging

Nuclear energy
The military
Law enforcement – forensic
Farming and fishing
Veterinary chemistry
Mining
Building materials

Polymers and plastics   Ceramics
Water supply   Automobiles
Coal, oil and gas   Aerospace

Chemistry groups, or classifies, substances into categories. We will go on to discuss, for example, the differences between elements, compounds and mixtures, but first we need to consider the most basic subdivision of all.

The three states of matter

Substances can be solids, liquids or gases. These are called the **three states of matter**.

The **kinetic theory** sounds complicated, but it is a very simple idea. 'Kinetic' means 'moving or having to do with movement'. The word 'cinema', for example, derives from the original description for moving pictures.

All substances are made of very small particles. These particles are constantly moving – this is the kinetic theory.

As you heat a substance, the particles move more rapidly – but not all the particles at a given temperature are moving at the same speed.

Water is a compound made by joining two hydrogen atoms to one oxygen atom – hence its formula, H_2O. When water is heated or cooled, it becomes steam or ice, but no chemical change occurs – it is still H_2O. What has altered is its state of matter – it has undergone a physical change.

At temperatures below $0\,°C$, water turns into a solid. Its molecules vibrate relatively slowly around fixed positions and a three-dimensional network or lattice is formed. Ice is a rigid structure that supports, for example, the weight of a skater. The lower the temperature, the more extensive the three-dimensional lattice becomes.

At temperatures above $0\,°C$, ice turns to liquid water. The molecules are now moving more rapidly and the three-dimensional network of water molecules breaks down. Liquids are random arrangements of particles. There are still forces that attract one molecule to another but these are weaker – so a liquid will flow. If you fill a jug with blocks of ice, there will be spaces between them, but think how astonished you would be if you poured water into a jug and it clung to the sides, leaving a hole in the middle.

Between $0\,°C$ and $100\,°C$, pure water remains liquid. However, the molecules move more and more rapidly as the temperature increases – they have more and more kinetic energy.

Your body temperature is about $37\,°C$. Water at, say, $70\,°C$ scalds because some of the kinetic energy carried by the water molecules is transferred to the molecules that make up your skin. These begin to move much more rapidly, chemical bonds are broken and we call the damaged tissue a burn.

At 100 °C, all the water molecules have enough kinetic energy to form a gas. In this third state of matter, the molecules move much more rapidly and the distances between the molecules increase dramatically. A kilogram of liquid water occupies a much smaller volume than a kilogram of steam.

The molecules of a gas are constantly colliding with each other and with any other object in their vicinity. Acting together, all these billions of collisions produce pressure. When you blow up a balloon, you are filling it with more and more molecules. These molecules collide increasingly often with the elastic skin of the balloon and with increasing force, so the balloon expands. At some stage, the balloon will burst – this will happen when the collision forces become strong enough to break the material of the balloon. You can burst a car tyre if you are careless with the air pump at a garage. Thick-walled metal vessels are needed to contain gases at very high pressure.

Evaporation versus boiling

If you fill a bucket with water and then lock it in your garden shed for 2 years, you will return to find an empty bucket. The water has not boiled, it will have evaporated. This happens because at any given temperature, some of the water molecules are always moving more rapidly than others. Some molecules will always have enough energy to escape the liquid surface to become water vapour.

Iron is a solid because the forces that hold iron atoms together in a very regular three-dimensional lattice are much stronger than the forces that hold water molecules together. A great deal of kinetic energy is needed to disrupt the iron lattice, therefore it only becomes liquid at 1,535 °C.

This argument in reverse explains why oxygen does not become a liquid until it is cooled to –183 °C. (See Table 2.1.)

Table 2.1 The melting and boiling points of iron, water and oxygen

	Melting point (°C)	Boiling point (°C)	State at 25 °C
Iron	1,535	2,750	solid
Water	0	100	liquid
Oxygen	–218	–183	gas

Remember, melting point is the temperature at which a solid changes to a liquid and boiling point is the temperature at which a liquid changes to a gas.

2 Elements and atoms

An **element** is a substance that cannot be broken down into simpler substances by chemical methods.

The smallest particle, or unit, of an element that can exist on its own – and take part in a chemical reaction – is an atom.

Our brains have evolved to cope with the universe as observed with the naked eye – a universe without microscopes, telescopes or other modern equipment. We all have trouble understanding numbers smaller or bigger than certain limits. This is a universal human characteristic because we were programmed thousands of years before the development of science. Probably the largest number we can all easily cope with is about a billion. In English, there is no common word for a bigger number.

Very large and very small numbers

A special system is used to describe very large and very small numbers – this is called **scientific notation**.

Table 2.2 Scientific notation

Number	Scientific notation
a thousand	10^3
a million	10^6
a billion	10^9
a thousandth	10^{-3}
a millionth	10^{-6}
a billionth	10^{-9}

So, a million, which we write as 1,000,000, is 10^6; and a millionth, written as $\dfrac{1}{1,000,000}$ is 10^{-6}.

Atoms are so small that it is almost impossible to understand how small they really are:

- The air in an empty milk bottle contains about 6×10^{21} oxygen atoms.

- An average wedding ring contains about 1.3×10^{22} gold atoms.

- A 10-stone person contains around 3×10^{27} atoms.

Until about 1900, it was thought that the atom was the ultimate unit of matter and that it could not be broken down into anything smaller or simpler. We now know that an atom is not the smallest thing there is, and there are many **subatomic particles**.

Under normal conditions, most atoms are very stable – they last for millions or billions of years and will not decay into subatomic particles. In the early part of the 20th century, experiments were devised to split the atom in the laboratory and three basic subatomic particles were discovered.

Three subatomic particles

The three basic particles have different properties (Table 2.3). This is the most important fact in chemistry.

Table 2.3 The three subatomic particles

Subatomic particle	Relative mass	Relative electrical charge
Proton	1	+1
Neutron	1	zero
Electron	$\dfrac{1}{1,840}$	−1

Atoms can be described as spheres with a small, extremely dense **nucleus** of **protons** and **neutrons**. **Electrons** orbit the nucleus, a bit like the planets around the Sun (Figure 2.1).

Nearly all the mass of an atom is concentrated in the nucleus, and the nucleus is a very small part of the total volume of the atom.

Figure 2.1 Model of an atom

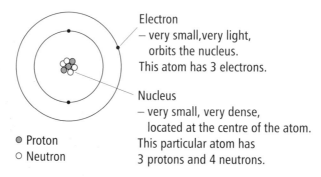

Electron
– very small, very light,
  orbits the nucleus.
This atom has 3 electrons.

Nucleus
– very small, very dense,
  located at the centre of the atom.
This particular atom has
3 protons and 4 neutrons.

● Proton
○ Neutron

Each element has a different kind of atom. These are different because each has a different combination of protons, neutrons and electrons. Two numbers are used to summarise the composition of any kind of atom: the atomic number and the mass number.

Atomic number and mass number

Atoms are electrically neutral – so the total number of protons, each with a positive charge, always equals the total number of electrons, each with a negative charge.

Each element has a different number of electrons; this is called the element's **atomic number**. The number of electrons determines the chemical properties of each element.

All elements except the lightest, hydrogen, also contain neutrons in the nucleus. There are no fixed rules that decide the number of neutrons, but generally, for the lighter elements, there are roughly equal numbers of protons and neutrons. Neutrons do not make any difference to the chemical properties of an atom, but they make atoms heavier.

The number of protons plus the number of neutrons in an atom is called its **mass number**.

Electrons are very light and their weight can be ignored in the calculation of mass numbers.

The first ten elements

Table 2.4 shows the numbers of protons, neutrons and electrons in atoms of the first ten elements.

Table 2.4   The first ten elements and their numbers of protons, neutrons and electrons

Element	Symbol	Protons	Electrons	Neutrons	Atomic number	Mass number
Hydrogen	H	1	1	none	1	1
Helium	He	2	2	2	2	4
Lithium	Li	3	3	4	3	7
Beryllium	Be	4	4	5	4	9
Boron	B	5	5	6	5	11
Carbon	C	6	6	6	6	12
Nitrogen	N	7	7	7	7	14
Oxygen	O	8	8	8	8	16
Fluorine	F	9	9	10	9	19
Neon	Ne	10	10	10	10	20

You will see from this that Figure 2.1 (page 42) shows one atom of the element lithium.

Adding or subtracting electrons completely changes chemical properties:

- Fluorine, atomic number 9, is a highly reactive poisonous gas. Neon, atomic number 10, is totally inert.

- Helium, atomic number 2, is a very light gas. Lithium, atomic number 3, is a silvery white metal.

- Carbon, atomic number 6, is usually a black solid. Nitrogen, atomic number 7, is a colourless gas.

Element symbols

Every element has its own symbol of one or two letters. The first or only letter is always upper case; the second is always lower case. Elements have different names in different languages, but all chemists throughout the world use the same symbols.

Some symbols are taken from Latin or other European languages and do not make immediate sense in English, as shown in Table 2.5.

Table 2.5   Elements and their symbols

Symbol	Atomic number	Name	Derivation
Be	4	Beryllium	
B	5	Boron	
Br	35	Bromine	
Ba	56	Barium	
Bi	83	Bismuth	
Na	11	Sodium	*Natrium*
K	19	Potassium	*Kalium*
Ag	47	Silver	*Argentium*
Sn	50	Tin	*Stannum*
Au	79	Gold	*Aurum*
Hg	80	Mercury	*Hydroargentium*
Pb	82	Lead	*Plumbom*

There are about 92 naturally occurring elements. Some of the heaviest are unstable, and their decay is called radioactivity. Uranium, atomic number 92, is the heaviest natural element. About a dozen elements heavier than uranium have been made artificially in very small quantities. All are unstable and highly radioactive.

Isotopes

Not all the atoms of each element are quite the same. **Isotopes** are different forms of the same element; they have the same number of protons but different numbers of neutrons. Isotopes have the same atomic number but different mass numbers.

All isotopes have identical chemical properties because they have the same number of electrons. Usually, one isotope is far more common than the others.

Heavier elements have more isotopes than lighter ones. Table 2.6 shows the isotopes of carbon.

Table 2.6 The isotopes of carbon

Isotope	Symbol	Protons	Electrons	Neutrons	Atomic number	Mass number
Carbon-12	C	6	6	6	6	12
Carbon-13	C	6	6	7	6	13
Carbon-14	C	6	6	8	6	14

Most carbon atoms are carbon-12. Carbon-13 and carbon-14 are less stable than carbon-12.

It is very difficult to separate one isotope from another. The hardest stage in making nuclear weapons is the separation of the various isotopes of uranium. Most uranium is the isotope with a mass number of 238; the nuclear industry uses uranium-235.

Abundance

Some elements are very much more abundant than others.

The universe is 78% hydrogen and 18% helium, the two simplest elements. All the other elements combined make up only 4% of all matter. Nine elements make up about 99% of the Earth's crust (Table 2.7).

Table 2.7 The elements making up the Earth's crust

Symbol	Element	Earth's crust (% by weight)
O	Oxygen	45
Si	Silicon	27
Al	Aluminium	8
Fe	Iron	6
Ca	Calcium	5
Mg	Magnesium	3
Na	Sodium	2
K	Potassium	2
H	Hydrogen	1
	All the others	1
	Total	100

Living organisms are mostly made of oxygen, carbon, nitrogen and hydrogen. Other elements like phosphorus, calcium, iron, sodium and potassium are present in very small quantities. Table 2.8 gives some examples.

Table 2.8   Some of the elements that make up living organisms

Element	Symbol	% mass in humans	% mass in cabbages	% mass in bacteria
Oxygen	O	63	77	74
Carbon	C	19	11	12
Hydrogen	H	9	9	10
Nitrogen	N	5	1	3
Calcium	Ca	1.5	–	–
Phosphorus	P	0.5	1	0.5
Everything else		2	1	0.5
Total		100	100	100

3 Electron arrangement

Electron arrangement is sometimes called electron configuration.

In all atoms, electrons orbit the nucleus – but they do this in a very precise way. The arrangement of electrons, or their configuration, is never haphazard.

You can imagine an atom as a series of spheres contained one inside the other, like the layers of an onion. At the centre of the atom is the nucleus, a very small, very dense ball containing all the protons and all the neutrons.

The nucleus is surrounded by a number of shells. The bigger the atom, the more shells it has. Electrons have to occupy one or more of these shells – they cannot exist in the spaces between the shells.

Larger atoms have many shells. We only need to look at the first four. The first shell, the one nearest to the nucleus, can only hold one or two electrons; the second and third shells can hold up to eight electrons; and the fourth shell can hold up to 18 electrons (see Figure 2.2).

Figure 2.2 shows an atom where the first four shells are full, therefore it has a total of 2 + 8 + 8 + 18 or 36 electrons.

Figure 2.2   Maximum capacity of electron shells

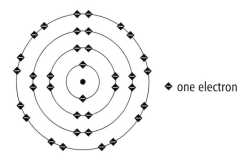

♦ one electron

The second rule of electron arrangement says that the inner shells must be full before electrons can begin to fill the next shell. Figure 2.3 shows the electron arrangement of the first three elements:

Figure 2.3   Electron arrangements of the first three elements

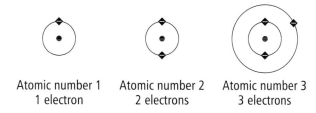

| Atomic number 1 | Atomic number 2 | Atomic number 3 |
| 1 electron | 2 electrons | 3 electrons |

Electron arrangement – the first 20 elements

We can extend this idea to show the electron arrangement of the first 20 elements (Table 2.9).

Table 2.9 Electron arrangement of the first 20 elements

Element	Symbol	First shell	Second shell	Third shell	Fourth shell	Atomic number = total number of electrons
Hydrogen	H	1	–	–	–	1
Helium	He	2	–	–	–	2
Lithium	Li	2	1	–	–	3
Beryllium	Be	2	2	–	–	4
Boron	B	2	3	–	–	5
Carbon	C	2	4	–	–	6
Nitrogen	N	2	5	–	–	7
Oxygen	O	2	6	–	–	8
Fluorine	F	2	7	–	–	9
Neon	Ne	2	8	–	–	10
Sodium	Na	2	8	1	–	11
Magnesium	Mg	2	8	2	–	12
Aluminium	Al	2	8	3	–	13
Silicon	Si	2	8	4	–	14
Phosphorus	P	2	8	5	–	15
Sulphur	S	2	8	6	–	16
Chlorine	Cl	2	8	7	–	17
Argon	Ar	2	8	8	–	18
Potassium	K	2	8	8	1	19
Calcium	Ca	2	8	8	2	20

Lithium	Li	2, 1
Carbon	C	2, 4
Sodium	Na	2, 8, 1
Calcium	Ca	2, 8, 8, 2

Electron arrangements are usually abbreviated to a string of figures, separated by commas.

4 The periodic table

The periodic table is a special kind of chart or diagram that groups together elements with similar properties. The elements are arranged in increasing order of atomic number. The periodic table of the naturally occurring elements starts with hydrogen, atomic number 1, and ends with uranium, atomic number 92.

The table is not a simple square or rectangle, but an unusually shaped grid of boxes. Each box represents a different element. The vertical columns are called **groups**. The horizontal rows are called **periods**.

Four pieces of information

Each box contains four pieces of information for each element, as shown in Figure 2.4:

- name
- symbol
- mass number
  or **atomic mass**
- atomic number

Figure 2.4   Information given for each element in the periodic table

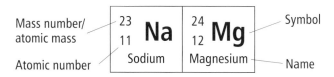

Sometimes the **atomic mass** is shown at the bottom of the box and atomic number at the top – there is no standardised layout.

Mass number and atomic mass

Looking at a full version of the periodic table, you might notice that the mass numbers for some elements are not whole numbers – how can this be?

Most elements occur as a mix of isotopes, but often one is much more abundant than all the rest. In these cases, the periodic table shows the mass number of the commonest isotope – for example, 12 for carbon, 14 for nitrogen and 16 for oxygen.

Sometimes there are two or three isotopes, each with quite high abundance. The best example is chlorine, symbol Cl.

About three-quarters of all chlorine atoms are Cl-35 and the other quarter are the heavier isotope Cl-37 (Table 2.10).

Table 2.10   The isotopes of chlorine

Isotope	Symbol	Protons	Electrons	Neutrons	Atomic number	Mass number
Chlorine-35	Cl	17	17	18	17	35
Chlorine-37	Cl	17	17	20	17	37

In these instances, the number given on the periodic table is the average of the common isotopes.

	Isotope	Abundance (%)
	Cl-35	75%
	Cl-37	25%
		100%
Average calculation		
	0.75×35	26.25
	0.25×37	9.25
		35.50

A detailed periodic table shows 35.5 in the chlorine box. This is the atomic mass for chlorine.

Periods and groups – rows and columns

Figure 2.5 is a simplified periodic table for the first 20 elements. The electron arrangement for each element is also shown in the boxes. You will see the direct connection between the layout of the periodic table and the electron arrangement of atoms.

Each period, or horizontal row, corresponds to an electron shell. As you move across the period the electron shell fills up.

Period 1 has two elements, hydrogen and helium. The first shell can hold two electrons.

Period 2 has eight elements, lithium to neon – the second shell can hold eight electrons.

Similarly, the third shell can hold eight electrons and period 3 has eight elements.

Each group, or vertical column, contains elements with the same number of electrons in the outer shell.

Group 1 elements have one outer shell electron. Group 2 elements have two electrons, and so on.

The elements on the extreme right of the periodic table all have full outer shells – this vertical column, group 8, is sometimes called group 0.

Figure 2.5   Simplified periodic table for the first 20 elements

Symbol
Name
Electron arrangement
Atomic no.

	Group 1	Group 2	Group 3	Group 4	Group 5	Group 6	Group 7	Group 0 (Group 8)
Period 1	H Hydrogen 1 Atomic no. 1							He Helium 2 Atomic no. 2
Period 2	Li Lithium 2,1 Atomic no. 3	Be Beryllium 2,2 Atomic no. 4	B Boron 2,3 Atomic no. 5	C Carbon 2,4 Atomic no. 6	N Nitrogen 2,5 Atomic no. 7	O Oxygen 2,6 Atomic no. 8	F Fluorine 2,7 Atomic no. 9	Ne Neon 2,8 Atomic no. 10
Period 3	Na Sodium 2,8,1 Atomic no. 11	Mg Magnesium 2,8,2 Atomic no. 12	Al Aluminium 2,8,3 Atomic no. 13	Si Silicon 2,8,4 Atomic no. 14	P Phosphorus 2,8,5 Atomic no. 15	S Sulphur 2,8,6 Atomic no. 16	Cl Chlorine 2,8,7 Atomic no. 17	Ar Argon 2,8,8 Atomic no. 18
Period 4	K Potassium 2,8,8,1 Atomic no. 19	Ca Calcium 2,8,8,2 Atomic no. 20						

This simplified table does not show mass numbers.

Symbols to learn

The periodic table is a reference document, not a list of names, symbols and numbers that you have to learn by heart. A few professional chemists can recite the table from memory but this is a party trick, not a necessity.

You do not have to learn atomic numbers, mass numbers or the sequence of the table, but you ought to know the symbols for the first 20 elements (Table 2.11).

The full periodic table

Figure 2.6 (page 54) is a full detailed periodic table. It looks complicated but its layout is based on exactly the same rules as the simplified version.

Hydrogen has one proton, one electron and no neutrons. Its properties are unusual and atypical, so it is often shown as an isolated box rather than as the first element in Group 1 – at the top left-hand corner of the table.

Table 2.11   Some element symbols

Element symbols you must learn		Element symbols which it is advisable to learn	
Hydrogen	H	Chromium	Cr
Helium	He	Manganese	Mn
Lithium	Li	Iron	Fe
Beryllium	Be	Cobalt	Co
Boron	B	Nickel	Ni
Carbon	C	Copper	Cu
Nitrogen	N	Zinc	Zn
Oxygen	O	Arsenic	As
Fluorine	F	Bromine	Br
Neon	Ne	Silver	Ag
Sodium	Na	Tin	Sn
Magnesium	Mg	Iodine	I
Aluminium	Al	Platinum	Pt
Silicon	Si	Gold	Au
Phosphorus	P	Mercury	Hg
Sulphur	S	Lead	Pb
Chlorine	Cl	Uranium	U
Argon	Ar		
Potassium	K		
Calcium	Ca		

This table shows atomic numbers at the bottom of the box and mass numbers or atomic masses at the top of the box. For all elements, except hydrogen, the mass number is always bigger than the atomic number.

This table gives the mass number for all elements of the commonest isotopes except for chlorine, Cl, atomic number 17 and copper, Cu, atomic number 29. These two show atomic masses of 35.5 and 63.5 – the averages of the relatively abundant isotopes.

Period 4 has 18 elements from potassium through to krypton; so does period 5, from rubidium through to xenon (pronounced 'zenon'). This reflects the number of electrons that can be held in the fourth and fifth shells.

You will notice that element number 57, lanthanum, is followed immediately by element number 72, hafnium, in the main body of the table. The missing 14 elements – called the lanthanum series – are shown as a separate row at the bottom of the table. This pattern repeats after element 89, actinium. Another row of 14 elements – the actinium series – is also shown separately.

The two series are shown separately because the electron arrangement rules get more complicated as atoms get larger. In very general terms, the sixth and seventh shells hold a maximum of 18 plus 14, or 32 electrons.

Artificial elements

The heaviest naturally occurring element is uranium, atomic number 92. You will find it as the third member of the actinium series. Elements heavier than uranium can be made artificially in laboratories. These are often named after famous chemists and physicists. For example, artificial element number 99 is einsteinium. Artificial elements are only manufactured in tiny quantities, sometimes just a few atoms.

The newest artificial elements are given temporary names and temporary symbols.

Most elements are metals

Most of the elements are solids at room temperature and the majority of them are metals. The transition metals are placed together as a central block because their electron arrangements are broadly similar.

Only bromine and mercury are liquids at room temperature.

There are 11 gaseous elements – hydrogen, nitrogen, oxygen, fluorine, chlorine and the six elements from helium down to radon in group 8 (or group 0).

Figure 2.6   The periodic table

TRANSITION ELEMENTS

1	2											3	4	5	6	7	0
																	4 **He** Helium 2
7 **Li** Lithium 3	9 **Be** Beryllium 4											11 **B** Boron 5	12 **C** Carbon 6	14 **N** Nitrogen 7	16 **O** Oxygen 8	19 **F** Fluorine 9	20 **Ne** Neon 10
23 **Na** Sodium 11	24 **Mg** Magnesium 12											27 **Al** Aluminium 13	28 **Si** Silicon 14	31 **P** Phosphorus 15	32 **S** Sulphur 16	35.5 **Cl** Chlorine 17	40 **Ar** Argon 18
39 **K** Potassium 19	40 **Ca** Calcium 20	45 **Sc** Scandium 21	48 **Ti** Titanium 22	51 **V** Vanadium 23	52 **Cr** Chromium 24	55 **Mn** Manganese 25	56 **Fe** Iron 26	59 **Co** Cobalt 27	59 **Ni** Nickel 28	63.5 **Cu** Copper 29	65 **Zn** Zinc 30	70 **Ga** Gallium 31	73 **Ge** Germanium 32	75 **As** Arsenic 33	79 **Se** Selenium 34	80 **Br** Bromine 35	84 **Kr** Krypton 36
85 **Rb** Rubidium 37	88 **Sr** Strontium 38	89 **Y** Yttrium 39	91 **Zr** Zirconium 40	93 **Nb** Niobium 41	96 **Mo** Molybdenum 42	99 **Tc** Technetium 43	101 **Ru** Ruthenium 44	103 **Rh** Rhodium 45	106 **Pd** Palladium 46	108 **Ag** Silver 47	112 **Cd** Cadmium 48	115 **In** Indium 49	119 **Sn** Tin 50	122 **Sb** Antimony 51	128 **Te** Tellurium 52	127 **I** Iodine 53	131 **Xe** Xenon 54
133 **Cs** Caesium 55	137 **Ba** Barium 56	139 **La** Lanthanum 57 *	178 **Hf** Hafnium 72	181 **Ta** Tantalum 73	184 **W** Tungsten 74	186 **Re** Rhenium 75	190 **Os** Osmium 76	192 **Ir** Iridium 77	195 **Pt** Platinum 78	197 **Au** Gold 79	201 **Hg** Mercury 80	204 **Tl** Thallium 81	207 **Pb** Lead 82	209 **Bi** Bismuth 83	210 **Po** Polonium 84	210 **At** Astatine 85	222 **Rn** Radon 86
223 **Fr** Francium 87	226 **Ra** Radium 88	227 **Ac** Actinium 89 †															

1 **H** Hydrogen 1

Lanthanum series:

140 **Ce** Cerium 58	141 **Pr** Praseodymium 59	144 **Nd** Neodymium 60	147 **Pm** Promethium 61	150 **Sm** Samarium 62	152 **Eu** Europium 63	157 **Gd** Gadolinium 64	159 **Tb** Terbium 65	162 **Dy** Dysprosium 66	165 **Ho** Holmium 67	167 **Er** Erbium 68	169 **Tm** Thulium 69	173 **Yb** Ytterbium 70	175 **Lu** Lutetium 71
232 **Th** Thorium 90	231 **Pa** Protactimium 91	238 **U** Uranium 92	237 **Np** Neptunium 93	242 **Pu** Plutonium 94	243 **Am** Americium 95	247 **Cm** Curium 96	245 **Bk** Berkelium 97	251 **Cf** Californium 98	254 **Es** Einsteinium 99	253 **Fm** Fermium 100	256 **Md** Mendelevium 101	254 **No** Nobelium 102	257 **Lr** Lawrencium 103

*58-71 Lanthanum series

†90-103 Actinium series

5 Compounds and mixtures

Only a few elements occur naturally in uncombined states. Generally these are the least reactive metals and some gases. For example:

Precious metals		Gases	
Copper	Cu	Oxygen	O_2
Silver	Ag	Nitrogen	N_2
Gold	Au	Argon	Ar
Platinum	Pt		

Most elements readily react to form compounds. A **compound** is two or more elements joined together by chemical bonds.

The properties of a compound are completely different from the properties of its component elements. For instance, sodium is a silvery metal and chlorine is a green poisonous gas, but sodium chloride is a white crystalline solid – common salt.

It is difficult to separate a compound back into its elements – because chemical bonds have to be broken.

The number and type of elements in a compound is fixed – every compound can be represented by a chemical formula.

Compounds and molecules

The smallest unit of an element is an atom. The smallest unit of a compound is a molecule.

Some examples of compounds:

Compound	Formula
Water	H_2O
Sodium chloride	NaCl
Carbon dioxide	CO_2
Copper sulphate	$CuSO_4$
Ammonia	NH_3
Methane	CH_4

A compound need not involve two different elements:

Oxygen atom	O	An atom of an element
Oxygen gas	O_2	A molecule of a compound
Ozone gas	O_3	A molecule of a compound

Nearly all familiar materials are **mixtures** – including most foods, drinks, healthcare, cosmetic and household goods. All living things are exceedingly complicated mixtures. There are no chemical bonds between the components of a mixture.

The proportions of the components of a mixture can be infinitely varied. A mixture has an ingredient list; it does not have a chemical formula.

Mixtures are easily separated

A mixture can be easily separated into its component parts.

Simple physical processes can be used to separate most mixtures (Table 2.12).

Table 2.12 Separating mixtures

	Mixture	Separation method(s)	Components	
			Elements	Compounds
1	Water and sugar	Evaporation	–	Water, H_2O Sucrose, $C_{12}H_{22}O_{11}$
2	Salt and sand	Solution Filtration Evaporation	–	Salt, NaCl Sand, SiO_2
3	Powdered iron and sand	Magnetic separation	Iron, Fe	Sand, SiO_2

A mixture can include any combination of elements and compounds. Unpolluted air, for example, has seven main components (Table 2.13).

Table 2.13 Composition of air

	Component		% by volume
Element	Nitrogen	N_2	78.08
Element	Oxygen	O_2	20.94
Element	Argon	Ar	0.93
Compound	Carbon dioxide	CO_2	0.03
Compound	Water vapour	H_2O	variable
Element	Krypton	Kr	trace
Element	Xenon	Xe	trace

Carbon dioxide content varies according to location, as does the water content of clean air. Natural volcanic activity can add sulphur dioxide, SO_2. Herbivorous animals produce methane, CH_4.

Writing chemical formulae

The rules for writing the formulae of compounds are straightforward and logical. The system uses element symbols, subscript numbers and sometimes brackets. The subscript number 1 is left out if a compound contains just one atom of a particular element – for example, H_2O, not H_2O_1, is the formula for water. Table 2.14 shows how it works.

Table 2.14 Formulae of some chemical compounds

Compound	Formula	Total number of atoms in one molecule of the compound
Water	H_2O	3
Hydrogen peroxide	H_2O_2	4
Sodium chloride	$NaCl$	2
Magnesium chloride	$MgCl_2$	3
Aluminium chloride	$AlCl_3$	4
Vanadium pentoxide	V_2O_5	7
Ammonium chloride	NH_4Cl	6
Ammonium sulphate	$(NH_4)_2SO_4$	15
Sodium hydroxide	$NaOH$	3
Calcium hydroxide	$Ca(OH)_2$	5
Octane	C_8H_{18}	26
Glucose	$C_6H_{12}O_6$	24

Some formulae include brackets. Calcium hydroxide could be written as CaO_2H_2, but the formula $Ca(OH)_2$ shows that one calcium atom is bonded to two OH groups.

For the same reasons, ammonium sulphate, $(NH_4)_2SO_4$, has a total of 15 atoms, not 10.

Be careful not to confuse atoms and compounds. A lower case letter in a formula is always part of an element symbol:

Co	=	one atom of cobalt
CO	=	one molecule of a compound called carbon monoxide

Compounds versus mixtures

It is important that you fully understand the differences between compounds and mixtures. A more detailed example may help.

Alcoholic drinks are basically mixtures of water and alcohol. Water and alcohol mix together in all proportions – a mixture might contain 99.99% water and 0.01% alcohol, or vice versa, or any other proportion. Different alcoholic drinks also contain small amounts of substances that give characteristic colours, flavours and aromas. This is why gin is different from dark rum, and cheap wine is different from more expensive bottles.

The weakest alcoholic drinks are roughly 2% alcohol and 98% water – typically, low alcohol beers and lagers. The strongest commercially available drinks are vodkas from Eastern Europe – some have alcohol contents approaching 40%.

Beers, stouts, lagers, ciders, wines, port, sherry, vermouth, liqueurs and spirits all have different alcohol contents. There are thousands of potentially different water/alcohol mixtures, even if we ignore the minor components that add taste, colour and smell.

Water is a compound with the formula H_2O. Alcohol is another compound, with the formula C_2H_6O, properly called ethanol. Figure 2.7 shows an alcoholic drink as a chemist would describe it.

Figure 2.7 An example of an alcoholic drink

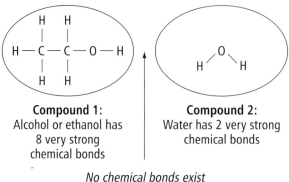

Compound 1:
Alcohol or ethanol has
8 very strong
chemical bonds

Compound 2:
Water has 2 very strong
chemical bonds

*No chemical bonds exist
between the two compounds
making up the mixture*

All water molecules have two hydrogen atoms and one oxygen atom. All ethanol molecules have two carbon atoms, six hydrogen atoms and one oxygen atom. These ratios are always the same.

Ethanol boils at 78°C and water boils at 100°C. Distillation can separate any water/alcohol mixture back into the pure compounds, although special methods are needed to make pure water from very concentrated solutions of alcohol.

Distillation is a physical process. It cannot break the eight chemical bonds in ethanol or the two chemical bonds in water.

The constituent carbon, hydrogen and oxygen atoms can be recovered from the water/alcohol mixture, but this involves a much more complicated series of chemical reactions.

In summary, a compound has a formula that never changes. A mixture has an ingredient list that is infinitely variable.

6 Ionic bonding

Compounds are two or more atoms joined together by chemical bonds. There are two main types – **ionic bonds** and **covalent bonds**. Here we discuss ionic bonding; covalent bonding is covered in the next topic.

Looking again at the periodic table (page 54), you will see that the nuclei and the inner shells of all the elements in group 1 are different, but all contain just one electron in an outer shell. For example:

Element	Symbol	Electron configuration	Atomic number
Lithium	Li	2, 1	3
Sodium	Na	2, 8, 1	11
Potassium	K	2, 8, 8, 1	19

The elements in group 1 are very similar. They are all low-density, silvery white metals. All react readily with water and many other elements.

Outer shell electrons

This introduces a very general idea in chemistry – that the properties of an element are largely determined by its outer shell electron configuration. The nucleus and the full inner shells make little difference to how an element reacts and what it will react with.

This pattern repeats across the periodic table. In group 7, for example, fluorine, chlorine, bromine and iodine have many properties in common because each has seven electrons in an outer shell.

The final group in the periodic table, group 8 or group 0, collects together some unusual elements. They all have full outer shells. Neon, for example, has the electron configuration 2, 8 and argon is 2, 8, 8.

These elements, called the inert gases or the **noble gases**, are exceedingly stable and do not usually react to form compounds. This stable, full outer shell configuration is the key to understanding chemical bonding.

Cations

The sodium atom, or any other atom in group 1, can achieve a stable state by losing or getting rid of one electron. When this happens, the sodium atom is no longer electrically neutral. The sodium nucleus takes no part in the process, so it still contains 11 protons and has a total electrical charge of $+11$. The 10 remaining electrons have a total charge of -10, and so the new particle has an overall charge of $+1$.

Charged particles are called **ions**. The sodium ion is written with a single positive sign, $^+$. Particles with one or more positive charges are **cations** (pronounced 'cat-eye-ons').

Tables 2.15 to 2.17 give details of sodium, magnesium and aluminium atoms and ions.

Table 2.15 Properties of a neutral sodium atom and a sodium ion

	Number of protons	Electron configuration			
		1st	2nd	3rd	Total
Neutral sodium atom, Na	11	2	8	1	11
Sodium ion, Na$^+$	11	2	8	zero	10

The magnesium atom has an atomic number of 12 and therefore an electron configuration of 2, 8, 2. Magnesium can also achieve the stable full shell structure but only if it loses two electrons rather than one, as shown in Table 2.16.

Table 2.16 Properties of a neutral magnesium atom and a magnesium ion

	Number of protons	Electron configuration			
		1st	2nd	3rd	Total
Neutral magnesium atom, Mg	12	2	8	2	12
Magnesium ion, Mg^{2+}	12	2	8	zero	10

This time, the magnesium ion is written as Mg^{2+} to show it has two positive charges.

Elements in group 3 can also form positive ions – the rules are the same as before. An example is aluminium, as shown in Table 2.17.

Table 2.17 Properties of a neutral aluminium atom and an aluminium ion

	Number of protons	Electron configuration			
		1st	2nd	3rd	Total
Neutral aluminium atom, Al	13	2	8	3	13
Aluminium ion, Al^{3+}	13	2	8	zero	10

The symbol Al^{3+} shows that the aluminium ion has three positive charges.

Removing electrons becomes progressively more difficult and the elements in group 4 very rarely form ions with four positive charges.

Anions

Shifting to the right-hand side of the periodic table, you can see that elements in group 7 can make a full outer shell if they accept one electron – 'filling the gap' – and elements in group 6 can achieve a stable state if they gain two electrons – 'filling two gaps'. Table 2.18 shows how chlorine and oxygen form ions:

Table 2.18 How chlorine and oxygen form ions

| | Nucleus | Electron configuration | | | |
		1st	2nd	3rd	Total
Neutral chlorine atom, Cl	17	2	8	7	17
Chlorine ion, Cl⁻	17	2	8	8	18
Neutral oxygen atom, O	8	2	6		8
Oxygen ion, O²⁻	8	2	8		10

Negatively charged ions are called **anions** (pronounced 'an-eye-ons').

Figure 2.8 summarises the formation of cations and anions.

Figure 2.8 The formation of cations and anions

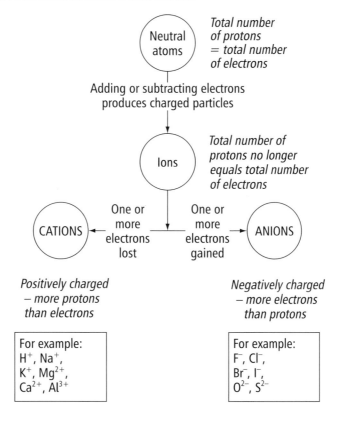

Swapping electrons

Sodium chloride, NaCl, is a compound made by the ionic bonding of one sodium atom and one chlorine atom. When the two atoms approach, under the right conditions, one electron moves from the outer sodium shell to occupy the single gap in the chlorine outer shell. The two atoms then bond in the same way as the north and south poles of a magnet snap together when the gap between them is sufficiently small.

Ionic bonding always involves the movement or swapping of electrons and the formation of ions – charged particles.

Figure 2.9 fully explains ionic bonding just by showing the outer electron shells because the inner shells and the nucleus do not change in any way.

Figure 2.9 Ionic bonding

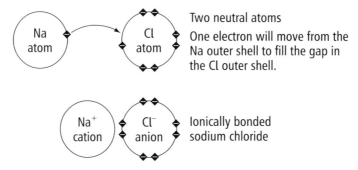

A neutral sodium atom has 11 electrons and a neutral chlorine atom has 17 electrons – a total of 28. Sodium chloride also has 28 electrons in all, but they are arranged differently, one electron having moved from the outer shell of Na to fill the gap in the outer shell of Cl. Ionic compounds are electrically neutral – the total positive charge on the cation must balance the total negative charge on the anion.

Compounds have completely different properties from their constituent elements. This is because chemistry is determined by **outer shell electron arrangement**. All chemical bonding produces new electron arrangements.

The simplest **ionic compounds** are those where a group 1 cation bonds with a group 7 anion. For example:

NaF	sodium fluoride	KF	potassium fluoride
NaCl	sodium chloride	KCl	potassium chloride
NaBr	sodium bromide	KBr	potassium bromide
NaI	sodium iodide	KI	potassium iodide

Some more ionic compounds

Just by looking at the periodic table, it should be clear that magnesium chloride is $MgCl_2$ – an ionic compound with three ions – and that aluminium chloride is $AlCl_3$ – an ionic compound with four ions (Figures 2.10 and 2.11).

Figure 2.10   Magnesium chloride – an ionic compound with three ions

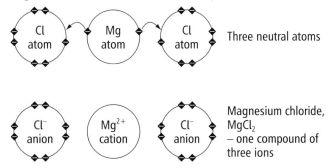

Figure 2.11   Aluminium chloride – an ionic compound with four ions

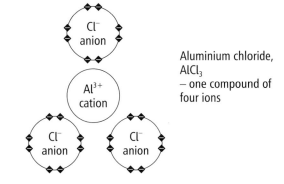

The formula for magnesium oxide is MgO – one magnesium atom wants to lose two electrons, one oxygen atom wants to accept two electrons (Figure 2.12).

Figure 2.12   Magnesium oxide – ionic bonding with two swapped electrons

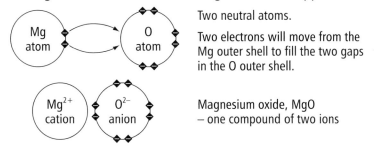

Strong ionic bonds

Most ionic compounds form giant three-dimensional lattices of alternating cations and anions. Ionic bonds are usually very strong and ionic compounds are often crystalline with very high melting points.

Some ionic compounds, like sodium chloride – common salt, dissolve in water. When this happens, the cations and anions separate and move freely through the solution. Solutions of ionic compounds conduct electricity because they contain charged particles.

7 Covalent bonding

Figure 2.13 shows a carbon atom. It is in group 4 of the periodic table, which tells us it has four outer shell electrons.

Figure 2.13   A carbon atom

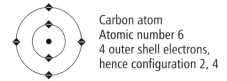

Carbon atom
Atomic number 6
4 outer shell electrons,
hence configuration 2, 4

To make an ion, carbon would have to gain four electrons to form the anion C^{4-}, or lose four electrons to give the cation C^{4+}. This process is not impossible, but it takes a great deal of energy.

Carbon and other elements in the middle of the periodic table make bonds by sharing electrons rather than by swapping them – this is **covalent bonding**.

The simplest covalent compound

The simplest covalently bonded compound is methane, CH_4. This is the main component of the natural gas we use for cooking and heating. In the UK, most of our natural gas is supplied from the oil fields of the North Sea.

Figure 2.14 shows carbon atom electrons as crosses and hydrogen atom electrons as dots. All electrons are identical – the dots and crosses are used just for clarity.

Figure 2.14   One methane molecule, CH_4

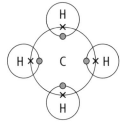

There is no need to show the nuclei or inner shells of the atoms because these take no part in covalent bonding – just like ionic bonding. Again, the outer shell electrons have been rearranged but in a different way.

Each covalent bond is a pair of shared electrons. These move into the space between the atoms, so that each nucleus is surrounded by a full shell.

In this example, carbon – when covalently bonded – has eight electrons and hydrogen has two electrons arranged around the nucleus. The positively charged nuclei are held together by a sandwich of negatively charged electrons (Figure 2.15).

Figure 2.15 Positively charged nuclei are held together by a sandwich of negatively charged electrons

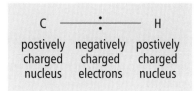

Nearly all of the compounds of carbon are covalently bonded. Carbon atoms can join together in very long chains and rings. Figures 2.16 and 2.17 show ethane and propane. These are constituents of lighter fuels and calor gas.

Figure 2.16 One ethane molecule, C_2H_6 **Figure 2.17** One propane molecule, C_3H_8

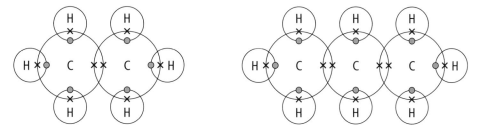

To save time, covalent compounds are usually written with a line standing for each single covalent bond – that is, for one pair of shared electrons, as in Figure 2.18.

Figure 2.18 Formulae for methane, ethane and propane

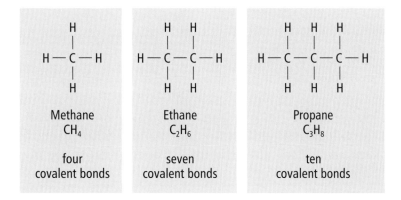

The formulae for methane, ethane and propane show that carbon always makes four covalent bonds and hydrogen always make one covalent bond. Nitrogen and oxygen also bond covalently.

Nitrogen and oxygen

Table 2.19 shows how easy it is to predict the number of covalent bonds needed to make a stable molecule.

Table 2.19 Number of bonds needed to make a stable molecule in four elements

Group	Element	Outer shell electrons	No. of covalent bonds needed for stability	Old outer shell plus shared electrons
1	Hydrogen	1	1	$1 + 1 = 2$
6	Oxygen	6	2	$6 + 2 = 8$
5	Nitrogen	5	3	$5 + 3 = 8$
4	Carbon	4	4	$4 + 4 = 8$

The formula for methane is CH_4, the formula for ammonia is NH_3 and the formula for water is H_2O. The dot and cross diagrams (Figures 2.19 and 2.20) show the covalent bonds that hold the ammonia and water molecules together.

Figure 2.19 Covalent bonds holding ammonia together

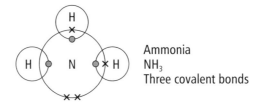

Ammonia
NH_3
Three covalent bonds

Figure 2.20 Covalent bonds holding water together

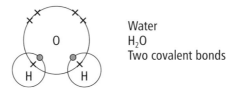

Water
H_2O
Two covalent bonds

The ammonia molecule has one pair of electrons not involved in making bonds and the water molecule has two pairs of non-bonding electrons. These are called lone pairs. They alter the three-dimensional shape of a molecule and usually make it more reactive.

Single molecules – not lattices

Most covalently bonded compounds exist as simple molecules, not as giant lattices like ionically bonded substances (Figure 2.21). Because covalent bonds are shared electrons, no ions are formed. There are strong bonds between the atoms of a covalently bonded compound, but not between the molecules themselves.

Figure 2.21   (a) Ionically bonded lattice. (b) Individual covalently bonded molecules

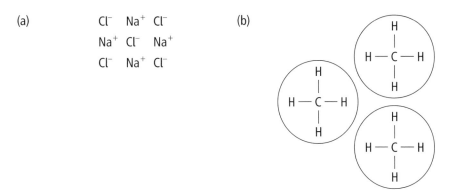

Most organic compounds are gases, liquids or waxy solids. They do not usually dissolve in water and they do not conduct electricity.

There are several exceptions to this general rule. A few covalently bonded substances form very regular lattices of covalent bonds. Diamond is the best example – this is a form of carbon where all the atoms are joined one to the other so that a single diamond is one giant structure. Diamonds are therefore very hard and very rigid.

Sand is mostly silicon dioxide, SiO_2. A grain of sand is a single giant covalently bonded molecule of alternating silicon and oxygen atoms.

8 Equations, reactions and solutions

The position of an element in the periodic table shows how many charges a cation or anion is likely to have.

Table 2.20   Cations and anions

	CATIONS					ANIONS	
	Group 1	Group 2	Group 3	Group 4	Group 5	Group 6	Group 7
No. of outer shell electrons	(1)	(2)	(3)	(4)	(5)	(6)	(7)
	H^+ Na^+ K^+	Mg^{2+} Ca^{2+}	Al^{3+}	*covalent* *compounds*		O^{2-} S^{2-}	F^- Cl^- Br^- I^-

Elements in groups 1, 2 and 3 are happy to lose one, two or three electrons to form cations with one, two or three positive electrical charges.

Elements in groups 6 and 7 are happy to gain one or two electrons to form anions with one or two negative electrical charges.

Elements in groups 4 and 5 can produce ions, but most of their compounds are covalent.

Elements in group 0 do not produce ions because they already have full outer shells of electrons.

Ionic compound formulae

If you know the charges on the ions you can predict the formulae of ionic compounds. For example:

Simple anions are named by adding '-ide' to the name of the atom.

HCl	$MgCl_2$	$AlCl_3$	Na_2O	Na_2S
$NaCl$	$CaCl_2$		MgO	CaS
KCl			Al_2O_3	

Some ions are made of groups of atoms that 'travel together'. These are **complex ions**. There are five important ones that you need to remember (see Table 2.21).

Table 2.21   The five important ions

Charge	Ion	Name
+1	NH_4^+	ammonium
−1	NO_3^-	nitrate
−1	OH^-	hydroxide
−2	SO_4^{2-}	sulphate
−2	CO_3^{2-}	carbonate

Formula	Name
NH_4Cl	Ammonium chloride
$(NH_4)_2SO_4$	Ammonium sulphate
$NaNO_3$	Sodium nitrate
$NaOH$	Sodium hydroxide
$CaCO_3$	Calcium carbonate
$Ca(OH)_2$	Calcium hydroxide
HCl	Hydrochloric acid
HNO_3	Nitric acid
H_2SO_4	Sulphuric acid

Again, if you remember the charges on the ions you can predict the formula of any ionic compound. Note the brackets in some formulae.

Chemical equations

Millions of different chemical reactions have been studied and every reaction can be summarised as a chemical equation. The rules are straightforward:

- The starting elements or compounds are shown on the left-hand side of the equation.

- The end products, which are what you have when the reaction is finished, are shown on the right-hand side of the equation.

- The equation has to balance – there must be the same number of atoms on each side of the equation.

In chemical reactions, old bonds are broken and new bonds are made. For example:

Calcium carbonate when strongly heated gives calcium oxide and carbon dioxide gas. This can be summarised as:

$$CaCO_3 = CaO + CO_2$$

Hydrochloric acid neutralises sodium hydroxide to form sodium chloride and water, again in summary:

$$HCl + NaOH = NaCl + H_2O$$

Sulphuric acid also neutralises sodium hydroxide, but the products are sodium sulphate and water. The equation for this reaction has to be balanced because two NaOH's are needed to react with one H_2SO_4:

$$H_2SO_4 + 2NaOH = Na_2SO_4 + 2H_2O$$

On heating, powdered iron and sulphur react together to give iron sulphide:

$$Fe + S = FeS$$

Relative atomic mass

Previously we have defined atomic mass as the weight of an atom. To be precise we should talk about relative atomic mass. The numbers in Table 2.22 actually describe how much heavier one atom is than another, not their absolute weights in grams, kilograms or whatever. For instance, two oxygen atoms would weigh the same as one sulphur atom.

Table 2.22   Relative atomic masses for some common elements

Element	Relative atomic mass
H	1
C	12
N	14
O	16
Na	23
Mg	24
Al	27
S	32
Cl	35.5
K	39
Ca	40

Formula mass

Just as elements have an atomic mass, compounds have a formula mass. This is simply the sum of all the atomic masses of the elements in the compound. Formula mass is often called molecular mass.

Formula mass calculations are just addition sums:

Formula	Calculation	Formula mass
H_2O	$(2 \times 1) + 16$	18
HCl	$1 + 35.5$	36.5
$CaCO_3$	$40 + 12 + (3 \times 16)$	100
Na_2SO_4	$(2 \times 23) + 32 + (4 \times 16)$	142
NaOH	$23 + 16 + 1$	40

Reacting quantities

Combining a balanced equation with formula masses, we can calculate reacting quantities. This is a fundamentally important idea in all laboratory work and throughout the chemical industry.

When magnesium carbonate is heated, it forms two new compounds – magnesium oxide and carbon dioxide. Knowing the atomic masses of magnesium, carbon and oxygen, we can work out formula masses and then reacting quantities.

Balanced equation	$MgCO_3$	=	MgO	+	CO_2
Formula mass calculation	$24 + 12 + (3 \times 16)$	=	$24 + 16$	+	$12 + (2 \times 16)$
Reacting quantities	84	=	40	+	44

Chemical reactions form new combinations of atoms. Nothing is added and nothing is taken away. Obviously, therefore, the total mass on the left-hand side of the equation must equal the total mass on the right-hand side of the equation.

This magnesium carbonate reaction will always take place in the same weight proportions, for example:

Mass of $MgCO_3$ heated	Mass of MgO produced	Mass of CO_2 produced
84 grams	40 grams	44 grams
84 tonnes	40 tonnes	44 tonnes
84 ounces	40 ounces	44 ounces

If you multiply or divide each term in an equation by the same number, the equation still balances. With this method, you can calculate reacting quantities for any starting mass of magnesium carbonate. For example:

Balanced equation	$MgCO_3$	=	MgO	+	CO_2
Reacting quantities	84 tonnes	=	40 tonnes	+	44 tonnes
Multiply throughout by 10	840 tonnes	=	400 tonnes	+	440 tonnes
Divide throughout by 4	21 tonnes	=	10 tonnes	+	11 tonnes
Divide throughout by 84	$\dfrac{84}{84}$	=	$\dfrac{40}{84}$	+	$\dfrac{44}{84}$
Equivalent to	1	=	0.476	+	0.524
Or	100%	=	47.6%	+	52.4%

Solution concentrations

Many compounds dissolve in water to form aqueous solutions – in this case water is the solvent. Different compounds have different solubilities. The solubility of most compounds increases as the temperature of the solvent increases.

Most drugs and medicines are administered as aqueous solutions – it is vitally important to know how strong or concentrated any particular solution is.

Concentrations are defined as a given mass of a substance dissolved in a fixed volume of a solvent. Any weight or volume measure could be used, like ounces per pint, but chemists and pharmacists use a standard system.

Solution concentrations are expressed in grams per litre – usually abbreviated to g/l. A litre is about 1¾ pints; an ounce is about 28 grams.

Concentrations are usually given as grams per litre, but there is a second system that you need to understand.

Moles

The **relative formula mass** of any compound expressed in grams is called one **mole** of that compound (Table 2.23).

Table 2.23 One mole of various compounds

Formula	Relative formula mass	One mole (g)
HCl	36.5	36.5
$CaCO_3$	100	100
Na_2SO_4	142	142
NaOH	40	40

One mole of a compound dissolved in one litre of water is called a 1M solution.

The concentration of any aqueous solution can be given as an M value. Take the example of hydrochloric acid. Pure HCl is a gas that dissolves easily in water to give hydrochloric acid. The more gas is dissolved into a given volume of water, the more concentrated the acid solution becomes. One mole of HCl; is 36.5 grams, and using this value we can work out the M value of any HCl solution (Table 2.24).

Table 2.24 Calculating M values of HCl

Weight of dissolved HCl gas (g)	Volume of water (l)	Concentration (g/l)	M value
36.5	1.0	36.5	1 M
36.5	2.0	18.25	0.5 M
3.65	1.0	3.65	0.1 M
0.365	1.0	0.365	0.01 M
73.0	1.0	73.0	2.0 M
100.0	1.0	100.0	2.74 M

9 Acids, alkalis and pH

Pure water is very largely a covalently bonded compound, but at room temperature, a few water molecules dissociate to give ions:

$$H_2O \quad = \quad H^+ \quad + \quad OH^-$$

water molecule   hydrogen ion   hydroxyl ion
(molecule)   (cation)   (anion)

We can show how this happens as a dot and cross diagram (Figure 2.22).

Figure 2.22 Dissociation

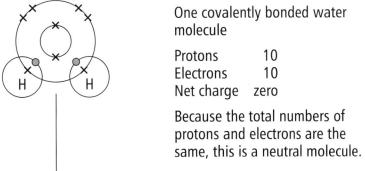

One covalently bonded water molecule

Protons   10
Electrons   10
Net charge zero

Because the total numbers of protons and electrons are the same, this is a neutral molecule.

Dissociation or ionisation.
One covalent bond breaks but both of
the electrons that had formed the bond
stay with the oxygen atom.

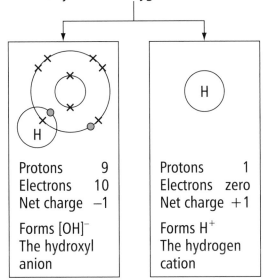

Protons   9
Electrons 10
Net charge −1

Forms [OH]⁻
The hydroxyl anion

Protons   1
Electrons zero
Net charge +1

Forms H⁺
The hydrogen cation

Hydrogen and hydroxyl ions

The **hydrogen ion** makes solutions acid. The **hydroxyl ion** makes solutions alkaline.

Pure water is neutral, not acid or alkaline, because the concentration of H^+ is the same as the concentration of OH^-.

An acid solution is one where the H^+ concentration is greater than the OH^- concentration.

An alkaline solution is one where the OH^- concentration is greater than the H^+ concentration.

There are three common strong acids. The equations show how they form ions:

Hydrochloric acid	HCl	$=$	H^+	$+$	Cl^-
Sulphuric acid	H_2SO_4	$=$	$2H^+$	$+$	SO_4^{2-}
Nitric acid	HNO_3	$=$	H^+	$+$	NO_3^-

These are strong acids – when added to water they dissociate completely to give the maximum possible concentration of H^+ ions. No molecules remain.

The more familiar acids like acetic acid, found in vinegar, and citric acid, found in lemons, are weak acids – this means that only a few of the acid molecules dissociate to give H^+ ions:

CH_3COOH	$\Leftrightarrow$	CH_3COO^-	$+$	H^+
(mostly molecules)		(a few ions)		(a few ions)
acetic acid		acetate anion		hydrogen cation

Some examples of alkalis are given below.

Sodium hydroxide fully ionises in water:

$NaOH$	$=$	Na^+	$+$	OH^-
sodium hydroxide		sodium		hydroxyl
(a strong alkali)		cation		anion

but ammonia only partly ionises in water:

NH_3	$+$	H_2O	$=$	NH_4^+	$+$	OH^-
ammonia		water		ammonium		hydroxyl
(a weak alkali)				cation		anion

The reaction of an acid with an alkali is neutralisation. For example:

$NaOH$	$+$	HCl	$=$	$NaCl$	$+$	H_2O
alkali		acid		a salt		water

The OH^- ions from any alkali react with the H^+ ions from any acid to give water.

The pH scale

A number called pH is used to measure the acidity or alkalinity of a solution. The p is always written lower case, the H always upper case; the pH scale goes from 0 to 14.

- A neutral solution has a pH of 7.0.

- Any solution with a pH less than 7 is acid.

- Any solution with a pH greater than 7 is alkaline.

- Very strong alkalis have a pH of 14.

- Very strong acids have a pH of 0.

The strength of earthquakes is measured using the Richter scale. In the UK, earthquakes measuring about 3 on the Richter scale are quite common, but they usually pass unnoticed and cause very little damage.

The most powerful and destructive earthquake recorded in recent times took place in Chile in 1960. It measured 9 on the Richter scale.

The Richter scale is logarithmic, not linear, which means that the 1960 Chilean earthquake was a million times more powerful than the typical British earthquake, not just three times more powerful. Each unit on the Richter scale represents a ten-fold increase (Table 2.25).

Table 2.25   The Richter scale

Richter scale	Relative destructive power
3	1
4	10
5	100
6	1,000
7	10,000
8	100,000
9	1,000,000

pH is a logarithmic scale

The pH scale is logarithmic in the same way as the Richter scale, but the lower the pH number the more acid the solution (Table 2.26).

The pH of any aqueous solution can be measured. All biological solutions like blood, sweat, tears and urine have a characteristic pH (Figure 2.23).

Table 2.26   The pH scale

pH scale	Relative acidity
7	1
6	10
5	100
4	1,000
3	10,000
2	100,000
1	1,000,000

Figure 2.23 The typical pH of some familiar solutions

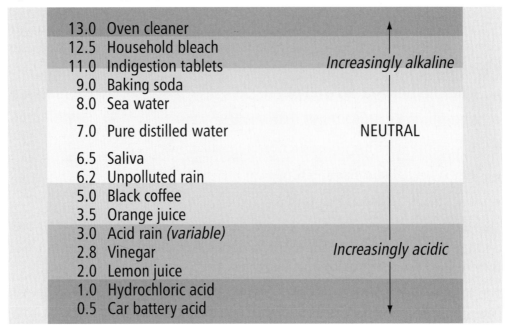

The blood pH in a normal adult varies between 7.35 and 7.45. Departures from this narrow range usually indicate some kind of disease or disorder.

Buffer solutions

A **buffer solution** is a mixture of compounds that maintains its pH despite accidental contamination by small amounts of acids or alkalis. Blood is a natural buffer solution.

As a very rough guide, solutions with a pH of between about 3 and 11 do not damage skin or other tissues. Many common foods, drinks, healthcare products, cosmetics and medicines are mildly acid or mildly alkaline. Many shampoos, for example, are formulated to give a pH of 5.5.

Measuring pH

The ability of a solution to conduct electricity varies with its pH. A pH meter is an electrical instrument designed to give a direct measure of acidity or alkalinity. More simply and cheaply, pH can be measured using pH **indicators**. Indicators are dyes that change colour at certain pH values (Figure 2.24). Indicators are usually sold as strips of paper coated with indicator dyes.

Universal indicator papers are coated with a mixture of six different indicator dyes. They give a range of colours and can be used to measure pH from 1 to about 11.

Figure 2.24 Various indicators

Universal indicator paper

pH	1	2	3	4	5	6	7	8	9	10	11
	←		acid			→	←		alkaline		→

Indicator											
Thymol blue	red	change			yellow			change		blue	
Methyl orange		red		change			yellow				
Methyl red		red			change		yellow				
Litmus		red				change			blue		
Bromo blue		yellow				change		blue			
PPT		colourless					change		pink		

Universal		red		orange	yellow	green	blue		violet		

Neutralisation

We can combine the ideas about pH and reacting quantities. Hydrochloric acid is a strong acid and sodium hydroxide is a strong alkali. Both dissolve easily and ionise completely in water:

$$HCl \xrightarrow{\text{water}} H^+ + Cl^-$$

no molecules   all ions in solution

$$NaOH \xrightarrow{\text{water}} Na^+ + OH^-$$

no molecules   all ions in solution

The reacting mass calculation shows that 36.5 g of HCl dissolved in water will exactly **neutralise** 40 g of NaOH dissolved in water.

$$HCl + NaOH \longrightarrow NaCl + H_2O$$
36.5 g + 40 g = 58.5 g + 18 g

very low   very high → resulting solution
pH   pH   pH 7.0

If 40 g of HCl in solution is added to 40 g of NaOH in solution, the resulting mixture will still be acidic, because 40 − 36.5 = 3.5 g of acid will still be left unneutralised.

$$HCl + NaOH \longrightarrow NaCl + H_2O + HCl$$
(36.5 + 3.5)   40 g   =   58.5 g   18 g   3.5 g
or 40 g

very low   very high →   resulting solution
pH   pH   mildly acidic

If 36.5 g of HCl in solution is added to, say, 44 g of NaOH in solution, the resulting solution will be alkaline – that is with a pH greater than 7.

10 Organic chemistry

In the 19th century, organic compounds were defined as those that could only be produced by plants and animals – wood, silk, sugar, urine, blood and milk, for example. We still use the terms 'organic' and 'organic compounds', but this now defines a special branch of chemistry – the study of carbon compounds.

Crude oil, and to a limited extent coal, are the main sources of the organic compounds we use in the chemical industry. All living things are exceedingly complicated assemblies of organic molecules, sometimes called **biological molecules**.

In total, about 10 million different compounds have been isolated and named. About 95% of these are organic. The very special properties of the carbon atom explain the huge number and variety of organic compounds.

Many atoms join together in pairs and triplets. Ozone is three atoms of oxygen, O_3, while hydrogen, oxygen, nitrogen and chlorine, for example, are diatomic gases in their normal states.

Carbon and silicon are the only elements that form long chains. Silicon can only do this if it alternates with oxygen atoms:

$$— Si — O — Si — O — Si — O —$$

Carbon – an exceptional element

Carbon is exceptional because it can join to itself to form chains and rings. In theory, there is no limit to the length or complexity of these structures. Carbon, in group 4, makes four covalent bonds. This also greatly increases the possible number of permutations and combinations.

Virtually all organic compounds are covalently bonded.

So far we have only looked at single covalent bonds. Carbon can also make double covalent bonds – two pairs of shared electrons – and occasionally triple covalent bonds – three pairs of shared electrons.

Hydrocarbons and homologous series

Organic compounds containing just hydrogen and carbon are called **hydrocarbons**. Crude oil is a variable hydrocarbon mixture. All the fuels we use for heating and transport are separated from crude oil by distillation, the critical stage in oil refining.

Carbon makes four bonds and hydrogen a single bond. Hydrocarbon structures can be thought of as an infinite number of jigsaws with an inexhaustible supply of two pieces (Figure 2.25).

Figure 2.25 A hydrocarbon structure

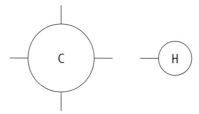

Previously we described methane as the simplest hydrocarbon. You can see from Figure 2.26 that this is just the first member of a similar family of hydrocarbons. These families of related compounds are called homologous series.

Figure 2.26 A family of hydrocarbons

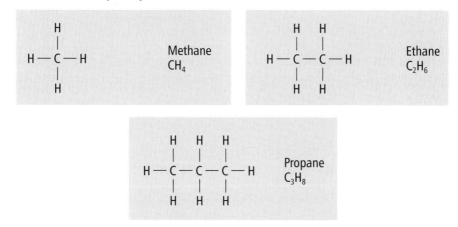

Isomers

The next member of the series is butane, a hydrocarbon with four carbon atoms. Figure 2.27 shows that there are two ways of linking four carbon atoms together, so there are two kinds of butane.

Figure 2.27 The two ways of linking four carbon atoms together

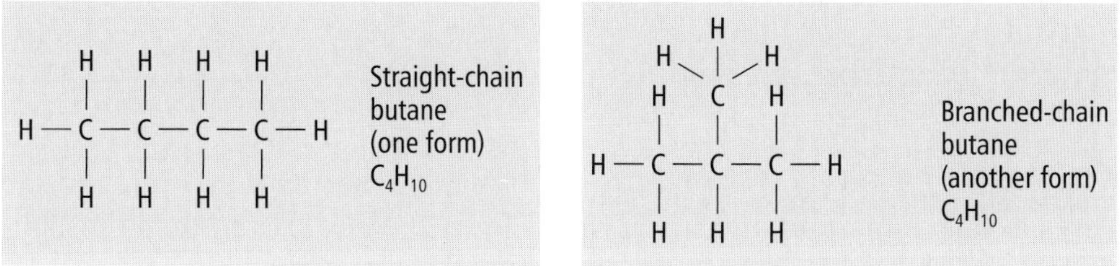

These are the two **isomers** of butane. Isomers are compounds with the same **molecular formula** but a different arrangement of atoms.

The more carbon atoms an organic molecule contains, the more isomers it has. The eighth member of this series is octane, the main component of petrol. Its formula is C_8H_{18}. It has 18 isomers.

Isomers have different chemical and physical properties.

Saturated and unsaturated

There are three different hydrocarbons with two carbon atoms, as shown in Figure 2.28.

Figure 2.28 Three different hydrocarbons with two carbon atoms

Ethane C_2H_6 (saturated)

Ethene C_2H_4 (unsaturated)

Ethyne C_2H_2 (unsaturated)

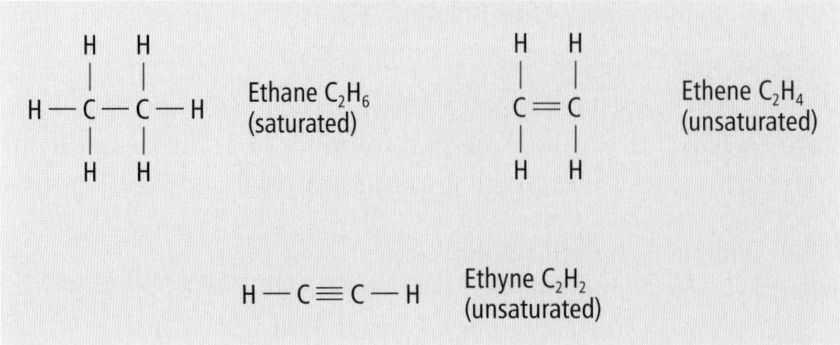

Many biological molecules have one or more carbon–carbon **double bonds**. These are described as **unsaturated**, because they are not saturated with hydrogen.

Very few biological molecules have carbon–carbon **triple bonds**.

Ring structures

As yet another source of variety, carbon atoms join together in rings. The most stable ring structures have five or six carbon atoms, as shown in Figure 2.29.

Figure 2.29 Ring structures with five or six carbon atoms

Cyclohexane
C_6H_{12}

Cyclopentane
C_5H_{10}

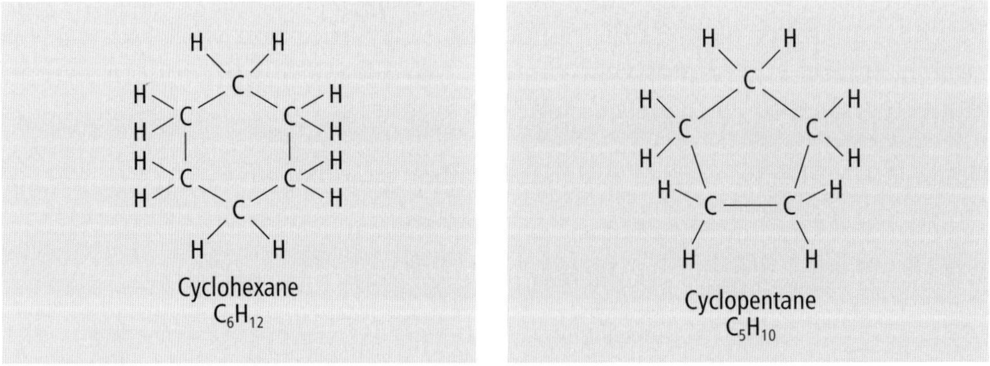

An especially important and stable ring is formed when six carbon atoms join together with alternating single and double bonds. This is benzene, C_6H_6 (Figure 2.30).

Figure 2.30   Six carbon atoms join together with alternating single and double bonds

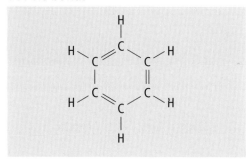

Figure 2.30 shows double and single bonds in fixed positions. In reality, the double and single bonds alternate so that pairs of electrons spread around the ring. This delocalised electron configuration is given a special symbol and is shown in Figure 2.31.

Figure 2.31   Delocalised electron configuration

Benzene, C_6H_6

All organic compounds contain carbon and hydrogen. Most also contain oxygen and many contain nitrogen.

More homologous series

Hydrocarbons can be seen as the parent molecules of many more families, or homologous series, of organic compounds (see Figure 2.32).

Figure 2.32   First two members of the alcohol homologous series

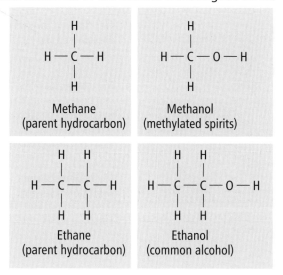

Methanol and ethanol are the first two members of the alcohol homologous series – all have an oxygen atom bonded to a hydrogen atom. This –OH is called a functional group.

Oxygen makes two covalent bonds and nitrogen makes three. It should now be clear why there are millions of different organic compounds.

There is an infinite number of ways of connecting together an inexhaustible supply of four components, as shown in Figure 2.33.

Figure 2.33 There is an infinite number of ways of connecting the four components

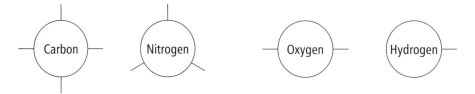

Describing and naming

Inorganic compounds are relatively simple and so are their names and formulae:

H_2O	water	$CuSO_4$	copper sulphate
H_2O_2	hydrogen peroxide	HNO_3	nitric acid

Because organic compounds can be much more complex, an orderly naming system has been developed and their formulae are usually written in shorthand.

Figure 2.34 takes alcohol as an example.

Figure 2.34 Different ways of showing the formulae of the organic compound alcohol

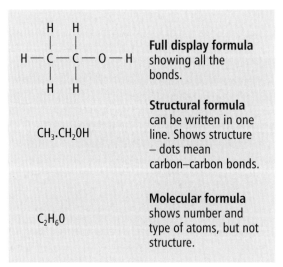

This compound is commonly called **alcohol** or ethyl alcohol. Its systematic name is ethanol.

Chapter 3
Biochemistry

National unit specification.
These are the topics you will be studying for
this unit:

1   Some more organic chemistry

2   Polymers

3   You are what you eat

4   Carbohydrates

5   Proteins

6   Enzymes

7   Lipids

8   Nucleic acids, DNA and RNA

As part of the assessment for this unit, you will also have to plan, conduct and report on a biochemistry experiment.

1 Some more organic chemistry

Biochemistry is the study of biological molecules and the chemical reactions that sustain life.

In this unit, we will be studying the structure and functions of the three most important groups of biological molecules – proteins, carbohydrates and lipids. All of these are complex organic compounds, but the rules that govern their shape, size and the way they are put together are straightforward and logical. First, we need to focus on a bit more organic chemistry.

What elements are we made of?

Carbohydrates contain carbon, hydrogen and oxygen only.

All lipids contain carbon, hydrogen and oxygen. An important subgroup of lipids also contains phosphorus.

All proteins contain carbon, hydrogen, oxygen and nitrogen. Some proteins also contain sulphur.

Virtually all the weight of humans and other living organisms is made up of four elements – carbon, hydrogen, oxygen and nitrogen. Small amounts of some other elements are also essential components of most living things:

Calcium

An adult human contains about 1.5 kg of calcium, mostly as bones and teeth. Calcium is also needed for blood clotting and for nerve and muscle function.

Iron

An adult contains around 4 g of iron, mostly in haemoglobin. A haemoglobin molecule has four iron atoms.

Sodium and potassium

Potassium and sodium ions regulate the water content of the body and are involved in the transmission of nerve impulses.

Iodine

An essential component of thyroxin, a hormone that controls the metabolic rate.

Magnesium

Magnesium ions are vital in the biochemical reactions that release energy to the body.

Trace elements

Very small quantities of a few other elements are essential to life. The most important are chromium, cobalt, copper, manganese, molybdenum, selenium and zinc.

Homologous series and functional groups

Because there are so many organic compounds, it is impossible to study each individually. They are grouped together into families with similar properties. These families are called **homologous series**.

The members of a homologous series have carbon skeletons of different lengths and shapes, but other groups of atoms are attached to the skeleton. Each homologous series has its own particular set of extra atoms – these are called functional groups.

We need to know some more about the most important homologous series and functional groups that occur in biological molecules.

Alcohols, diols and triols

A compound whose name ends in –ol always contains an OH group. Alcohols contain one OH group, **diols** contain two OH groups and **triols** contain three OH groups.

Like all organic compounds, alcohols, diols and triols have systematic names that describe the length of the carbon skeleton and the type of functional group, or groups, attached to the skeleton.

Lipids have structures based on propan-1,2,3-triol.

CH_3OH	methanol
$CH_3.CH_2OH$	ethanol
$CH_3.CH_2.CH_2OH$	propan-1-ol
$CH_3.CH.CH_3$ $\quad$ OH	propan-2-ol
$CH_3.CH.CH_2$ $\quad$ OH OH	propan-1,2-diol
$CH_2.CH.CH_2$ OH OH OH	propan-1,2,3-triol

Carboxylic acids

Some biological molecules include the **carboxylic** acid functional group.

The most familiar is acetic acid, found in vinegar.

The functional group in carboxylic acids is:

The hydroxyl group is the same as that in alcohols but there is also an oxygen atom double bonded to the carbon atom. The carboxylic acid functional group is usually written as –COOH.

The first members of the carboxylic acid homologous series are water-soluble. Solubility decreases as the carbon skeleton gets longer. Carboxylic acids with a total of 16 or 18 carbon atoms are widely found in animal fats and plant oils – these are the long chain fatty acids.

$H.COOH$	methanoic acid, also called formic acid
$CH_3.COOH$	ethanoic acid, also called acetic acid
$CH_3.CH_2.COOH$	propanoic acid (3 carbon atoms)
$CH_3(CH_2)_{14}COOH$	palmitic acid (16 carbon atoms)
$CH_3(CH_2)_{16}COOH$	stearic acid (18 carbon atoms)

The principal sources of palmitic and stearic acid are animal fats, especially beef and milk. For these two, the carbon chain has no double bonds and they are saturated fatty acids.

Oleic acid, principally derived from olive oil, has 18 carbon atoms, like stearic acid, but there is a double bond between carbon atom 9 and 10. This is a monounsaturated fatty acid.

Linoleic acid, made from sunflower oil, also has 18 carbon atoms, but there are two double bonds – one between carbon atoms 9 and 10, and another between carbon atoms 12 and 13. This is a polyunsaturated fatty acid.

Amines and amino groups

The ammonia molecule is one nitrogen atom joined to three hydrogen atoms, NH_3.

If one of the hydrogen atoms is replaced by a carbon chain, then the resulting organic compound is called an amine. The first three members of the amine homologous series are:

CH_3NH_2	methylamine
$CH_3.CH_2NH_2$	ethylamine
$CH_3.CH_2.CH_2NH_2$	propylamine

–NH_2 is the amino functional group. It can be argued that the amino acids are the most important group of biological molecules. Amino acids contain an amino group and a carboxylic acid group bonded to a central carbon atom. The general formula of an amino acid is:

The central carbon atom has to make four bonds, like all carbon atoms:

- Bond one – to a carboxylic acid group.

- Bond two – to an amino group.

- Bond three – to a hydrogen atom.

- Bond four – to a carbon chain or ring – group X.

There are 20 different naturally occurring amino acids. Each has a different group X. We will look at amino acids in more detail later.

All proteins are made by joining amino acids together in a precise sequence. Different proteins have different chain lengths and different sequences of amino acids. With 20 amino acids to choose from, it can be seen that there is a huge variety of possible proteins.

Five- and six-membered rings

Many biological molecules include five or six atoms joined together in a ring. There are five important ones that you should be able to recognise:

The cyclohexane ring is six carbon atoms joined together by single bonds, written as a hexagon symbol:

The cyclopentane ring is five carbon atoms joined together by single bonds, written as a pentagon symbol:

The benzene ring is six carbon atoms joined together by alternating double and single bonds, written as:

or

The pyranose ring is five carbon atoms and one oxygen atom, all joined by single bonds, usually written as:

The furanose ring is four carbon atoms and one oxygen atom, joined by single bonds, usually written as:

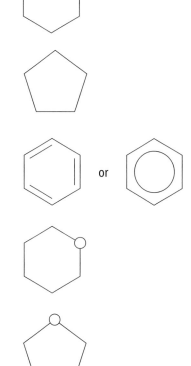

2 Polymers

A **polymer** is a big molecule made by joining together a number of smaller molecules.

The first manufactured polymer – polythene – was made by accident in 1933. Since then, hundreds of different commercial polymers have been manufactured and sold in huge tonnages. Many familiar objects are made from polymers – all plastics and all artificial fibres are **man-made polymers**. For example:

Polythene

PVC

Polypropylene

Polystyrene

Acrylic fibres

Perspex®

Polyurethane

Silicones

Polyester

Nylon

Lycra®

Synthetic rubber

Natural polymers are made inside the cells of living organisms. The human body is largely composed of proteins – all proteins are polymers. Enzymes that control the speed of chemical reactions in living organisms are polymers. The nucleic acids, DNA and RNA, are also polymers.

Most carbohydrates are polymers. These form the structure of plants and act as food stores for all plants and animals.

Natural polymers are more complicated than man-made ones, but the chemistry that determines their shape, size and function is identical.

Some polymer definitions

You will need to be familiar with some special terms used to describe all types of polymer – man-made and naturally occurring (Table 3.1).

Table 3.1   Terms used to describe polymers

Term	Explanation
Macromolecule	A big molecule. All polymers are macromolecules.
Monomer	The single small molecule or molecules that link together to give a polymer.
Homopolymer	A polymer where all the monomers are the same molecule.
Copolymer	A polymer built up from two or more different monomers.
Stereoregular polymer	Polymers with a defined orderly arrangement of monomers. All natural polymers are stereoregular.
Link or linkage	The bonds, atoms or groups of atoms that join one monomer to another in a polymer.
Degree of polymerisation	The number of monomers in a particular polymer.
Repeating unit or residue	The name given to the monomer once it is part of the polymer chain.

Addition polymers

There are two ways in which monomers can bond together to form a polymer chain – addition and condensation. Nearly all naturally occurring polymers are **condensation polymers**. Manufactured polymers can be formed by addition or condensation reactions.

There are several hundred different manufactured addition polymers. The two most important are polythene and PVC.

Addition polymers are made from monomers that have a carbon-carbon double bond.

Under high temperatures and pressures, and with the right catalyst, the double bonds open out to form a very long chain molecule with a backbone of carbon-carbon single bonds, as shown in Figure 3.1 (overleaf).

The naming of polymers can be confusing. Many monomers have an old name and a new one. Some polymers are patented and have tradenames like Lycra®, Tactel®, Acrilan® and Perspex®. Europeans and Americans often have different names for the same polymers.

Figure 3.1 Monomers and their resultant addition polymers

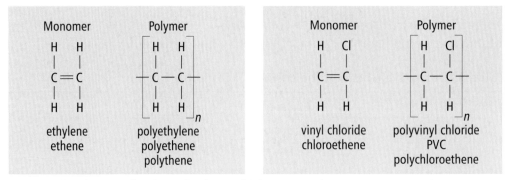

n = the degree of polymerisation, which can vary between 1,000 and 10,000

Most addition polymers are mixtures of molecules with different degrees of polymerisation – that is, of different chain lengths. The polymer chains themselves are irregular, often with branches of different lengths attached at random intervals along the main chain.

Condensation polymers

Condensation polymers are more complicated. Naturally occurring condensation polymers have exceedingly regular shapes, structures and compositions.

Most artificial fibres are manufactured condensation polymers – the best examples are polyester and nylon.

Two different monomers are used as raw materials to make polyesters – a dicarboxylic acid and a diol.

A dicarboxylic acid is any molecule that has a carboxylic acid group at each end:

$$HO - \overset{\overset{\textstyle O}{\|}}{C} - \boxed{X} - \overset{\overset{\textstyle O}{\|}}{C} - OH$$

A diol is a molecule with an hydroxyl group at each end:

$$HO - \boxed{Y} - OH$$

The polymer is formed when the hydroxyl group of one monomer reacts with the carboxylic acid group of the other monomer. This reaction releases a molecule of water (Figure 3.2).

Figure 3.2 Formation of a condensation polymer

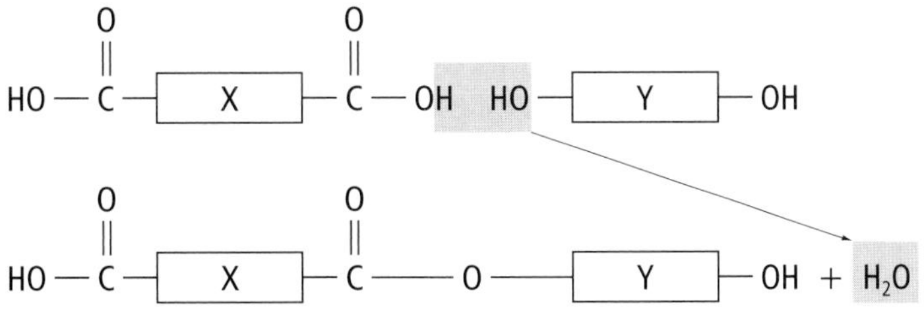

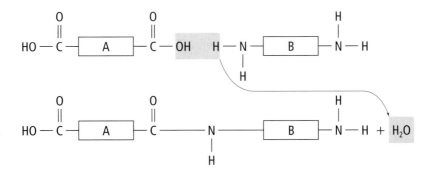

This process repeats and a long chain is formed with alternating monomer units.

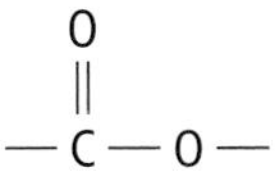

$$\overset{O}{\underset{||}{-C-O-}}$$ is called an ester link, hence polyester.

Again, two different monomers are used to make nylon – a dicarboxylic acid and a diamine:

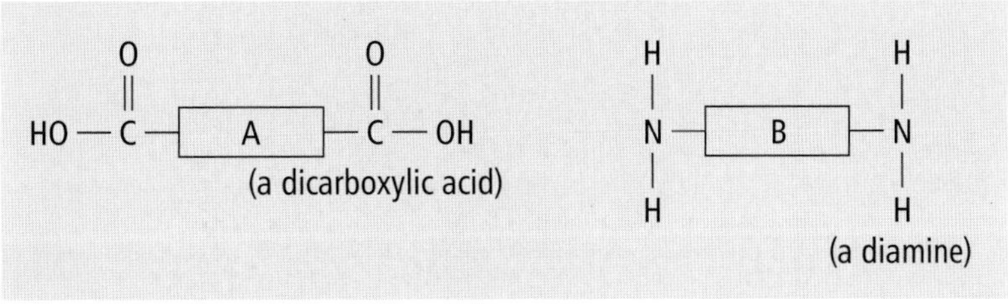

The polymer is formed when the carboxylic acid group of one monomer reacts with the amine group of the other monomer (Figure 3.3).

Figure 3.3 Formation of nylon

This process repeats, and a long chain is formed with alternating monomer units.

Amino acids

An amino acid has two functional groups – an amino group at one end of the molecule and a carboxylic acid group at the other end:

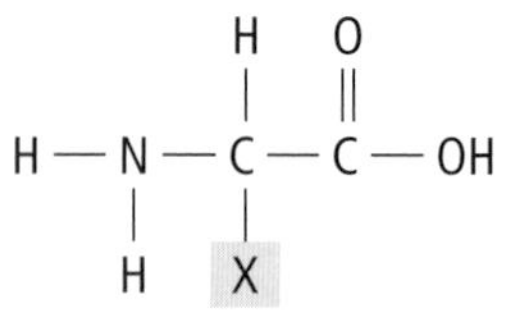

There are 20 different amino acids. Each has a different arrangement of atoms at position X.

Proteins are condensation polymers of amino acids. The carboxylic acid end of one amino acid bonds to the amine group end of another amino acid. The **polymer link** is identical to that found in nylon (Figure 3.4).

Figure 3.4 Formation of a protein

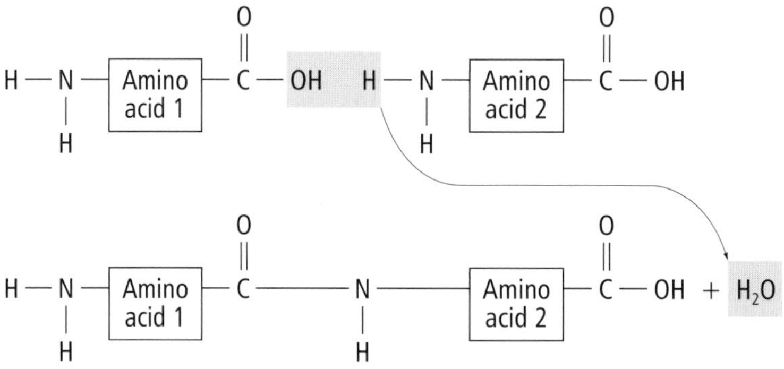

Once again, this process repeats and long chain condensation polymers can be formed.

Nylon, polyester and other manufactured condensation polymers are made from two different monomers and the resulting polymer chain can only have alternating monomer units. For example:

A — B — A — B — A — B — A — B — A — B — and so on.

Amino acids and proteins

When a living organism makes a protein, it has 20 different amino acids to choose from – that is, 20 different monomers. These monomers can be arranged in billions of different combinations and sequences. Each combination makes a different protein, with a different function.

The proteins that make up the human body are condensation polymers of between 50 and about 1,000 amino acids.

Haemoglobin is a good example of a complex protein. Its formula is

$$C_{2952} H_{4664} O_{832} N_{812} S_8 Fe_4$$

Its molecular weight is about 65,000.

It has four amino acid chains, two with 141 amino acids and two with 146 amino acids. That is 574 amino acids in all.

The four polymer chains are folded into a complex three-dimensional shape. Sulphur atoms form bridging links that hold the four chains together.

The four iron atoms sit at the centre of the molecule. These bond with oxygen molecules and transport oxygen around the body.

The peptide link

The polymer links in nylon and in proteins are chemically identical:

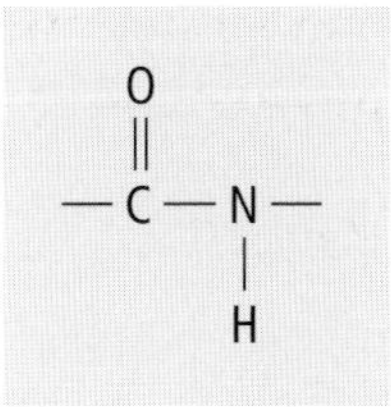

In manufactured polymers like nylon this group of atoms is called the amide link, but in proteins it is called the **peptide link**.

The word 'peptide' is used to describe amino acid polymers of different chain lengths:

Number of amino acids	Biochemical name
2	dipeptide
3	tripeptide
4 to 20	peptide
21 to 49	polypeptide
50 to 1,000	protein

3 You are what you eat

Table 3.2 shows the typical chemical composition of an adult:

Table 3.2   Chemical composition of an adult

	Human (% by mass)
Proteins	18
Lipids	18
Carbohydrates	1
Other molecules and ions	4
Biological molecules	41
Water	59
Total	100

In very general terms, the food we eat serves two purposes: it is used to build, maintain and repair the body's structures; and it provides fuel or energy for the life processes.

Again, in very general terms, proteins are ingested and broken down into their component amino acids. These amino acids are then reassembled to form the different kinds of proteins that make up the human body. Animals and plants use lipids and carbohydrates to store energy. When we eat them, we 'steal' their food stores.

Water

The main component of all living things is water. Most mammals are about 60% water and plants are typically between 80% and 95% water.

Water is vital to life because:

- It acts as an efficient solvent for smaller biological molecules and a transport medium to circulate these molecules around the body.

- It is a good insulator and prevents rapid temperature changes.

- It takes part in many vital biochemical reactions.

- Through **hydrogen bonding**, it determines the three-dimensional structure of many larger molecules – especially proteins.

Water is a covalently bonded molecule. This means there is a pair of shared electrons between the oxygen atom and each of the two hydrogen atoms.

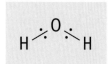

The electron pairs are more strongly attracted to oxygen than they are to hydrogen. They are therefore closer to the central oxygen atom than the two hydrogen atoms. We describe this as polarisation and water has two polarised covalent bonds.

Polarisation means that the oxygen atom has a small negative charge and the hydrogen atoms have a small positive charge.

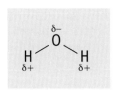

In liquid water, and in many molecules that contain an OH group, the slightly negative oxygen atom on one molecule is attracted to the slightly positive hydrogen atom on an adjacent molecule. This attraction is called hydrogen bonding.

Hydrogen bonds are weaker than ordinary covalent or ionic bonds but they are still strong enough to hold the different parts of a large biological molecule together in a stable three-dimensional shape.

In this unit, we will look at each of the major groups of biological molecules in turn. These are:

- carbohydrates
- proteins
- enzymes
- lipids
- nucleic acids

It helps briefly to outline the sources, structures and functions of these compounds before we turn to the detail.

Carbohydrates

Carbohydrates contain carbon, hydrogen and oxygen only. The hydrogen and oxygen atoms are always present in a 2:1 ratio – as in water, H_2O.

carbo = carbon; *hydrate* = water

Most carbohydrates have names ending in *–ose*. The commoner carbohydrates have traditional names as well as scientific ones. Table sugar is properly called *sucrose*, for example.

The most important carbohydrate is glucose. Its formula is $C_6H_{12}O_6$.

There are several isomers of glucose, but the most important has a single-ring structure.

Carbohydrates with a single ring or monomer, like glucose, are called **monosaccharides**.

Two monomers can join together to form a second group of carbohydrates called **disaccharides**.

Monosaccharides and disaccharides are freely soluble in water and are commonly called sugars.

Compounds with many saccharide units joined together by condensation polymerisation are called polysaccharides.

Starch and glycogen are polysaccharides. They are polymers with between 30 and several thousand saccharide units.

The ultimate carbohydrate is **cellulose**. This is a straight-chain polymer of about 6000 saccharide units. Cellulose is the structural material of plants. Wood and cotton are both mostly cellulose.

Some examples of carbohydrates:

Monosaccharides	glucose, fructose
Disaccharides	sucrose, maltose, lactose
Polysaccharides	starch, glycogen, cellulose

In all living organisms, carbohydrates are used to provide energy.

Polysaccharides act as food stores: starch in plants and glycogen in animals.

Proteins

Proteins are a highly variable group of biological molecules.

All proteins are condensation polymers of the 20 amino acids.

The function of a protein is largely determined by its three-dimensional shape.

Different sequences of amino acids produce different proteins.

Some proteins contain two or more different polymer chains held together by hydrogen bonds, or other bridging groups of atoms.

Polymer chains, called **polypeptide** chains in proteins, can be folded, pleated or coiled into complex shapes.

Proteins have many functions, for example:

- *Structural proteins* – cartilage, skin, hair, horns, hooves and feathers.
- *Contractile proteins* – muscles.
- *Enzymes* – all enzymes are proteins.
- *Transport proteins* – which carry vital compounds through the body, like haemoglobin.
- *Immunoproteins* – antibodies are proteins.

Enzymes

Catalysts increase the rate of a chemical reaction without being used up by the reaction. Most inorganic chemical reactions use catalysts, but they also usually need very high temperatures, very high pressures and extreme pH conditions.

Enzymes are biological catalysts. They allow biochemical reactions to take place at body temperature, atmospheric pressure and in **aqueous** solutions with pH values close to 7.0.

Enzymes are millions of times more efficient than most man-made catalysts.

There are many different enzymes. Each will only catalyse one biochemical reaction or group of reactions.

Enzyme-catalysed reactions are very 'clean' – no unwanted by-products are formed.

The function of an enzyme is determined by its three-dimensional shape.

An inhibitor is a compound that inactivates an enzyme.

All enzymes are proteins. Most enzymes have names ending in –*ase*.

Lipids

Fats, oils and waxes are known collectively as **lipids**.

Fats are mostly of animal origin and are solids at room temperature. **Oils** are mostly of vegetable origin and are liquids at room temperature.

All lipids are insoluble in water.

Lipids are the high-energy, long-term food stores for animals and plants.

Lipids are also the structural component of cell membranes, and they act as protective coatings and insulators in plants and animals.

Unlike proteins, enzymes and many carbohydrates, lipids are not polymers.

The most important lipids are triglycerides. These are compounds formed by the reaction between a triol and three long chain carboxylic acids.

DNA and RNA

DNA, deoxyribonucleic acid, carries all of a living organism's genetic information.

DNA has a double helix structure. Each of its two strands is a very complicated condensation polymer.

It is a self-replicating molecule – it can make exact copies of itself – and it passes genetic information from one generation to the next.

The sequence of monomer units in the DNA polymer is called the genetic code.

DNA contains all the information needed to synthesise proteins.

Energy values

Carbohydrates, lipids and proteins provide energy. In many societies, alcohol is also a significant energy source.

The energy content of foods is measured in kilocalories per gram or in kilojoules per gram. One calorie is 4.18 joules.

Lipids are the most concentrated energy source (Table 3.3).

Table 3.3   Energy sources

| | Energy content | |
	kJ/g	kcals/g
Lipids	37	8.9
Carbohydrates	17	4.1
Proteins	17	4.1
Alcohol	30	7.1

Most foods are mixtures of carbohydrates, lipid and proteins. Nearly all foods also contain water – which has no energy value.

Some foods contain indigestible polysaccharides, usually called fibre or **roughage**.

The most energy-rich foods are pure lipids like lard, beef dripping, olive oil and corn oil.

Some 'foods' have no energy content. The best examples are low-calorie soft drinks, where all the sugar is replaced with artificial sweeteners.

It follows that all foods have an energy content of between zero and 8.9 kilocalories per gram, or 890 kilocalories per 100 g.

4 Carbohydrates

In the leaves of green plants, carbon dioxide and water combine to form **glucose** – a monosaccharide. Water is absorbed through plant roots and carbon dioxide is taken in from the atmosphere. This process, known as **photosynthesis**, needs energy from sunlight and chlorophyll as a catalyst:

$$6CO_2 \quad + \quad 6H_2O \quad \xrightarrow[\text{sunlight}]{\text{chlorophyll}} \quad C_6H_{12}O_6 \quad + \quad 6O_2$$
$$\text{glucose}$$

Photosynthesis also releases oxygen into the atmosphere.

All life on Earth depends on photosynthesis – it is by far the most important of all chemical reactions.

The food chain

Thousands of glucose molecules are polymerised inside plants to form the very large molecules called cellulose. Cellulose makes up the structural framework of plant materials.

Glucose molecules are also combined in a different way to give smaller polymers called **starch**. Plants store starch in seeds, fruits, roots and tubers to act as a food store.

Herbivorous animals eat plants. The starch, and for some animals the cellulose as well, is broken down, back into its component glucose molecules.

Some of the glucose is used immediately by animals, but most is transported to the liver, where it is converted into another polysaccharide, glycogen. **Glycogen** is often described as animal starch.

Animals use glucose as a primary energy source. It is carried around the body in the bloodstream, where it is oxidised – eventually to give carbon dioxide and water. This process, called **respiration**, is precisely the reverse of photosynthesis:

$$C_6H_{12}O_6 \quad + \quad 6O_2 \quad \longrightarrow \quad 6CO_2 \quad + \quad 6H_2O$$
$$\text{glucose} \qquad\qquad \text{oxygen} \qquad\qquad \text{carbon}$$
$$\text{from air} \qquad\qquad \text{dioxide}$$
$$\text{exhaled}$$

Animals also convert glucose into lipids and amino acids by a series of biochemical reactions. In this way, herbivores make their essential lipids and proteins.

Directly and indirectly, carbohydrates – specifically the glucose molecule – are the ultimate source of most of our food.

The original source of virtually all the world's energy is the Sun. Photosynthesis traps light energy from the Sun and stores it in the chemical bonds of the glucose molecule. This energy is later released when the glucose molecule bonds are broken to give carbon dioxide and water, as shown in Figure 3.5.

Figure 3.5   Fundamental biochemical energy

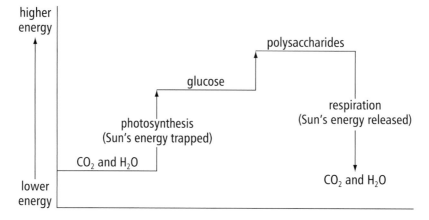

Monosaccharides

There are many different monosaccharides. The commonest and most important have five or six carbon atoms. Those with five carbon atoms are called pentoses, those with six carbon atoms are called hexoses.

pent = five, *hex* = six, *-ose* = carbohydrate

Glucose is a hexose. The molecular formula for glucose is $C_6H_{12}O_6$ and its **structural formulae** are shown in Figures 3.6 and 3.7.

Figure 3.6   Structural formula of glucose (straight-chain form)

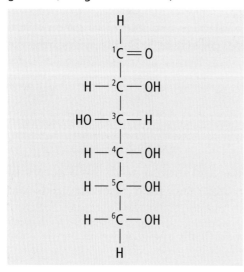

Because glucose has six carbon atoms, the straight-chain form can readily switch into a ring structure. Carbon atom number 1 joins to the oxygen atom on carbon atom number 5. Carbon atom 6 is left as a branch, not as part of the ring.

Figure 3.7   Structural formula of glucose (ring form)

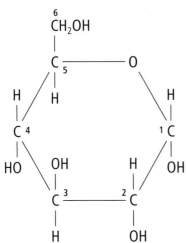

When monosaccharides form disaccharides and polysaccharides, the monosaccharide is always present as the ring form.

Disaccharides

Disaccharides are formed when two monosaccharides are joined together in a condensation reaction.

The polymer link is called a glycosidic link. It is simply an oxygen atom forming a bridge between the two halves of the disaccharide (Figure 3.8).

Figure 3.8   Formation of a glycosidic link

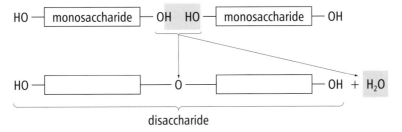

disaccharide

The diagrams show three common disaccharides:

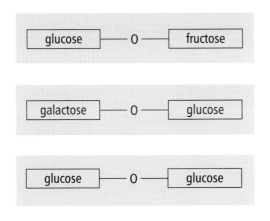

This disaccaride is sucrose – common table sugar, derived from cane or beet.

This disaccaride is **lactose** – found in the milk of mammals.

This disaccharide is maltose – found in barley and some other cereals.

Polysaccharides

The four most important polysaccharides all use the glucose molecule as their monomer. They are:

- amylose starch
- amylopectin starch
- glycogen – animal starch
- cellulose

For simplicity, diagrams of polysaccharides often use a simple hexagon to represent the glucose monomer; the oxygen atom in the glycosidic link is sometimes not shown.

Amylose is an unbranched chain of about 300 glucose units. The links are made between carbon atom 1 and carbon atom 4 of each glucose molecule:

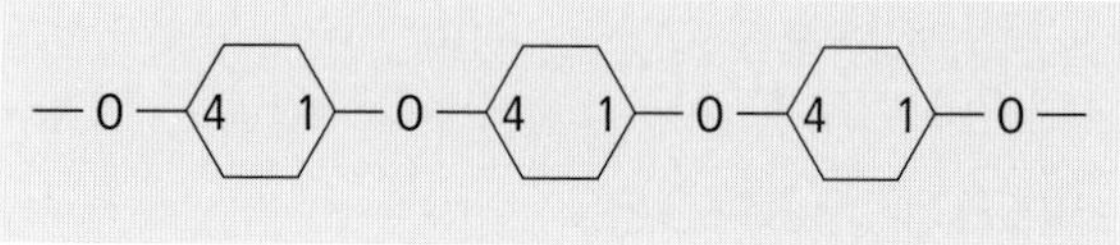

The orientation of the glucose rings around the polymer links produces a helical or spiral molecule. The spiral structure is stabilised by hydrogen bonds.

Amylopectin is a branched-chain polymer. The main chain has the same structure as amylose, but there are branches at intervals of about 30 glucose units on the main chain.

The main chain links are between carbon atom 1 and carbon atom 4. The branches are formed by links between carbon 1 and carbon 6.

Amylopectin is a very large molecule, typically with hundreds of thousands of glucose units:

Figure 3.9 Amylopectin

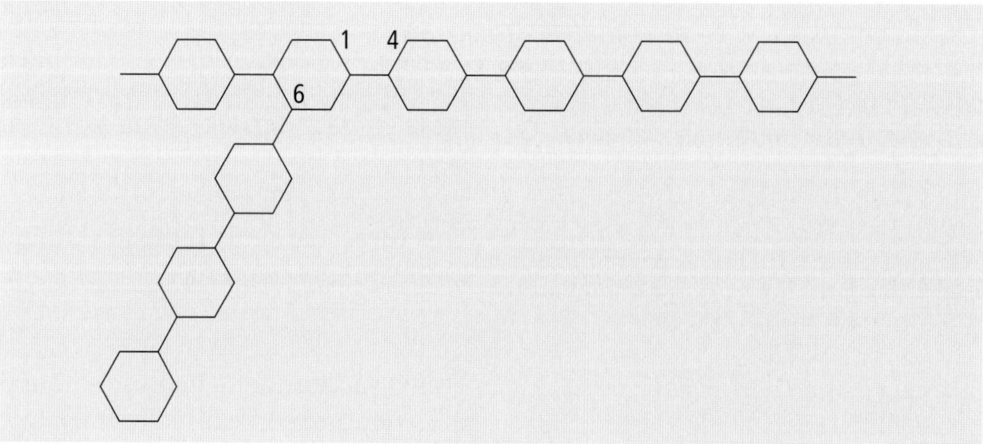

Starch is the glucose storage polymer used by all plants. Starch is stored as insoluble starch grains in tubers, roots, seeds and fruits. Plant starch is typically 30% amylose and 70% amylopectin.

The two polymers are compact and do not take up much space inside plant cells.

Starch is easily converted back to glucose by the appropriate enzymes when energy is required.

Glycogen is the animal equivalent of plant starch. Glycogen is stored in the liver and muscles of most animals.

Glycogen's structure is very similar to amylopectin, but the branches are shorter and occur at intervals of about 10 glucose units on the main chain. Glycogen, like amylopectin, is a very large compact molecule.

Cellulose

Plants have rigid cell walls that support and protect the contents of the cell. Cellulose fibres are the main components of the cell wall.

Cellulose is an unbranched polymer of many thousands of glucose units. Because the glucose involved in cellulose is a different isomer from the glucose involved in starch, the cellulose polymer is a straight chain, not a spiral.

Strands of the cellulose polymer are tightly crosslinked by hydrogen bonds to form bundles called microfibrils, which then bond together to form fibres. A typical plant cell wall has several criss-crossed layers of cellulose fibres.

Virtually all animals can digest monosaccharides, disaccharides and plant starches, because their bodies contain the right enzymes to break the glycosidic links found in these molecules.

The glycosidic links in cellulose are different and need a group of enzymes called **cellulases** to break this polymer down into glucose.

Many mammals do not produce cellulase and therefore cannot use grass or other sources of cellulose directly as food.

Ruminant animals like cows can, however, digest grass and other celluloses because in a part of their alimentary canal, called the rumen, there are billions of bacteria that produce cellulase enzymes.

The bacteria in the rumen turn the cellulose into glucose, which the animal can then use directly as food.

Cellulose is important in the human diet, not as a food source, but as roughage to provide bulk.

Figure 3.10 Simplified carbohydrate cycle

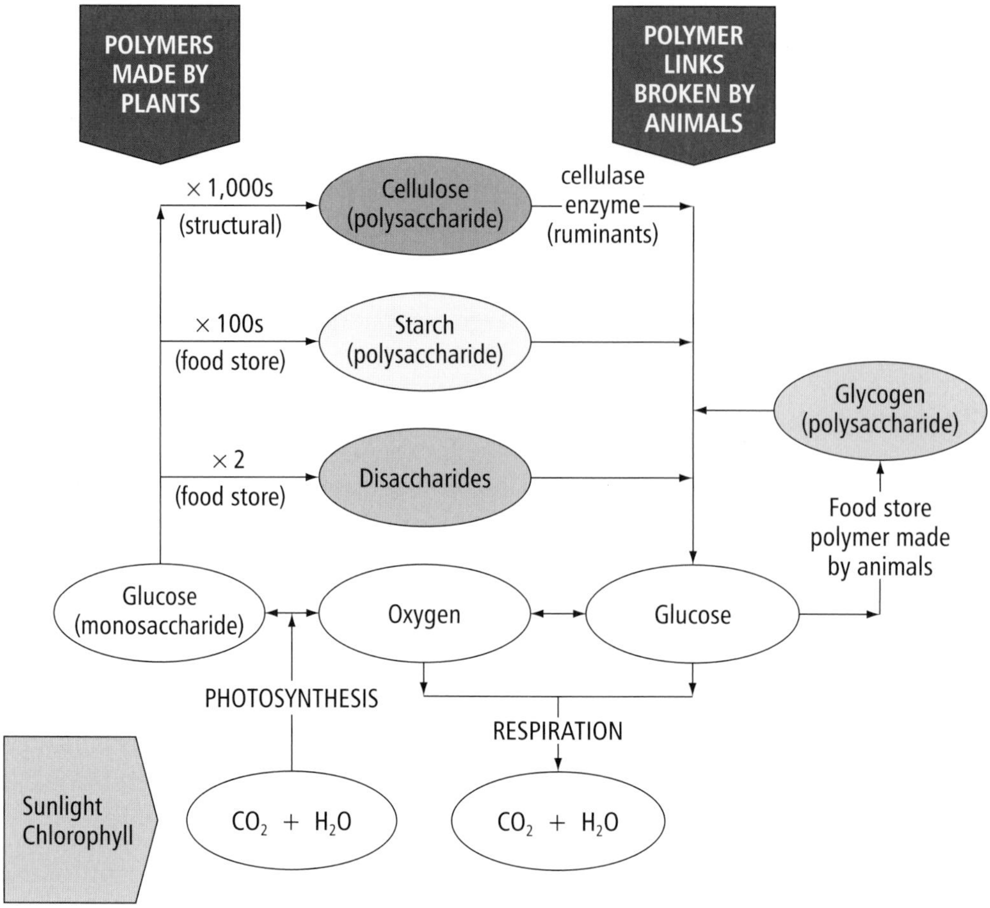

5 Proteins

Proteins are condensation polymers of **amino acids**. Different species have different proteins and for a particular species a range of proteins perform many different functions. Given below (Table 3.4) are some examples of human proteins.

Table 3.4   Various human proteins

Protein	Function	Location
Myosin	Muscle contraction	Muscle tissue
Actin	Muscle contraction	Muscle tissue
Insulin	Glucose release	Blood, pancreas
Immunoglobins	Antibodies	Blood, lymph
Collagen	Structural	Skin, tendon
Keratin	Structural	Hair, nails
Haemoglobin	Oxygen transport	Blood
Ferritin	Iron storage	Marrow, liver, spleen

Many proteins have names ending in -in or -en.

Enzymes are also proteins. These are dealt with in the next topic.

General formula of amino acids

All amino acids have the same general formula. Each has a hydrogen atom, an amino group and a carboxylic acid group attached to the same central carbon atom:

$$\text{H} - \underset{\underset{\text{H}}{|}}{\overset{\overset{\text{H}}{|}}{\text{N}}} - \underset{\underset{\text{X}}{|}}{\overset{\overset{\text{O}}{||}}{\text{C}}} - \overset{\overset{\text{O}}{||}}{\text{C}} - \text{OH}$$

Different amino acids have different groups of atoms at position X.

There are many possible amino acids, but only 20 have ever been found in living organisms.

The 20 different amino acids

You certainly do not have to remember the names, structures or formulae of the amino acids. However, the 20 different molecules are excellent illustrations of how organic compounds are put together and of the most important functional groups.

Remember, we are looking just at the fourth group attached to the central carbon atom:

The other three are the same for all 20 amino acids.

Glycine is the simplest – group X is just a single hydrogen atom. Another five amino acids have increasingly complex hydrocarbon chains, and are shown in Figure 3.11.

Figure 3.11   Display formulae and structural formulae of five amino acids

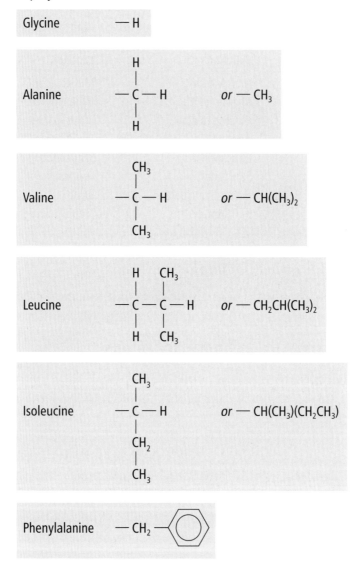

You can see that leucine and isoleucine are isomers – their molecular formulae are the same, but the carbon skeleton arrangements are different. Phenylalanine combines a carbon chain and a benzene ring.

Another three amino acids include the hydroxyl group, –OH. Remember, oxygen forms two covalent bonds.

Serine $\quad -C-O-H \quad or -CH_2OH$

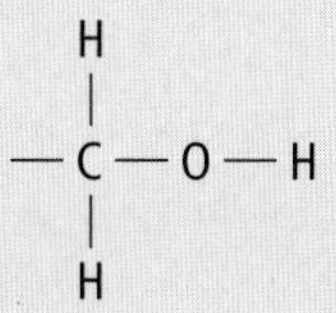

with:
- H above the C
- H below the C

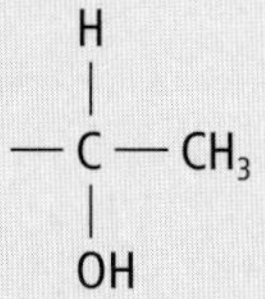

Threonine $\quad -C-CH_3 \quad or -CH(OH)CH_3$

with:
- H above the C
- OH below the C

Tyrosine $\quad -CH_2-\bigcirc-OH$

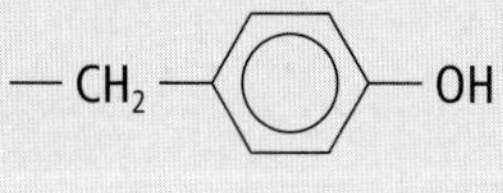

Two have carboxylic acid groups at position X:

Aspartic acid $\quad -C-C\begin{smallmatrix}O\\OH\end{smallmatrix} \quad or -CH_2COOH$

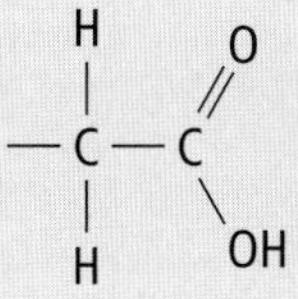

with:
- H above the first C
- H below the first C

Glutamic acid $\quad -CH_2CH_2COOH$

Two more amino acids have a single sulphur atom. Like oxygen, sulphur makes two covalent bonds.

Cysteine $\quad -C-S-H \quad or -CH_2SH$

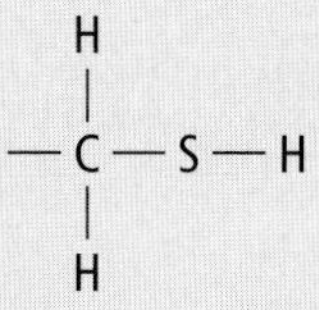

with:
- H above the C
- H below the C

Methionine $\quad -CH_2CH_2SCH_3$

Asparagine and glutamine include an amino group $-NH_2$ at position X and a carboxyl group. This is an oxygen atom double bonded to a carbon atom:

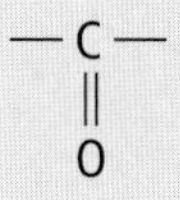

$$-C-\\ \|\\ O$$

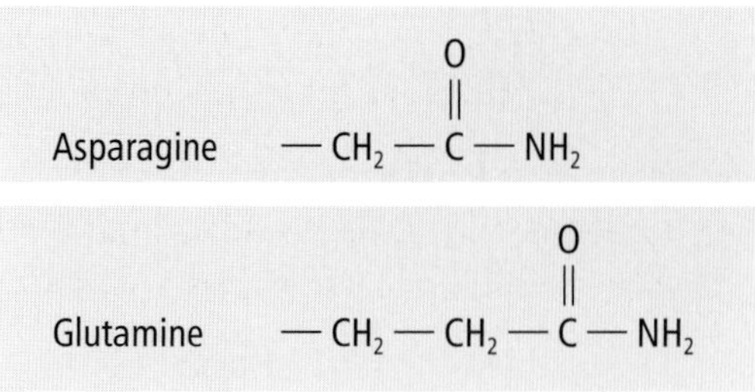

Asparagine $-CH_2-C-NH_2$ with O double-bonded to C

Glutamine $-CH_2-CH_2-C-NH_2$ with O double-bonded to C

Lysine has a single amino group at the end of a straight four carbon atom chain:

Lysine $-CH_2CH_2CH_2CH_2NH_2$

Cystine and arginine include several different functional groups. Cystine has two sulphur atoms bonded together:

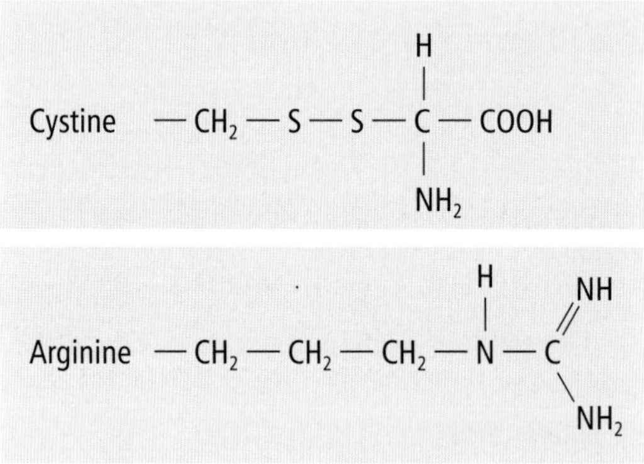

Cystine $-CH_2-S-S-C-COOH$ with H above C and NH_2 below C

Arginine $-CH_2-CH_2-CH_2-N-C$ with H above N, and C double-bonded to NH and single-bonded to NH_2

The two most complex amino acids are histidine and tryptophan, which both have ring structures made of carbon and nitrogen atoms:

The five-membered ring looks complicated but it makes sense if you add up the covalent bonds – carbon makes four, nitrogen three and hydrogen a single bond.

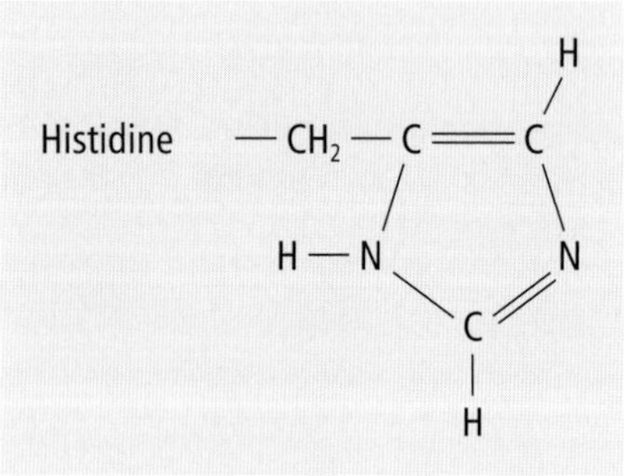

Histidine $-CH_2-C=C$ (five-membered ring with $H-N$, N, and C with H)

Tryptophan has a double ring:

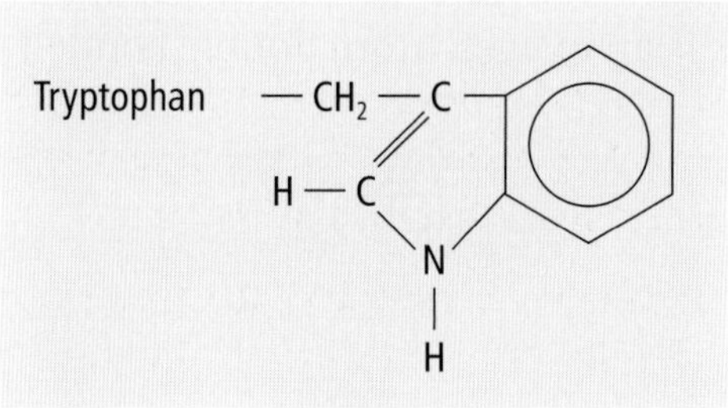

Tryptophan $-CH_2-C$ (double ring structure with $H-C$, N, H)

Each amino acid has a characteristic shape. Some are more or less spherical, others are long-chain molecules. Five give aqueous solutions that are not neutral.

As the names suggest, aspartic acid and glutamic acid form acid solutions, i.e. with a pH below 7. Arginine, lysine and histidine form alkaline solutions with a pH above 7.

A typical protein has several hundred amino acids joined together in a precise sequence. Proteins are therefore large, complicated and highly variable molecules.

Protein foods are taken into the body and a range of enzymes break down their peptide links to turn the food protein back into its component amino acids. In other words, the polymer is turned back into monomers.

Using another set of enzymes, these amino acids are reassembled to produce human proteins that grow, repair and maintain our bodies. New polymers are manufactured.

Eight essential amino acids

12 of the 20 amino acids can also be synthesised from very simple molecules inside the body. The other eight cannot, because we do not have the appropriate enzymes. These eight are called the essential amino acids and they must be ingested.

The eight essential amino acids are:

- valine
- leucine
- isoleucine
- threonine
- lysine
- methionine
- phenylalanine
- tryptophan

Human infants cannot synthesise histidine. This can be seen as a ninth essential amino acid.

Many foods contain proteins. The highest quality protein foods have a significant percentage of total protein, but they also have proteins with a large proportion of the eight essential amino acids.

Eggs, milk, beef and chicken are high quality proteins. Soya, rice, wheat, nuts and maize are lower quality.

Protein shape and structure

Biological molecules are large and complicated. Biological function depends on three-dimensional shape and structure. Unless a biological molecule is exactly and precisely the right shape, it will not perform properly, or will not perform at all.

Sickle cell disease is a good example of how a disease or disorder can be caused by an apparently trivial change in protein composition.

Normal haemoglobin is a nearly spherical protein molecule made up from 574 amino acids. Sometimes just one of the 574 amino acids is copied wrongly. Instead of glutamic acid, this abnormal form of haemoglobin has a valine molecule.

The replacement of one glutamic acid by one valine produces a haemoglobin molecule that is sickle-shaped – a bit like a crushed ping-pong ball – rather than spherical.

Sickle haemoglobin can transport oxygen around the body, but it does so less efficiently than normal spherical haemoglobin.

Individuals with sickle cell disease suffer from severe anaemia and other conditions, where the decay products of the sickle cells accumulate in the tissues and blood vessels.

All proteins contain at least one polypeptide chain. Some have two or more.

The shape and structure of a protein can be studied at four levels:

Primary structure

This is the sequence of amino acids in each polypeptide chain.

Secondary structure

Often the chains form spirals or sheets rather than linear arrangements; these secondary structures are usually held together by hydrogen bonds.

Tertiary structure

Helical chains and sheets can then be folded or coiled again to give fibres, globules or other regular three-dimensional shapes. Again, hydrogen bonding is involved, but some tertiary structures are held together by bridging atoms.

Quaternary structure

Many proteins consist of two or more polypeptide chains. The quaternary structure describes the way these chains are held together.

Denaturing

The disruption or breaking down of a protein's structure is called **denaturing**.

The peptide links that join amino acids together are strong covalent bonds and these can only be broken at high temperatures or by extremes of pH.

However, the bonds that determine the protein's secondary, tertiary and quaternary structures are relatively weak and can be broken more easily.

There are many everyday examples of protein denaturation, such as:

- The souring of milk or the curdling of milk when vinegar is added.
- Boiling or frying eggs.
- Cooking meat and fish.
- Perming hair.

Amino acid sequencing

Insulin is a relatively small biological molecule. We can use it as another example to summarise how amino acids come together to make proteins.

Insulin is a hormonal protein. It controls the level of glucose in the bloodstream. Insulin is made up of two amino acid polymers, or polypeptide chains. The A chain has 21 amino acids; the B chain has 30 amino acids – that is 51 in all.

Figure 3.12 (overleaf) shows the structure of the A chain. There are 20 different natural amino acids. The insulin A chain uses 11 of these, with some repeats.

Biochemistry

Figure 3.12   Insulin – A chain

1	GLY
2	ILE
3	VAL
4	GLU
5	GLN
6	CYS
7	CYS
8	THR
9	SER
10	ILE
11	CYS
12	SER
13	LEU
14	TYR
15	GLN
16	LEU
17	GLU
18	ASN
19	TYR
20	CYS
21	ASN

Amino acid symbol	Position	Full name of amino acid
GLY	1	Glycine
ILE	2, 10	Isoleucine
VAL	3	Valine
GLU	4, 17	Glutamic acid
GLN	5, 15	Glutamine
CYS	6, 7, 11, 20	Cysteine
THR	8	Threonine
SER	9, 12	Serine
LEU	13, 16	Leucine
TYR	14, 19	Tyrosine
ASN	18, 21	Asparagine

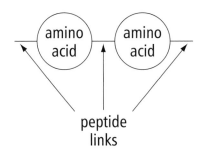

peptide links

112

6 Enzymes

Enzymes are proteins, therefore their **primary structures** are determined by amino acid sequencing in polymer chains. Nearly all enzymes are water soluble.

Every chemical reaction has a characteristic rate. Some reactions proceed very rapidly – explosions of compounds like TNT are the best examples. Other reactions take place very slowly – the rusting of iron and steel, for example, can take months or years.

The rate of all reactions increases with increasing temperature. A temperature increase of $10\,°C$ roughly doubles the rate of most reactions.

When one or more of the **reactants** is in solution, increasing the solution's concentration will also increase reaction rates.

Catalysts

Another way of increasing reaction rates is to add a catalyst to the reaction mixture. A **catalyst** is a substance that increases the rate of a reaction, but is not used up by it.

The modern chemical industry depends on catalysts. The commonest are metals like iron, vanadium and platinum. The manufacture of essential basic chemicals like ammonia and sulphuric acid would not be commercially viable without catalysts. The oil industry and the production of man-made polymers are also totally dependent on catalysts.

Even with catalysts, most commercial chemical reactions also need high temperatures and pressures. Temperatures of up to $1000\,°C$ and pressures of 400 atmospheres are commonplace.

The living world can be seen as a huge chemical industry. Starting with the simplest molecules like carbon dioxide, water, oxygen and nitrogen, every living organism manufactures a massive range of complex biological molecules. The output of the 'living chemical industry' has been measured in billions of tonnes per year.

Most living things cannot tolerate sustained temperatures much above $45\,°C$, pressures greater than normal atmospheric pressures, or extremes of pH.

Enzymes – biological catalysts

Biological reactions have to take place in aqueous solutions, usually at low reactant concentrations.

The characteristic rates of biological reactions under these mild conditions are very slow. Without biological catalysts, life would be impossible.

Enzymes are very much better catalysts than man-made ones. They work at body temperatures, ordinary pressure and moderate pH.

The efficiency of a catalyst is measured by its turnover number – this is the number of molecules reacted per molecule of catalyst per minute. A typical enzyme has a turnover number of about 5 million; commercial catalysts rarely have turnover numbers greater than 20,000. Enzymes are a hundred to a thousand times more efficient than manufactured catalysts.

Enzymes are specific – they will only catalyse the reaction of one molecule or one type of molecule.

Enzyme-catalysed reactions do not produce unwanted by-products. They are 'clean' reactions.

Enzyme-catalysed reactions are easily controlled by concentration and pH changes inside living cells. Inside a cell, an enzyme must be able to distinguish one molecule from another, with complete accuracy. For example, the enzymes that catalyse the production of proteins have to be able to tell one amino acid from another. If one enzyme acted on two or more amino acids, then a protein with the wrong primary sequence would be assembled.

Each enzyme has a target molecule. This molecule is called the enzyme's substrate.

The lock and key model

Enzymes are large spherical molecules made by the coiling, bundling and folding of one or more polypeptide chains.

The surface of the enzyme molecule is not completely smooth and uniform. There are one or more clefts or dents in the structure, with a particular and precise three-dimensional shape. This is called the **active site** and can be seen as equivalent to a lock.

Part of the **substrate** molecule has a group of protruding atoms with a shape that precisely fits the active site. This part of the substrate molecule acts like a key.

The key and the lock fit together – in other words, the enzyme and the substrate form a temporary chemical bond.

The active site acts as a catalyst and the substrate molecule splits into two parts.

The two new molecules can no longer bond with the active site and they are released into the cell.

The enzyme's active site is unchanged, and it is ready to accept another substrate molecule.

The making and breaking of the temporary enzyme-substrate bond proceeds very rapidly and one enzyme molecule can catalyse a 'conveyor belt' of substrate molecules. This is why turnover numbers for enzymes are so high.

The lock and key model explains the specific action of enzymes. Only one key will fit a particular lock because all the other keys are the wrong shape (Figure 3.13).

Figure 3.13   The lock and key model

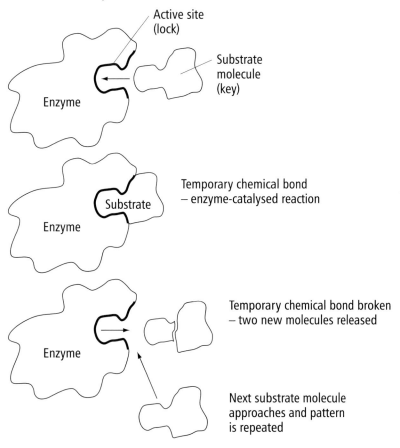

Reaction rates

The rate of an enzyme-catalysed reaction changes according to temperature, pH, concentration of the enzyme and concentration of the substrate.

Some compounds can greatly reduce the reaction rates of enzyme-catalysed reactions or stop them altogether. These compounds are called **inhibitors**.

The kinetic theory says that all molecules are moving and that the higher the temperature, the faster they move.

For two molecules to react, they have to collide. Faster moving molecules collide more often – this is why reaction rates increase with temperature.

At temperatures of around 0°C, most enzyme-catalysed reactions are very slow. This is why fridges and freezers prevent food spoilage.

Between 0°C and about 40°C, reaction rates increase rapidly – roughly doubling for each 10°C change.

Reaction rates begin to decrease at temperatures beyond 40°C. The tertiary structure of the enzyme begins to break down, changing the shape of the active site.

Above 65°C, most enzymes are completely denatured and enzyme-catalysed reactions stop.

All enzymes have an optimum operating temperature. This is the temperature at which the catalysed reaction reaches its maximum rate.

Extreme pH values denature most enzymes and prevent enzyme-catalysed reactions.

Small changes in pH can change the ionisation of enzymes and substrates, so all enzyme-catalysed reactions have an optimum pH as well as an optimum temperature.

A few specialist enzymes work best at very low pH. For example, the enzyme pepsin breaks down proteins in the very acidic conditions of the stomach.

A series of experiments can be conducted using a fixed enzyme concentration and gradually increasing concentrations of substrate. A graph of reaction rate against substrate concentration has a characteristic shape, as shown in Figure 3.14.

Figure 3.14 Reaction rate against substrate concentration

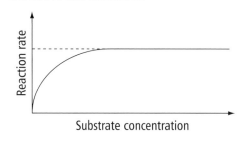

At first, the reaction rate increases because there are more and more substrate keys available to fit a fixed number of enzyme locks.

At some higher substrate concentration, the reaction rate levels out and cannot be increased, no matter how much extra substrate is added to the reaction mixture.

This maximum reaction rate is called V_{max}.

At V_{max}, every enzyme lock is occupied by a substrate key, so adding yet more substrate cannot accelerate the reaction rate. This is sometimes called the saturation point.

At V_{max}, substrate molecules 'form a queue' at each active site and a new substrate molecule can only occupy the site when the previous molecule leaves. The reaction rate then depends only on how quickly the temporary bonds between the substrate and the enzyme are broken. The V_{max} situation is very much like a crowded supermarket, with all the tills working and a queue at every till.

Inhibition

An inhibitor is a molecule that slows or stops an enzyme-catalysed reaction. This inhibition can be reversible or permanent.

Some compounds that permanently inhibit enzyme reactions are amongst the most dangerous toxins known. The nerve gas sarin inhibits the enzymes involved in nerve impulse transmission. Even at low concentrations, sarin causes paralysis and death.

Reversible enzyme inhibition is an essential biochemical process. This kind of inhibition is used to stop enzyme-controlled reactions at an appropriate point in metabolic pathways. A metabolic pathway is a series of enzyme-catalysed reactions that together produce an essential biological molecule.

A competitive inhibitor for a particular enzyme is a molecule whose shape is very similar to the substrate molecule.

The inhibitor binds to the enzyme's active site but does not take part in the catalysed reaction.

The inhibitor competes with the substrate to fill the enzyme's active sites. This slows the reaction (Figure 3.15).

A non-competitive inhibitor still binds to the enzyme, but to part of the enzyme molecule away from the active site.

Non-competitive inhibitors alter the shape of the enzyme active site so that it cannot bind with the substrate molecule.

Figure 3.15   Enzyme inhibition

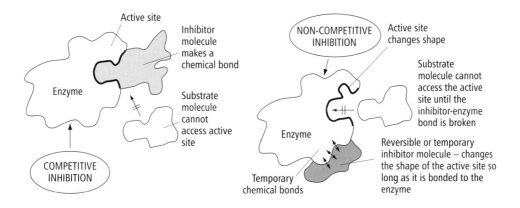

Commercial enzymes

A modern biological washing powder contains four kinds of enzyme:

- An enzyme that breaks down human proteins like blood, sweat, urine and so on.

- An enzyme that breaks down starch-based stains.

- A third type of enzyme that digests lipids to remove fat and grease marks.

- A fourth enzyme that breaks the bonds in cellulose. These enzymes are advertised as fabric conditioners, because they remove the stray ends of fibres produced by wear and tear on the fabric.

Different combinations of enzymes are used for wash temperatures of 40°C, 50°C and 60°C.

Some people develop rashes after wearing clothes washed in biological detergents. Enzyme residues can sometimes react with the proteins in skin tissues to cause soreness and irritation.

7 Lipids

Fats, oils and waxes are collectively called lipids.

Fats and oils are the highest energy foods. They also act as long-term energy reserves for animals and plants. Lipids and carbohydrates have different functions – carbohydrates are short-term energy stores.

	kJ/g	kcals/g	Index
Lipids	37	8.9	100
Carbohydrates	17	4.1	46

Fats form protective layers, typically on plant leaves and around the kidneys of mammals. In mammals, fats also provide an insulating layer under the skin.

Lipids are the structural components of cell membranes. Some hormones are lipids.

Solid fats and liquid oils

Fats are solid at room temperature. Oils are liquid.

Warm-blooded animals have body temperatures of about $38\,^{\circ}C$. These temperatures are above the melting points of most fats. This means they can be transported around the body as liquids.

Plants cannot keep themselves warm at low temperatures. Plant oils must therefore have lower melting points.

Fish and some marine mammals are a special case. Fish that live in the polar and temperate regions have to be able to thrive at water temperatures close to $0\,^{\circ}C$. Many fish oils have very low melting points.

Lipid melting points depend on their chemical structure.

Lipid chemistry

Lipids are not polymers. They are smaller, simpler molecules than polysaccharides, proteins or enzymes.

Lipids are insoluble in water.

Lipids are formed by the combination of one triol with three long-chain carboxylic acids in a condensation reaction (Figure 3.16). These lipid molecules are also called triglycerides.

Figure 3.16 Formation of a lipid

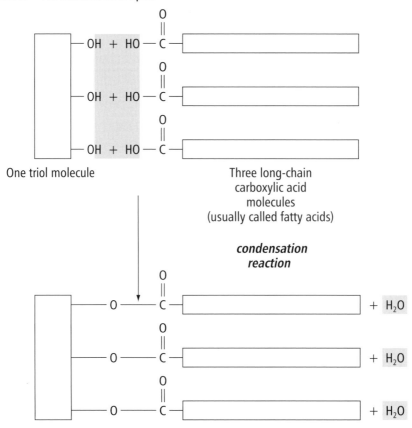

One triol molecule

Three long-chain carboxylic acid molecules (usually called fatty acids)

condensation reaction

Three water molecules are released for each triglyceride formed.

Lipids from different sources have slightly different structures.

The triol is nearly always propan–1,2,3–triol. The common name for this compound is glycerol.

$$CH_2 - OH$$
$$CH - OH$$
$$CH_2 - OH$$

All lipids are made from three long straight-chain carboxylic acids. The chains are never branched and no lipid has ever been discovered that includes a carboxylic acid with an odd number of carbon atoms.

Carboxylic acids of different chain lengths are found in living organisms:

- 16 carbon atoms
- 18 carbon atoms
- 20 carbon atoms
- 22 carbon atoms

Different lipids are made from different combinations of three carboxylic acids. All three can be the same, two can be the same and the third different, or three different acids can be present.

Saturated and unsaturated

'Saturated' means saturated with hydrogen.

Saturated fatty acids have only carbon-carbon single bonds in their chain. The lipids made from these acids are called saturated fats.

Some fatty acids have one double bond as part of their chain. The vegetable fatty acid, oleic acid, has 18 carbon atoms in all, and there is a carbon-carbon double bond between the ninth and tenth carbon atoms. The fats and oils made from these acids are monounsaturated.

Most vegetable oils and all fish oils are compounds derived from fatty acids with two or more double bonds. Some fish oils contain fatty acids with five or six carbon-carbon double bonds. These oils are **polyunsaturated**.

The greater the number of double bonds, the lower the melting point of the lipid.

Lipids are an essential component of the human diet. Our bodies are designed to store fat as a long-term energy reserve to fall back on in times of famine and food shortage.

Weight for weight, lipids contain more than twice as many calories as proteins and carbohydrates.

Most societies see protein foods as higher status and higher quality than carbohydrates, but nearly all animal protein foods are also high in saturated fats.

With increasing prosperity, the proportion of fat in the diet increases and energy expenditure tends to decrease as we get less exercise.

High fat consumption, especially of saturated animal fats, has been linked with many major diseases and disorders.

As a general rule, the longer the carbon chain in a molecule, the less likely it is to be water-soluble. The carboxylic acid with two carbon atoms is acetic acid and this dissolves readily in water to make vinegar. Lipids are made from carboxylic acids with between 16 and 22 carbon atoms. For this reason, lipids are not water-soluble.

Lipids will, however, dissolve in some organic solvents. Dry cleaners use these solvents to remove fat, oil and grease stains from clothes.

Phospholipids

All cells are surrounded by partially permeable membranes, which control the passage of food and waste into and out of the cell. Membranes are also found inside a cell, where they surround its various internal compartments.

The main components of cell membranes are a special group of lipids called **phospholipids**.

In a phospholipid, the third carboxylic acid chain is replaced by a small group of atoms. The composition of this third group varies, but it always includes oxygen, nitrogen and phosphorus – hence the name phospholipid.

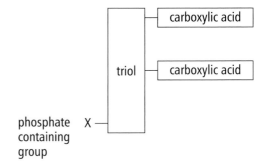

Like all molecules, phospholipids are electrically neutral, but with phospholipids the distribution of electrical charge varies considerably along the length of the molecule.

Phospholipids have a small ionically bonded or polar head, and a long covalently bonded or non-polar tail. Figure 3.17 shows a phospholipid more or less to scale.

Figure 3.17 A phospholipid

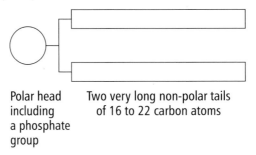

Polar head including a phosphate group

Two very long non-polar tails of 16 to 22 carbon atoms

Phospholipid molecules have two special properties:

- They always line up together – with all the heads pointing in the same direction.

- The polar heads are attracted to water. The non-polar tails are repelled by water.

When a phospholipid is added to water it forms a thin skin on the water's surface. This is a monolayer. The molecules arrange themselves with their heads in the water and their tails pointing upwards into the air.

If more phospholipid is added, the molecules group together to form spheres called micelles. In a micelle, the heads point outwards to form the surface of the micelle and the non-polar tails group together in the centre of the sphere.

Cell walls are double or bimolecular layers of phospholipids. These structures are strong enough to contain water and the dilute solutions that make up the contents of a cell.

Animals store energy in two ways, as lipids and as the carbohydrate glycogen. Table 3.5 shows how the structure and functions of the two molecules differ.

Table 3.5 Animal food stores

	Glycogen	Lipids
Structure	Branched-chain polysaccharide polymer	Triglyceride molecules
Efficiency and function	Short-term concentrated energy store	Long-term highly concentrated energy store
Storage	Compact insoluble granules	Water-insoluble droplets
Storage site	Liver and muscles	Subdermal layer
Energy per gram	4.1 kcals/g	8.9 kcals/g
Oxygen need	Some glucose can be released in the absence of oxygen – instant energy	Cannot be metabolised without oxygen – – long-term energy

8 Nucleic acids, DNA and RNA

For this unit, you only need to understand the basics of DNA's structure and functions. These notes are a simplified outline only.

DNA was first isolated by a Swiss biochemist in 1869. At that time, its structure could not be determined and its significance was not realised.

In 1944, it was shown to be involved in the passing of genetic information from one cell to another. Previously, it was thought that the genetic material was a special kind of protein.

Watson and Crick

Between 1951 and 1953, a group of four scientists working at London and Cambridge universities put together the calculations and experiments that eventually led to the discovery of the general structure of DNA. English physicist Francis Crick and American zoologist James Watson published their discovery on 25 April 1953.

Watson and Crick used two main methods. Both demonstrate the fundamental importance of three-dimensional shape in understanding how biological molecules work:

- X-ray photography – when a beam of X-rays is shone at a crystalline molecule, some of the rays hit atoms and are reflected, others pass through the spaces between atoms. The resulting picture, called an X-ray diffraction pattern, can be used to calculate the distances between atoms and the bond angles between groups of atoms.

- Molecular model building – the atoms and groups of atoms that make up a **macromolecule** have to fit together in a precise pattern, a bit like a three-dimensional jigsaw. The molecule will not work, or will not be stable, if pieces are in the wrong place, or if pieces are missing, or if pieces are duplicated wrongly.

Watson and Crick used molecular models made from cardboard, tinplate and wire to test the various structures suggested by X-ray diffraction. None of their models cost more than a few pounds to make, but without them, the discovery of DNA's structure would have been impossible.

The genetic molecule

DNA is deoxyribonucleic acid. RNA is ribonucleic acid. They are called **nucleic acids** because they are found in the nuclei of cells.

DNA and RNA are long straight-chain condensation polymers.

The molecular and structural formulae of DNA and RNA must be able to explain all the facts of genetics:

- The molecule has to be self-replicating. In other words, it must be able to make copies of itself, and the copying mechanism has to be very, very accurate.

- One generation must be able to pass DNA molecules to the next.

- DNA and RNA have to control the making, or synthesis, of proteins – the working parts of all living things.

The molecular and structural formulae of DNA and RNA also ought to be able to explain two more observations about living things:

- Individuals of the same species have differences that cannot be explained by diet and environment.

- There are millions of species. Some are very similar, some are very different. Dogs and foxes have much in common, but it is easy to tell an elephant from an onion.

The double helix

In the late 1940s and early 1950s, the most prominent biochemist in the world was Linus Pauling. In 1952, Pauling published a paper suggesting that protein polymer chains often wound themselves into a spiral – usually called a helix. Pauling was the first chemist to describe the secondary and tertiary structures of proteins.

Using Pauling's model of the protein helix, Watson and Crick took X-ray photos of DNA, looking for a similar structure. There were four possibilities: a single spiral, as in some proteins, or a structure based on two, three or four spirals.

They found that DNA was a double helix. Two spirals are wound together and the distance between the two is the same at every point along its length. The basic structure of DNA looks like a spiral staircase, with one strand as the left handrail and the other as the right handrail.

The two strands were found to be a simple condensation polymer made from alternating phosphate and sugar monomers.

The sugar in DNA is a pentose, five atoms in a ring, called deoxyribose – hence deoxyribonucleic acid.

— phosphate — sugar — phosphate — sugar —

Four bases

The discovery of the double helix was a major step forward, but two problems remained.

The phosphate sugar backbone is very simple and very regular. A simple molecule, no matter how big, cannot explain why the DNA of individuals and species varies.

DNA contains nitrogen; the polymer strands contain only carbon, oxygen, hydrogen and phosphorus.

Nitrogen containing compounds must be present and they must explain the variability of DNA between individuals and species.

A solution of ammonia, NH_3, has a pH of more than 7 – it is an alkali.

If one or more of the hydrogen atoms in ammonia is replaced by an organic group – that is, a chain or ring of carbon atoms – the new molecule is called an organic base. Base is another word for alkali.

DNA contains four different organic bases.

The four bases have cyclic structures.

The four bases found in DNA are called adenine, cytosine, guanine and thymine. These names are abbreviated to A, C, G and T.

Thymine and cytosine are smaller molecules, with a single six-membered ring structure. Figure 3.18 shows simplified structural formulae for these molecules.

Figure 3.18 Thymine and cytosine

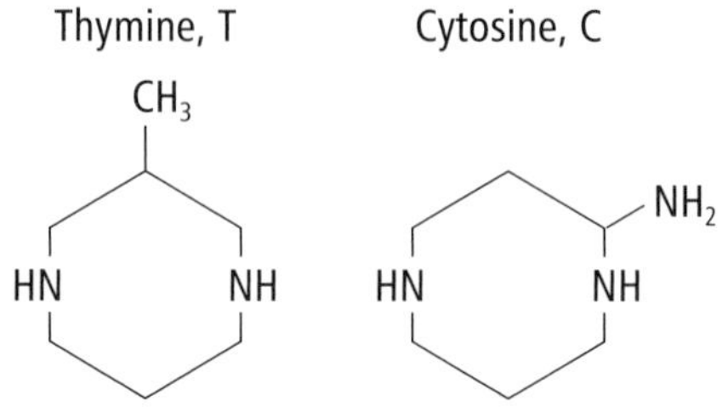

Adenine and guanine are larger molecules with a six-membered ring joined to a five-membered ring. Their simplified structural formulae are shown in Figure 3.19.

Figure 3.19 Adenine and guanine

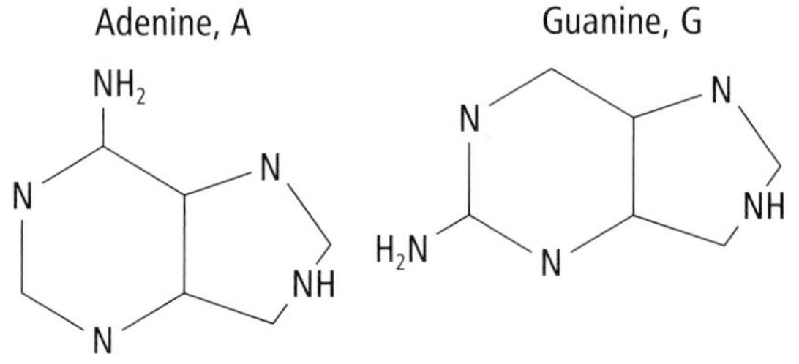

Base pairing

All life on Earth depends on the following:

- The four bases can bond together to form two base pairs.

- The two pairs of bases join together using hydrogen bonds.

- Cytosine can only join to guanine because this pairing needs three hydrogen bonds.

- Adenine can only join to thymine because this pairing need two hydrogen bonds.

Additionally, the cytosine–guanine pair is exactly the same length as the adenine–thymine pair.

A	┄┄┄┄	T
G	════	C
T	┄┄┄┄	A
C	════	G

Handrails and steps

The double helix backbone is similar to the handrails of a spiral staircase. The base pairs fit horizontally between the two 'handrails' like the 'steps' of the staircase.

In each 360° turn of the double spiral, there are exactly ten base pairs – or ten 'steps of the staircase'.

Because the two permitted base pairs are the same length, the DNA molecule is regular and stable – the distance between the two spirals is always the same, no matter how long the molecule becomes.

The two strands of DNA are held together by the hydrogen bonds linking the two sets of base pairs.

At the beginning of the reproductive cycle, the hydrogen bonds are broken and the DNA molecule 'unzips' to make two single strands.

Figure 3.20   One DNA strand

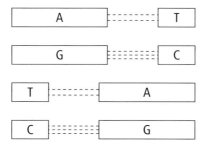

☐ = C or T, shorter single-ring bases

▭ = G or A, longer double-ring bases

phosphate
sugar

P
S — T
P
S — C
P
S — G

The base can be
A, C, G or T

P
S — BASE

Figure 3.20 shows a tiny stretch of one DNA strand with the base sequence

T, C, G

Inside the cell nucleus, this single strand of DNA comes into contact with a 'soup' of simpler molecules. This soup, amongst many other things, contains four different monomer molecules:

These monomers then bond with the single DNA strand to rebuild a new second strand and reform the double helix.

Replication

Because A will only bond with T, and G will only bond with C, the new double helix is an exact copy of the old one (Figure 3.21).

Figure 3.21 Replication of DNA

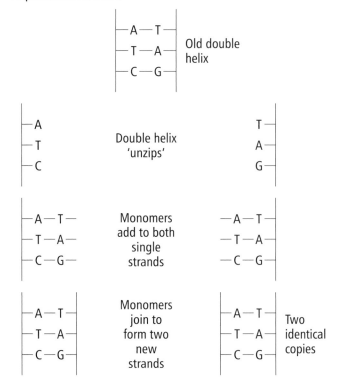

RNA is different

Watson and Crick discovered the structure of DNA but not the sequence of reactions that allow DNA to build proteins – the working parts that make species and individuals differ one from another.

DNA does not directly make proteins. **RNA** molecules and enzymes are involved in copying the base sequence from DNA, moving this information around the cell and making the proteins themselves.

RNA is similar to DNA, but there are three important differences:

- The sugar is ribose, not deoxyribose – hence ribonucleic acid.
- A base called uracil replaces the thymine found in DNA. Uracil and thymine are virtually identical.
- RNA exists as single strands, not double spirals.

There are different kinds of RNA, and the building of proteins also involves hundreds of different enzymes. The detail is horrendously complicated, but the central principle is incredibly simple.

DNA molecules are enormous. Generally, the more complicated the organism, the longer the DNA molecule becomes:

Organism	Number of base pairs – 'spiral staircase steps'
Bacteria	About 5 million
Humans	About 3 billion

The DNA molecule can be seen as an 'instruction manual' written with an alphabet of four letters – A, C, G and T.

The sequence of letters is continuous and without punctuation marks. For even the simplest organisms, there are billions and billions of possible combinations.

RNA copies the DNA sequence, but it replaces thymine with uracil, so the 'instruction manual' still uses four letters – A, C, G and U.

The triplet code

RNA reads the DNA code in groups of three bases.

Each group of three bases, or triplet, says "make an amino acid".

For example:

- GUU says "make valine".
- GCU says "make alanine".
- AGC says "make serine".

In this example, the RNA sequence GUUGCUAGC would make a tripeptide valine–alanine–serine.

A typical protein might have a polypeptide chain of 100 amino acids – the RNA code for this protein would then be a sequence of 300 bases.

Protein synthesis is exact because the same code of three bases always makes the same amino acid; and the sequence of triplets controls the order in which the amino acids are joined together.

There are also triplet codes for 'start' and 'stop'.

The sequence of bases that codes for one polypeptide chain is called a gene.

In higher animals, the DNA is packaged into chromosomes, each of which is thought to be a single molecule of DNA.

It is difficult fully to explain the structure of DNA, base pairing and the genetic code with diagrams alone. Many websites include three-dimensional representations of DNA that make replication and genetic coding much easier to visualise and understand. Key words such as 'DNA', 'double helix', 'base pairs' and 'genetic code' will give a selection of websites when entered into any decent search engine.

Chapter 4
Diet

National unit specification.
These are the topics you will be studying for this unit:

1 The balanced diet concept
2 Weights and measures
3 Energy
4 Fats and oils
5 Sugars and starches
6 Protein
7 Dietary fibre, NSP
8 Water and other drinks
9 Vitamins
10 Minerals
11 Malnutrition

You will find it helpful to read or reread Chapter 3, Biochemistry, before you begin this unit.

1 The balanced diet concept

In Europe and North America, a typical large food superstore offers something like 15,000 different food and drink products. The UK food manufacturing and distribution industries are amongst the most efficient in the world, and many of us now have easy access to an affordable choice of food that would have astonished our grandparents.

Diet has become a major concern, perhaps bordering on an obsession, for the mass media in developed societies. We are constantly bombarded with dietary advice – much of it ill-informed, contradictory and inconsistent.

This unit is about the science of diet. It has very little to do with dieting or the latest unsubstantiated claims for eating programmes that produce miraculous overnight benefits.

Humans are omnivores

We have evolved to become **omnivorous** animals. Our bodies are designed to work best on a diet where no one food group predominates. The concept of a sustainable balanced diet is central to an understanding of diet and health.

Figure 4.1 shows the basic subdivision of a balanced diet into macronutrients, water, fibre and micronutrients. Macronutrients are lipids, carbohydrates and proteins – the major food groups that we need in relatively large amounts. Vitamins and minerals are the micronutrients. These are an essential part of a balanced diet, but they are only needed in very small quantities.

There is no human biological need for alcohol, but it has been included as a fourth macronutrient because it can be a significant component of some Western diets.

All the dietary recommendations and most of the statistics in this unit are taken from a UK government report (*Dietary Reference Values for Food Energy and Nutrients for the United Kingdom*, HMSO, 1991). This report, although published some time ago, is still recognised by government, the health professions and the food industry as the best available information source on health and diet in the UK.

Figure 4.1   The balanced diet concept

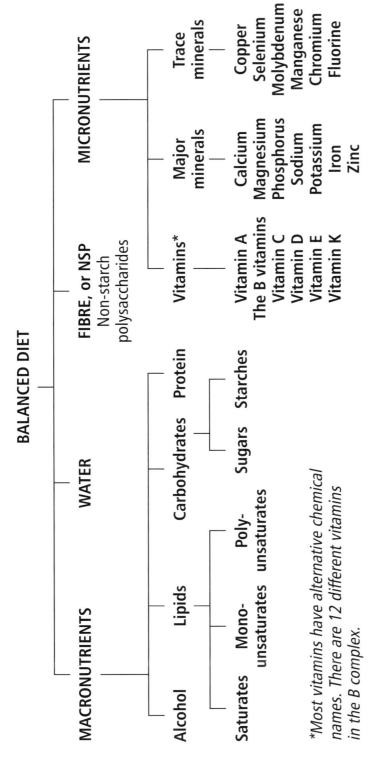

BALANCED DIET

MACRONUTRIENTS   **WATER**   **FIBRE, or NSP**   **MICRONUTRIENTS**
Non-starch
polysaccharides

Alcohol   **Lipids**   **Carbohydrates**   **Protein**   **Vitamins***   **Major minerals**   **Trace minerals**

Saturates Mono- Poly-   Sugars Starches   Vitamin A   Calcium   Copper
           unsaturates unsaturates   The B vitamins   Magnesium   Selenium
                                                Vitamin C   Phosphorus   Molybdenum
                                                Vitamin D   Sodium   Manganese
                                                Vitamin E   Potassium   Chromium
                                                Vitamin K   Iron   Fluorine
                                                             Zinc

*Most vitamins have alternative chemical
names. There are 12 different vitamins
in the B complex.

2 Weights and measures

The units of measurement used generally in science are discussed fully in the Appendix, page 269.

This is the ingredient list for a recipe for pheasant with cream and apples:

1 plump young oven-ready hen pheasant

Half an onion, chopped finely

4 Cox's apples

1 tablespoon butter

1 tablespoon oil

Half a glass dry cider

7 fl. oz double cream

Salt

Freshly milled black pepper

(Serves two people)

This produces a very good meal but it is no use to a dietician because so much information is missing:

- How much does the plump young hen pheasant weigh?

- How big is a tablespoon?

- What kind of butter, and what kind of oil do we use?

- Do we use big onions and big apples, or medium ones, or small ones?

- How big a glass should we use to measure out the cider?

- How much salt and how much pepper do we use?

- The recipe serves two people – but is that two 18-stone rugby players or two 7-stone ballet dancers?

- Presumably, the pheasant dish will be served with something else. Will this be a huge pile of chips, or a small, delicate portion of steamed broccoli?

- How many calories, how much fat, how much protein and how much carbohydrate does this meal contain?

Science is about measurement

Cooking is an art, the study of diet is a science. All sciences are based on accurate measurement.

Two different weight systems are widely used – the old imperial system of pounds and ounces and a second system, based on grams and kilograms.

The metric system was first introduced in France and has now spread to most of the rest of the world. Amongst large countries, only the USA still uses imperial weights.

Scientists throughout the world use the metric system.

Kilograms and grams

The commonest metric weight unit is the gram – abbreviated to a small letter g, for example, 35 g.

The gram is a small weight unit. There are about 28 grams to an ounce and 454 grams to a pound.

Most food quantities are given in grams. For example, a tin of beans normally contains 420 grams of product.

Any weight, no matter how big or small, can be expressed in grams, but the numbers can get inconveniently large or may have to be shown as tiny decimals, which are difficult to understand.

Larger weights are usually given in kilograms, kg.

The prefix 'kilo' means multiply by 1,000.

$$\text{One kilogram} \ = \ 1,000 \text{ grams}$$

$$1\,\text{kg} \qquad \ = \ 1,000\,\text{g}$$

Larger food quantities and body weights are usually shown as kilograms. For example:

	kilograms	grams
Bag of sugar	1	1,000
Big bag of potatoes	5	5,000
7 lb newborn baby	3.18	3,180
7-stone ballet dancer	44.5	44,500
12-stone man	76.2	76,200
18-stone rugby player	114	114,000

One kilogram is about 2.2 pounds (lb).

Milligrams and micrograms

Smaller weights can also be shown in grams, but these usually work out as awkward decimals.

Another prefix is used for smaller quantities. The prefix 'milli' means divide by 1,000.

Many vitamins and minerals are essential to a healthy diet but they are only needed in small amounts. The dosages of most medicines are also given in milligrams.

	milligrams	grams
Daily requirement of vitamin C	40	0.04
Daily requirement of calcium	700	0.7
One paracetamol tablet*	500	0.5
One ibuprofen tablet*	200	0.2
*active ingredient		

A third prefix is occasionally used to describe very small weights. The prefix 'micro' means divide by one million (1,000,000):

$$\text{One gram} = 1,000,000 \text{ micrograms}$$

$$1\,g = 1,000,000\,\mu g$$

Trace minerals and a few vitamins are measured in micrograms:

	micrograms	grams
Daily requirement of vitamin A	600	0.0006
Daily requirement of iodine	140	0.000 14

Litres and millilitres

All drinks and some foods like soup and milk are measured by volume, not by weight.

The imperial volume measurement system uses gallons, pints and fluid ounces. The metric system is based on litres and millilitres.

The prefix 'milli' always means divide by 1,000, therefore:

$$\text{One litre} = 1,000 \text{ millilitres}$$

$$1\,l = 1,000\,ml$$

Food and drink volumes can be shown in litres, or millilitres, or both:

	litres	millilitres
Can of soft drink	0.33	330
Carton of milk	0.50	500
Bottle of wine	0.75	750
Large carton of orange juice	1.5	1500

Different liquids have different densities – the same volume of different liquids will have different weights.

Water is used as the reference standard for liquid densities:

- One millilitre of water weighs one gram.

- One litre of water, 1,000 ml, therefore weighs one kilogram, 1,000 g.

Nearly all drinks and liquid foods are dilute solutions of nutrients in water, so the assumption that one litre weighs one kilogram is close enough to calculate energy values.

For example:

1. One bottle of wine is 750 ml.

2. One bottle of wine is therefore 750 g.

3. Wine is 10% alcohol and 90% water.

4. Water has no calories.

5. Pure alcohol has 7 calories per gram.

6. A bottle of wine contains 10% of 750 g or 75 g of pure alcohol.

7. 75 g of pure alcohol contains 75 × 7, equal to 525 calories.

8. Therefore, one bottle of wine contains 525 calories.

9. A generous glass of wine is 150 ml – that is, five glasses to a bottle.

10. Therefore, one glass of wine has 525/5 or 105 calories.

Calories and joules

Some foods and drinks are highly flammable. A Christmas pudding covered in brandy can be set alight, so can a glass of sambucca, and sugar will burn explosively if it is thrown onto a fire.

Your body burns all its food to produce energy in exactly the same way, but this happens slowly and is very closely controlled. The release of energy is gradual over a period of hours rather than concentrated into a few seconds.

Different foods contain different amounts of energy – fat has the most per gram, proteins and carbohydrates contain less.

If the total weight and composition of any diet is known, then its energy value can be calculated precisely.

Most food weights are measured in kilograms or grams and most drink volumes are measured in litres or millilitres. The energy content of food is measured in kilocalories or calories.

The **calorie** is a very small amount of energy, so it is convenient to work with **kilocalories**:

$$\text{One kilocalorie} = 1{,}000 \text{ calories}$$
$$1\,\text{kcal} = 1{,}000\,\text{cal}$$

The word calorie in everyday language refers to kilocalorie.

Another unit of energy is used in chemistry and physics – this is the **joule** or the **kilojoule**:

$$\text{One calorie} = 4.18 \text{ joules (J)}$$
$$\text{One kilocalorie} = 4.18 \text{ kilojoules (kJ)}$$

Throughout this unit, we will use kilocalories as the unit of food energy.

Nearly all packaged foods have to show their energy content in kilocalories and in kilojoules per 100 g of product. For example:

- 454 g jar of sweet pickle
- Energy content 551 kJ/130 kcal per 100 g

Manufacturers are allowed to round energy contents shown in kilocalories – so the calculation 1 kcal = 4.18 kJ does not always apply exactly on food labels.

Variables and variation

We all know people who can eat as much as they like and never seem to put on weight – and we all know others who put on three pounds if they even look at a bacon sandwich. These differences are real and scientifically proven, not just fantasy or jealousy.

All humans are the same species, but all of us, except identical twins, are different.

Anything that can vary is called a variable. There are two types of variables:

- discrete variables
- continuous variables

Table 4.1 gives some examples of discrete variables for people:

Table 4.1   Examples of discrete variables

Discrete variables	Possibilities
Gender	Two possibilities – male or female
Pregnancy	Two possibilities – pregnant or not pregnant
ABO blood group	Four possibilities – A, B, AB or O

Discrete variables are things you can count in whole numbers – you cannot be just a little bit pregnant, your blood group cannot be mostly AB.

Continuous variables are more common and more familiar, and include:

- height
- weight
- intelligence
- hair colour

You could, for example, collect together 1,000 women who know that their weight is 57 kg or about 9 stone. If, however, each of these women were weighed accurately enough, then each would be different. For example, woman number one might weigh 57.3124 kg and woman number 1,000 might weigh 57.3126 kg.

The needs for energy and nutrients are very good examples of continuous variables.

The normal distribution

Provided the sample is big enough, most continuous variables show the same pattern – it does not matter what the continuous variable is. Statistical calculations used to calculate variation can be complicated, but the basic ideas are simple common sense.

Height is the most commonly used example of a continuous variable.

In this example of how heights vary, our sample is all adult Swedish men (Figure 4.2). Obviously, different figures would apply if the sample was, for example, Japanese women or Irish boys.

Figure 4.2   The normal height distribution in adult Swedish men

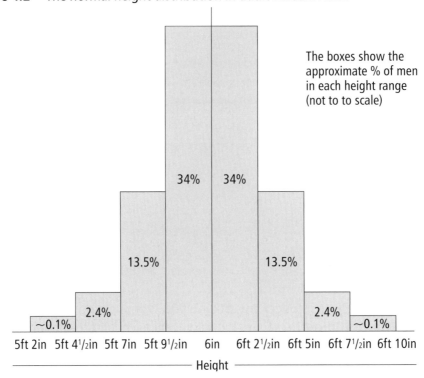

The boxes show the approximate % of men in each height range (not to to scale)

34%   34%

13.5%   13.5%

2.4%   2.4%

~0.1%   ~0.1%

5ft 2in   5ft 4½in   5ft 7in   5ft 9½in   6in   6ft 2½in   6ft 5in   6ft 7½in   6ft 10in

——— Height ———

The average height of Swedish men is 6 ft.

The height distribution is symmetrical – 50% are taller than 6 ft, 50% are shorter than 6 ft.

Most men have heights quite close to the average – 68% of the sample are between 5 ft 9½ in and 6 ft 2½ in.

There are fewer men who are much taller or much shorter than the average. The greater the departure from the average, the smaller the group becomes. For example, only 0.1% of Swedish men – that is, one in a thousand – is taller than 6 ft 7½ in.

This kind of pattern is called the **normal distribution** and it accurately describes very many kinds of continuous variation patterns.

It is common sense that different continuous variables will have different averages or mean values. Again for Swedish men:

- Average height 6 ft.

- Average waist measurement, say, 35 in.

- Average IQ, say, 100.

Again, it is obvious that some things are more variable than others. For example, weight varies more than hair colour.

There are limits to any variation – no Swedish adult men are 4 in tall, and none are 12 ft tall, for example.

The standard deviation

Any continuous variable can be described using just two numbers:

- The arithmetic mean, commonly called the average.

- The **standard deviation**.

You may have noticed a pattern in the height illustration – each height band covers a range of 2½ in. This value is the standard deviation in height for Swedish men.

The greater the value of the standard deviation, the more variable a characteristic becomes. For example:

- If the standard deviation was zero inches, then every Swedish man would be 6 ft tall – this kind of thing never happens in the real world.

- If the standard deviation was 1 in, then only one Swedish man in a thousand would be taller than 6 ft 3 in.

- If the standard deviation was 4 in, then there would be a lot more very tall and very short Swedes.

Table 4.2 shows the general rules for continuous variables with a normal distribution.

Table 4.2 Continuous variables with a normal distribution

Range	% of sample within this range	% rounded
Average ± 1 standard deviation	68.26	68
Average ± 2 standard deviations	95.46	95
Average ± 3 standard deviations	99.73	99.7
Average ± 4 standard deviations	99.994	100

For most practical purposes, the rounded numbers are used. The normal distribution rules sometimes become unreliable at the two extremes.

Dietary reference values

Calcium is an essential component of a balanced diet – without enough of it, bones and teeth do not develop properly. Complete absence of calcium is lethal.

Many experiments and trials have given figures for the average calcium requirement for different groups of people. However, even similar groups need different amounts of calcium – because this is a continuous variable.

Women between the ages of 19 and 50, who are not pregnant or not breast-feeding, have been shown to need an average calcium intake of 550 mg per day.

Trials have also shown that the standard deviation for this group of women is 75 mg per day of calcium.

If the average and the standard deviation are known, then sensible advice can be given concerning how much calcium is needed for a healthy balanced diet.

Dietary reference value is the collective word used to describe any recommended or suggested intake of food, drink, nutrient or fibre. There are three main kinds of dietary reference values. Figure 4.3 uses calcium to show how the system works.

Figure 4.3   Calcium requirements

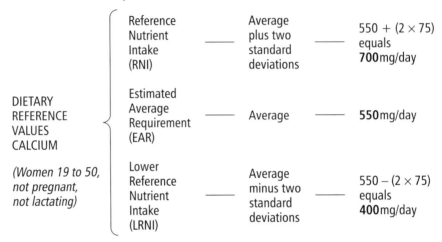

Dietary advice for most nutrients is usually based on the RNI or **reference nutrient intake**. This quantity is enough, or more than enough, for 97.5% of the group concerned.

In the UK, the dietary recommendation for total energy intake, or calories, is only given as an EAR, or average need.

3 Energy

Energy comes in many different forms. One form can be converted to another: a battery turns chemical energy into electrical energy; a car engine turns the chemical energy in petrol into heat and the energy needed to move the vehicle.

Nearly all the energy that surrounds us comes directly or indirectly from the Sun. The Sun can be described as a huge natural nuclear power station, turning nuclear energy into heat and light.

The Sun's energy reaches the Earth by radiation – sometimes called solar radiation or solar energy. Some of this radiation is visible, like sunshine, some, like ultraviolet and infrared, is invisible to the human eye.

Plants use solar energy directly – they do not need to eat. Photosynthesis traps solar energy and stores that energy in the chemical bonds of glucose and other molecules.

Some animals eat plants. These animals, known as **herbivores**, are using the Sun's energy indirectly.

Carnivorous and omnivorous animals eat plants and/or other animals. These are using solar energy at second or third hand. Humans are omnivorous animals.

Food is, at the most basic level, a store of solar energy. At the moment, while you are reading this, your body is using energy at the rate of about 2 kcals per minute.

Most of this energy is being supplied by the food you have eaten in the last 24 hours. If you have eaten potatoes in the last day or so, for example, then you are using the solar energy that fell on a potato field many months or possibly a year or more ago.

The conservation of energy

Energy can be converted from one form to another, but it cannot be created or destroyed – this is the conservation principle.

The conservation principle means that food energy calculations are always just simple arithmetic – put another way, your body is a completely accurate calorie counter. It never forgets and it never gets the sums wrong.

If you eat more calories than you use, the extra calories will be stored – your weight will increase.

If you eat fewer calories than you need, your body will make up the difference by using some of the store – your weight will reduce.

A difference of 3,130 kcals is equivalent to about 1 lb of stored fat. The time period does not matter – your brain can forget the 28 chocolates you ate on Boxing Day, your body cannot.

If, in 1 week, you eat 17,000 kcals, but use just 14,000 kcals, then during that week your weight will increase by about a pound. If, in 1 year, you eat 730,000 kcals but use up 727,000 kcals, then your weight will increase by 1 lb over the year.

Food energy values

Energy is stored in the chemical bonds of the food we eat. Different kinds of food have different kinds of chemical bonds, so they store different quantities of energy per gram.

Biochemists and food scientists have calculated the energy values of nearly all foods with great accuracy. Approximate values in kilocalories are used by dieticians – only scientists use the precise values:

Food	Energy per gram		
	kJ	precise kcal	approx kcal
Lipids	37	8.85	9
Carbohydrate	17	4.07	4
Protein	17	4.07	4
Alcohol	30	7.13	7
Fibre	zero	zero	zero
Water	zero	zero	zero

A few micronutrients provide energy, but they are eaten in such small quantities that their calorie values can be ignored.

Sugars and sweeteners are a special case. Our bodies are programmed to like sweet things, because sweetness suggests that a food is fresh and wholesome. Many natural plant toxins are compounds called alkaloids – these are exceedingly bitter. Decaying plant and animal foods taste bitter and smell bad. We have evolved to recognise these signals.

All sugars have the same energy value but their sweetness varies. Food and drink manufacturers use different combinations of sugars for different products and different markets. Sugars include glucose, isoglucose, HFCS, corn syrup, dextrose, fructose, lactose and sucrose. Modified food starches also contribute sweetness.

Artificial sweeteners have a sweet taste but contain few calories or no calories at all. They are used as sugar substitutes to reduce cost, calories or the health problems that come with excess sugar consumption. Three artificial sweeteners are commonly used: saccharin and acesulfame-K have no calories; a third product, called aspartame, is a very simple protein, so it contains 4 calories per gram. Weight for weight, aspartame is about 200 times sweeter than sugar, so its calorie contribution is insignificant. A 330 ml can of diet soft drink contains about 0.165 g, or 165 mg of aspartame – this contributes less than 1 calorie.

Very few real foods are 100% fat, protein or carbohydrate. The two common exceptions are lard, which is virtually pure fat, and white sugar, which is more or less pure carbohydrate.

Most foods are mixtures of the three main macronutrients, water and micronutrients. Foods that are rich in starch usually also contain fibre.

Foods are natural products. Their composition varies according to origin, season, freshness and degree of processing.

Manufactured foods are produced to closely controlled specifications for energy and nutrient content.

Calorie calculations and declarations

The energy content of any food can be calculated by simply adding up the calories provided by the amount of fat, carbohydrate and protein it contains. Take bread as an example.

A family-sized white sliced loaf weighs 800 g. There are 20 slices, so each average slice weighs 40 g.

The manufacturer has to show the energy and nutrient content of its product per 100 g. This law makes sure that different brands and different pack sizes can easily be compared.

The label on the loaf says:

Typical analysis	per 100 g
Energy	1,037 kJ (244 kcal)
Protein	8.3 g
Carbohydrate	49.2 g
(of which sugars)	(1.1 g)
Fat	1.6 g
(of which saturates)	(0.3 g)
Fibre	2.8 g

Manufacturers are not obliged by law to tell their customers how much water their products contain – so most do not. Some consumers think that adding water is 'cheating'.

Anything in the bread that is not a macronutrient or fibre must be water, so the water content of the bread can be calculated easily:

Typical analysis	per 100 g
Protein	8.3 g
Carbohydrate	49.2 g
Fat	1.6 g
Fibre	2.8 g
Total of above	61.9 g
'Undeclared water'	38.1 g
Total	100.0 g

The manufacturers say that their bread contains 244 kcals per 100 g. We can check their calculations:

Constituent	per 100 g	kcals per gram	kcals per 100 g
Protein	8.3 g	4	33.2
Carbohydrate	49.2 g	4	196.8
Fat	1.6 g	9	14.4
Fibre	2.8 g	zero	zero
Water	38.1 g	zero	zero
Total	100.0 g	–	244.4

We have confirmed that 100 g of bread contains 244 kcals, so a whole 800 g loaf contains 8 × 244 or 1,952 kcals. Each slice contains 1,952/20, equivalent to 97.6 kcals or about 100 kcals.

Cooking and processing

Preparing, processing and cooking food usually alters its calorie content, and sometimes its nutritional value. Three things can happen:

- Water or a nutrient can be removed.

- Water or a nutrient can be added.

- Heat can alter the properties of some nutrients.

Adding or removing lipids makes the greatest difference to food energy values. Removal is more difficult than addition. Visible fat can be trimmed from meat, and grilling partly separates proteins and lipids. Cooking with fat or oil dramatically increases energy values.

Prolonged heating of unsaturated oils can change their chemical

	kcals/100 g
Boiled or baked potatoes	85
Roast potatoes	140
Chips	240
Fresh bread	240
Fried bread	505

composition – more of this later.

Adding sugar obviously increases calories. Most fresh fruits are water plus 10% to 15% fructose, glucose or sucrose. Fresh peaches have 30 kcals per 100 g, peaches canned in syrup have 90 kcals per 100 g.

Extended boiling or stewing of fruits and vegetables destroys their vitamin C content. The vitamin is unstable and steam volatile – again, more of this later.

Dry rice and dry pasta are about 10% water. This increases to about 70% after cooking.

Trimming, coring and peeling fruits and vegetables reduces their fibre content.

Water removal concentrates nutrients and increases their energy value on a weight for weight basis. Bread contains about 40% water, toast is around 20% water. Fresh plums have 40 kcals per 100 g, prunes have 160 kcals per 100 g.

Four energy needs

Modern medical trials can precisely determine the calorie requirement for any individual under any set of circumstances. These procedures are rarely necessary. Instead, theoretical calculations are used to give average calorie needs for similar groups of people with similar lifestyles.

Your body does four things with the energy it takes in from food and drink. Total energy need is calculated by adding these four components together:

- Basal metabolic rate, **BMR**.
- Physical activity level, **PAR**.
- Thermogenesis.
- New tissue synthesis.

We need to look at each of these in turn.

Growth and repair

Protein foods are needed to produce and repair all the working parts of the body.

Adults use only about 100 to 150 kcals/day to repair or replace dead and damaged tissues. This very small energy need is usually added to the base metabolic rate in total energy estimates.

Infants up to the age of around 6 months convert about 30% of their total calorie intake into new tissue. Thereafter, the percentage of total calories used for growth reduces rapidly.

Recent research is beginning to suggest that diet quality in the first 6 months of infancy greatly influences adult health, vulnerability to many diseases and even life expectancy. The benefits of breastfeeding may be very much greater than the medical profession previously suspected.

Keeping warm

Human body temperature is maintained at 37°C. Variations of more than about ±2°C for extended periods are harmful and eventually fatal. The year-round average temperature in the UK is something like 10°C. Food energy is needed to provide enough heat to bridge this 27°C gap. This heat production is called **thermogenesis**.

Thermogenesis is not usually a major component of total energy requirement because appropriate clothing minimises heat losses. Living and working in very cold climates can, however, increase food needs by as much as 3,000 kcals/day. No food is needed for thermogenesis if the ambient temperature is maintained at 37°C.

Base metabolic rates

The energy used for new tissue synthesis and thermogenesis is small and can be ignored in estimates of total calorie-need for most individuals.

Most people use most of their food energy just to keep their body chemistry working. This minimum energy-need corresponds to complete physical inactivity and is called the base or **basal metabolic rate**, abbreviated to **BMR**. An adult sleeping soundly in a room heated to 37°C uses energy at very close to his or her basal metabolic rate.

Basal metabolic rates vary with gender, age and body weight (Table 4.3).

Table 4.3 Basal metabolic rates

Age range	Male kcals/day	Female kcals/day
0–3 months	390	370
4–6 months	490	460
7–9 months	590	545
10–12 months	655	615
1–3 years	880	830
4–6 years	1,225	1,105
7–10 years	1,405	1,240
11–14 years	1,585	1,320
15–18 years	1,970	1,510
19–50 years	1,820	1,385
51–59 years	1,820	1,360
60–64 years	1,700	1,360
65–74 years	1,665	1,360
75+ years	1,500	1,290
Pregnancy (add)	–	200*
Lactation (add)	–	570
*last 3 months only		

Some of these BMR figures are surprising:

- BMR is a large proportion of typical total calorie requirement.

- There is a significant gender difference – adult women need about three-quarters of an adult man's calories to fuel their body chemistry. Women are smaller, but also more efficient.

- The BMR for a teenage boy is likely to be about 40% greater than his mother's.

- Pregnant women should not 'eat for two', but breastfeeding women need significantly more calories.

- BMR slows considerably after age 60 for men – less so for women.

Physical activity

Any physical activity uses energy.

Physical activity has two characteristics – intensity and duration. Duration is more important than intensity in energy-use.

In the year 1900, more than 80% of adult men in the UK had jobs involving high or very high physical activity. By the year 2000, this proportion had fallen to around 5%.

Women's employment patterns have altered and 'housekeeping' now involves much less physical effort than it used to – even if the chores are shared between the sexes.

Public and private transport have mostly replaced walking.

Many people have replaced work-related physical activity with leisure exercise, but generally, Western societies are much less active than they used to be.

Total energy needs

Depending on the duration and intensity of an individual's physical activity averaged over a typical 24-hour period, a physical activity number can be estimated for a range of lifestyles:

Physical activity level ratio	Example
1.4	Car-owning student – no regular exercise
1.5 to 1.6	Junior nurse with two young children – occasional car user, swims twice a week
1.7 to 1.9	Marathon-running teenage bricklayer

Total energy requirement is then estimated by multiplying the appropriate BMR by the physical activity ratio. For example, using simple figures:

$$2,000 \text{ kcals/day} \times 1.5 = 3,000 \text{ kcals/day}$$
$$(\text{BMR}) \qquad (\text{PAL}) \qquad (\text{total energy need})$$

Table 4.4 shows the range of total calorie requirements that apply for most people.

Table 4.4 Average calorie requirements

Male 19 to 50 years			Female 19 to 50 years not pregnant or breastfeeding		
BMR kcals/day	PAL	Total kcals/day	BMR kcals/day	PAL	Total kcals/day
1,820	1.4	2,550	1,385	1.4	1,940
1,820	1.5	2,730	1,385	1.5	2,080
1,820	1.6	2,910	1,385	1.6	2,220
1,820	1.7	3,095	1,385	1.7	2,355

Correct energy content is the first requirement for a balanced diet, but it cannot be the only requirement. Extremely unbalanced diets are actually life-threatening, even if their calorie content is precisely matched to an individual's needs.

Food	Weight containing 2,000 kcals
Olive oil	220 ml
Butter	270 g
Chocolate	340 g
Red wine	4 bottles
Whole milk	2.9 l
Prunes	1.2 kg
Medium-sized apples	30 apples

A typical adult woman needs something like 2,000 kcals/day. Each of the bizarre daily diets shown in the table supplies this amount of energy.

All of these would be exceedingly dangerous in the long term.

Energy density

Animals like cows and elephants spend nearly all their waking hours eating – their bodies are large and their food has relatively few calories per gram. Herbivores have low **energy density** diets.

Adaptation to an omnivorous diet is an evolutionary improvement.

Omnivorous animals survive even if their usual or regular food source becomes exhausted or unavailable.

Fats and protein foods have high energy densities. Less time is needed to gather or catch food; more time can be given to other activities.

Humans are the ultimate omnivores, but the constant temptation of manufactured, very energy-dense foods in Western societies easily leads to excessive energy intakes.

4 Fats and oils

It is likely that the ideal human diet ought to contain relatively low levels of fats and oils and that most of these lipids should be vegetable oils, not animal fats. This cannot be proved, but evidence from the natural diet of the great apes and from the variation of human diet by region mostly points in the same direction.

Western diets probably contain much more fat than our bodies were designed, by evolution, to cope with. In the UK, fats and oils provide around 38% of total calorie intake, and the 'natural' calorie contribution from lipids might be as low as 10%.

Western disease

There is a group of diseases and disorders that are much more common in the West than in developing countries – coronary heart disease, stroke, obesity, hypertension, diabetes and some cancers.

Many of these Western diseases have been linked with high-lipid diets and especially with high animal fat intake. The linking evidence is very strong but not totally conclusive in all situations. Research is sometimes conflicting and dietary advice can be confusing.

Western lifestyles are also characterised by physical inactivity, excessive total calories, smoking, stress and pollution. It is difficult to be totally certain that fat, on its own, is a major risk.

However, fat consumption increased steadily through the course of the 20th century in the West – so did the rates of the typical Western diseases.

Immigrants tend to suffer from the disease pattern of their adopted country, not their place of birth. Heart disease and some cancers are rare in Japan, but widespread amongst Japanese immigrants in the USA. Diabetes is uncommon in rural India, Pakistan and Bangladesh, but is very common in some groups of older Asian women who have lived in the UK for many years.

Sexual equality has led to many women adopting 'male' diets and lifestyles. The incidence of Western disease is increasing in women and the gender gap is narrowing.

Finland once had the highest intake of animal fat in the world – up to 50% of total calories consumed. It also had the world's highest level of coronary heart disease. Government education programmes have led to lower fat intakes, and the level of heart disease in Finland has fallen dramatically.

Saturated and unsaturated lipids

All animals and nearly all plants produce lipids as long-term food stores. Lipids are compounds made from one molecule of a triol and three **fatty acids**:

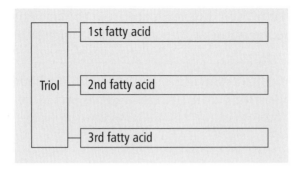

Different plants and different animals make use of different types and different combinations of fatty acid to make their particular lipids.

Some kinds of fatty acid are thought to be more damaging to health than others.

Fatty acid molecules are long-chain organic compounds. Those found in nature contain 16, 18, 20 or 22 carbon atoms linked together. There is little conclusive evidence that chain length has any influence on health or disease.

Carbon atoms can be linked together with single bonds or double bonds. Depending on the types of carbon–carbon bond they contain, fatty acids can be placed into one of three groups:

- Saturated fatty acids – only single bonds.

- Monounsaturated fatty acids – one double bond.

- Polyunsaturated fatty acids – two or more double bonds.

Figure 4.4 shows the differences for fatty acids with 16 carbon atoms.

Cis and trans isomers

Two molecules are isomers if they have the same molecular formula but their atoms are joined together in a different way.

The more carbon atoms a molecule contains, the more isomers are possible.

Fatty acids contain between 16 and 22 carbon atoms – each can exist as different isomers.

A carbon–carbon double bond is rigid, and unsaturated compounds come in two forms called cis and trans isomers. Figures 4.5 and 4.6 show the two types for a monounsaturated fatty acid with 16 carbon atoms.

Cis is pronounced like the 'sis' in 'sister' or 'cistern'.

Figure 4.4   Fatty acids – differences

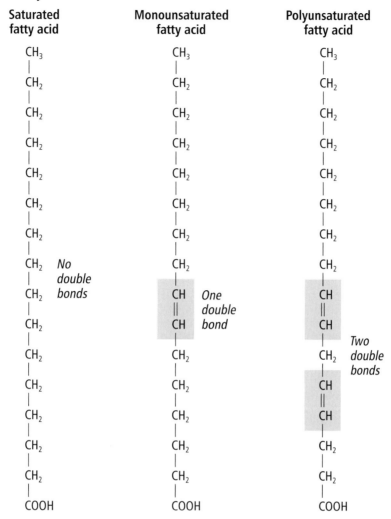

Figure 4.5   Cis isomer (same side)

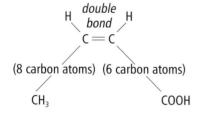

It can be seen that cis and trans isomers have different shapes and therefore different biological functions. Natural unsaturated lipids are nearly always cis isomers, but some kinds of industrial processing convert the cis form into the trans isomer.

Figure 4.6   Trans isomer (opposite sides)

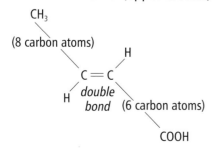

Cis unsaturated fatty acids are thought to be beneficial to health, but trans isomers have been linked with heart disease.

Margarines are made from vegetable and fish oils. Some margarine manufacturing processes turn cis isomers into trans isomers.

Prolonged heating of vegetable oils converts cis fatty acids to the trans isomers. Repeated reuse and recycling of deep fry oils should be avoided.

Figure 4.7 summarises the different kinds of lipid.

Figure 4.7   The different kinds of lipids

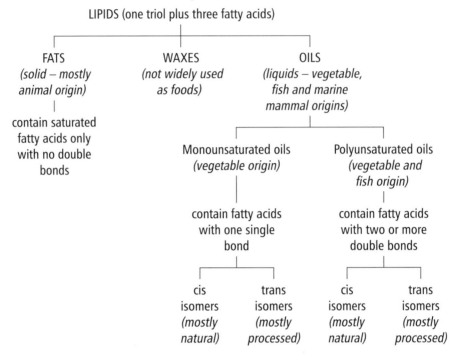

Essential fatty acids

More than 100 different fatty acids have been found in naturally occurring lipids; some are much more common than others, but only two are an essential component of the human diet. These are the **essential fatty acids**, EFAs.

A minimum intake of about 5 g per day of the EFAs is needed to avoid major health problems, but deficiency is rare, because:

- EFAs are widely distributed in many common foods, although vegetable oils are richer sources.

- The average Western diet contains about 15 g/day of fatty acids.

- EFAs can be stored in the body. A typical European has a reserve of about 750 g or around 6 months' supply.

As an exception to these general rules, EFAs are vital in the diet of newborns and infants up to the age of around 6 months.

The brain is more than 50% lipids by weight and EFAs are essential for neurological growth and development.

Breast milk from properly nourished mothers is rich in EFAs, but formula foods can be deficient. The importance of EFAs is still being researched – there is no evidence that high consumption is harmful.

Coronary heart disease

The UK has one of the world's highest rates of coronary heart disease (CHD). The problem is multifactorial – this means that CHD has many causes and that there are interactions amongst these causes. The factors for CHD may include:

- gender
- age
- weight
- excess overall calorie consumption
- excess sugar consumption
- excess lipid consumption
- excess saturated lipid consumption
- vitamin deficiency
- mineral deficiency
- hypertension
- smoking
- lack of exercise
- emotional and psychological stress
- genetic predisposition
- pollution

Obviously, this very long list will include major influences as well as less important ones, and there is close linkage amongst some groups of factors.

At the most basic level, the root causes of CHD are gender and poverty. After the menopause, female rates of CHD begin to approach those of men and poverty can be linked to most of the other factors. Men living in Glasgow and Sunderland have the highest UK rates of heart disease; the lowest incidence is found amongst women from Surrey.

Cholesterol

Excess consumption of saturated fats is thought to be the largest single cause of CHD. The evidence comes from many statistical surveys and, most importantly, a mechanism that links saturated fat intake with CHD has been identified.

In general terms, cholesterol is transported around the body attached to a group of molecules that contain a lipid chemically bonded to a protein. For obvious reasons, these compounds are called lipoproteins. There are three kinds of lipoprotein:

- VLDL – very low density lipoproteins
- LDL – low density lipoproteins
- HDL – high density lipoproteins

CHD begins when the arteries are narrowed by deposits of cholesterol-rich lipids. LDL releases more cholesterol than HDL or VLDL.

Saturated fat consumption increases the production of LDL; unsaturated fats probably decrease the body's ability to make LDL.

A great deal of research has been directed towards the possible connections between fat consumption and other major Western diseases. The risks, mechanisms and causes of stroke are more or less identical to those for CHD.

It is possible that high fat consumption is involved in breast, bowel, pancreatic and prostate cancer, but the multifactorial problem greatly confuses the issue. However, no disease or disorder has ever been linked to sensible low-fat diets.

Many diseases show great variation between districts, countries, regions and even continents. Only two reasons can explain these differences – genetics, in the widest sense, and environment.

There are proven genetic and racial differences in predisposition to some diseases. African men tend to have high rates of hypertension independently of diet.

Some environmental factors are obvious. There are proven links between air pollution and bronchitis, and between water quality and very many infectious diseases.

Diet is part of the environment, and diets differ markedly from place to place.

The greatest sufferers from Western diseases are generally the poorer people in the richer countries. CHD rates peak in North America, north-west Europe and Australia. White South Africans also have very high rates of CHD.

The Mediterranean diet

Across Europe, rates of CHD, strokes and hypertension are highest in Scotland and northern England, and lowest in Greece and southern Italy. The Mediterranean diet is often said to be the healthiest in the world, but it is difficult to disentangle the beneficial effects of diet and general lifestyle.

Beef, pork, milk and dairy products are virtually absent from the traditional Mediterranean diet. Protein consumption is relatively low and based on fish, with a little lamb and goat meat.

Sugar consumption is low, but the mainstay of the diet is complex carbohydrate foods like pasta and bread. Fibre intake is high.

Compared with most of Europe, the Greeks and southern Italians eat huge quantities of fruit and vegetables.

Alcohol consumption is high, but very little beer or spirits is drank. Most alcohol is taken as locally produced red wine.

There is virtually no saturated fat intake. Olive oil is the major lipid.

Prolonged cooking, stewing, frying and baking is not a major feature of the diet.

Non-diet environmental factors may be relevant. Southern Italy and most of Greece is not prosperous and there are fewer cars than in most of Europe. Regular exercise is unavoidable. Climate makes a difference – there is a link between cold wet weather and heart disease.

There is probably nothing protective about Greek or Italian genes. Northern Italian cities like Milan and Turin have relatively high rates of CHD.

Dietary recommendations

Table 4.5   The current dietary recommendations for lipids

Lipid type	% of total calorie intake	For an adult non-active woman	
		kcals/day	g/day
Saturated	11	215	24
Cis-monounsaturated	13	250	28
Cis-polyunsaturated	7	135	15
Trans – all types	2	40	5
Total lipids	33%	640 kcals/day	72 g

Dietary advice is given as averages for large groups of people (Table 4.5). Individual needs, risks and tolerances will be different from these averages.

However, an individual diet that departs dramatically from the average recommendations over many years is almost certainly a health risk.

Informed adults are free to make choices and it is impossible to be good all the time.

Some dietary recommendations are more important than others. The single most important piece of advice is to minimise consumption of saturated fats.

Virtually all packaged foods show total fat and unsaturated fat content on their product labels. This is by far the best guide. Many processed foods contain more fat than you might expect.

The easiest way to eat too much saturated fat is to rely on fast food like fish and chips, burgers, pizza, and Indian and Chinese takeaways. Fats are cheaper than protein and increase palatability. A big burger and regular fries has 810 calories. A deep pan 10″ pizza has between 1,200 and 1,400 calories.

All fats and vegetable oils have 900 kcals/100 g – this includes lard, beef dripping, olive oil, sunflower oil, corn oil, groundnut oil, soya oil and all blended products.

Butter is 85% fat; margarines vary between 40% and 70% fat.

Nuts and crisps have very high fat contents – between 40% and 65% total fat.

Protein foods vary considerably in fat content and fat type. Turkey, chicken and white fish have the least, pork and bacon the most (Table 4.6).

Table 4.6   Fat content of various protein foods

	Typical fat content, %
White fish	2
Shellfish	2
Turkey	3
Chicken	5
Duck	10
Eggs	11
Oily fish	15
Beef	10 to 20
Lamb	15 to 25
Cheese	~35
Processed meats	25 to 40
Pork and bacon	25 to 50

Generally, the higher the total fat, the greater the proportion of saturates.

Fruits, vegetables, salads, cereals and complex carbohydrate foods usually have very little fat. Avocados and olives are an exception, with about 20% fat.

5 Sugars and starches

There are three kinds of carbohydrate, each with a different role in the diet:

- **Sugars** are monosaccharides and disaccharides. They dissolve in water and have a sweet taste.

- Starches are polysaccharides. They are insoluble in water and are the main constituent of starchy foods like potatoes, rice and pasta. Starches are often called complex carbohydrates.

- **Fibre** is mostly cellulose, another kind of polysaccharide. It cannot be digested by humans. Fibre is properly called non-starch polysaccharide or NSP. Fibre is discussed in detail in Topic 7.

Sugars

Sugars are the simplest carbohydrates.

Compounds with a single ring structure are called monosaccharides. The commonest monosaccharides are glucose and fructose.

Compounds with two ring structures joined together are disaccharides – sucrose and lactose are the most abundant.

Solutions of monosaccharides or disaccharides are often indistinguishable without chemical analysis; all have a clean, sweet taste.

Different plants produce different kinds of monosaccharide and disaccharide.

Sugars that form part of the natural cell structure of plants are called **intrinsic sugars**.

Sugars that are not part of natural cell structures are called extrinsic or, more usually, added sugars.

An apple contains intrinsic sugars, commercial apple juices have **extrinsic sugars**. The great majority of added sugar in the UK diet is sucrose.

Sucrose is a disaccharide made in plant cells by bonding one glucose molecule to one fructose molecule. The sweet component of most fruits is the monosaccharide fructose.

Most plants store their food as starch polysaccharides, but there are two major exceptions:

- Sugar cane is a tropical crop. It is a member of the grass family and it stores sucrose inside the canes or stalks.

- Sugar beet is a temperate crop that resembles turnips, swedes and beetroots. Sucrose is stored in its roots or tubers.

- When ripe for harvest, beet and cane plants contain between 15% and 20% by weight of sucrose. Pure beet and pure cane sugars are identical.

Hidden sugar consumption

Sucrose is grown and refined in huge tonnage. In the West and many developing countries, sucrose is the cheapest source of calories, unless rice is the main staple food. In the UK, a 1 kg bag of sugar costs about 60 p – this works out as 67 calories for a penny. Best fillet steak provides about 3 calories for a penny.

Generally in the UK, we are buying less packet sugar for sweetening hot drinks and home baking, but this reduction has been matched by an increase in sugar consumed as part of processed food. Sugar is a major ingredient in soft drinks, sugar confectionery, chocolate, cakes, biscuits and canned food. Even savoury canned food like baked beans and soups can contain 2% to 8% added sugar.

UK sugar consumption averages 95 g per person per day and provides about 18% of total calories. Only 26% of this is bought as packet sugar.

Breast or bottle-fed infants derive 40% of their total energy needs from lactose – a disaccharide, sometimes called milk sugar. In the UK, pre-school children get about 30% of their total energy from sugar.

In the UK, sugar consumption varies significantly with gender and class. Poorer people eat the most.

Dental caries, or tooth decay, is directly linked to sucrose. Tooth decay is rare in societies with sucrose consumption below 60 g per person per day. Children, young teenagers and the elderly are most at risk.

Intrinsic sugars in fruits and vegetables are not a major cause of tooth decay. Fluoridation of the water supply greatly reduces the problem.

There is an essential human need for carbohydrates but not for sugars. All our carbohydrate could come from starch, although this kind of diet would be difficult to maintain.

No current medical opinion puts restrictions on recommended consumption of intrinsic sugars. This means that fruits and vegetables can be eaten more or less without limit. Lactose behaves like an intrinsic sugar and is thought to be more beneficial than sucrose – again, no dietary restrictions are currently recommended.

The recommended maximum intake of extrinsic sugars, essentially added sucrose, is 60 g/day, providing roughly 10% of total calories.

There is no proven link between sugar consumption at current UK levels and diabetes, for normal individuals. Diabetes is, however, linked with obesity and therefore excess total calorie intake. Sugar is often taken as extra calories and in this way can be seen as a factor in diabetes.

Some people and families are genetically predisposed to diabetes and should avoid high sucrose consumption.

Starch

Starches are polysaccharides. They are polymers made by joining many glucose molecules together. Glucose is the monomer, starch is the polymer. There are two kinds of starch:

- Amylose is a straight-chain polymer. Molecules vary in length – the shortest have chains of about 30 glucose units, the longest around 3200 glucose units.

- Amylopectin is a much bigger, more complicated molecule. The chains are longer, with branches at intervals along the main chain.

Different plants produce starch with different proportions of amylose and amylopectin.

When heated with water, starch granules swell and burst. Cooked starches are more easily digested than raw starch.

Glucose is stored in the muscles, and as glycogen in the livers and muscles of animals. Glycogen is sometimes called animal starch, and its chemical structure is similar to amylopectin.

The brain, nervous system and red blood cells can be damaged within minutes if their glucose supply is interrupted – so the body controls blood glucose concentration within very close limits.

Sugars are broken down into glucose more rapidly than starch, because starch molecules are disassembled one unit at a time.

Sugars cause a rapid increase in blood glucose concentrations; starches have a more gradual effect. Some kinds of starch can be broken down into glucose more rapidly than others.

Many researchers believe that 'slow release' starches are more beneficial than 'rapid release' starches and sugars, because their digestion needs less insulin and causes smaller swings in blood glucose levels. These theories are not proven, and the minority view says that normal individuals can cope with all kinds of carbohydrate.

Starch provides about 80% of the world's calories. The main starch crops are rice, maize, millet, sorghum, wheat, barley, oats and potatoes.

UK consumption of starches is highly variable, but averages around 24% of total calories.

High-starch diets are beneficial provided other nutrients, especially vitamins, are present in sufficient amounts. Third World malnutrition usually results from vitamin and protein deficiency, not excess starch.

Breast milk does not contain starch, while some formula milks do.

Starch is likely to be a better source of calories for active children than sugars or fats, but children generally eat more sugar than adults.

Most starch foods also have significant quantities of fibre; sugars do not contain fibre.

Dietary recommendations

Current dietary advice combines recommendations for all carbohydrate – that is, sugars plus starch (Table 4.7).

Table 4.7 The current dietary recommendations for carbohydrates

Carbohydrate	% of total calories	For a woman aged 19 to 50 kcals/day	g/day
Extrinsic or added sugars	10	195	50
Intrinsic sugars, milk sugars and starch	37	720	180
Total digestible carbohydrate	47%	915 kcals/day	230 g

There is a significant difference between actual carbohydrate consumption in the UK and the recommendations for a balanced diet (Table 4.8).

Table 4.8 Comparing recommendations and actual carbohydrate consumption

	Actual % of total calories	Recommended % of total calories
Added sugars	18	10
Natural sugars, milk sugars and starch	24	37
Total carbohydrate, excluding fibre	42%	47%

These differences can be translated into simple dietary advice:

- Many people eat nearly twice as much added sugar than they ought to. Most of this will be as part of processed foods, not as sugar added to tea and coffee. Full-sugar soft drinks, sweets, chocolate and cakes are the highest added sugar processed foods.

- Low-calorie soft drinks are a sensible alternative, but in moderation.

- Most people ought to eat much more fruit, vegetables, salads and fruit juice. Later we will discuss the many other benefits of fruit and vegetables.

- Starch consumption ought to be increased; there is little dietary difference between the main starch foods – essentially potatoes, rice and pasta are equally beneficial.

- Overall consumption of carbohydrates should be higher. For most people, this means they ought to eat less saturated fat and more starch.

Carbohydrate foods

Packaged foods have to show sugar, starch and total carbohydrate content – this is always a reliable guide.

One teaspoon of sugar is about 4 or 5 g of sucrose and 16 to 20 kcals.

Full-sugar soft drinks contain between 5% and 12% added sugars. Tonic water has the least, full-sugar colas have the most. Sometimes, sucrose is replaced with glucose, isoglucose or a product called high-fructose corn syrup. All of these substitutes are equivalent to sucrose in calories and health effects.

Diet soft drinks have no sugars, but sometimes very high caffeine contents.

Fruits contain between 8% and 20% intrinsic sugars. Eat as much as you like. Read the label carefully on shop-bought fruit juices – some have added sucrose.

Sugar confectionery is more or less pure sucrose. Many popular mints are 98% sugar. Wine gums and hard gums are around 60% sugar.

Chocolate is 60% sugar. Dark chocolate has less fat than milk chocolate, but just as much sugar.

Sugar is a preservative, and many canned foods, pickles and sauces have a surprisingly high sugar content. Read the label.

Jams and marmalades are about 70% sugar.

Vanilla ice cream is 25% sugar. Some flavoured ice creams can be 45% sugar. Sorbets have much less sugar, typically around 12%.

Potatoes, rice and pasta are about 10% water and 90% starch when raw, and around 65% water and 35% starch after cooking.

It is very difficult to eat too much cooked plain starch, but preparation makes a big difference. Fried rice is a high calorie food, so is mashed potato with butter, and so are chips and things like hash browns. Plain pasta is the best choice.

Pizza dough is high starch and relatively low calorie. Bought-in pizzas are high calorie foods because nearly all the toppings are rich in saturated fats.

Bread is good, but butter adds calories and saturated fat. Jam has added sugar.

- One slice dry bread = 100 kcals
- One slice bread and butter = 220 kcals
- One slice bread, butter and jam = 270 kcals

Most people add twice as much butter to toast than they do to untoasted bread.

6 Protein

Protein deficiency is rare in the UK and in most developed countries. Poorly fed infants and some on specialised diets – like vegans and strict vegetarians – run a risk of deficiency, but most adults eat significantly more protein than the minimum need (Table 4.8).

Table 4.8 Calories derived from protein

	UK men and women aged 19–50 years (% of total calories derived from protein)
Estimated average requirement	7.2%
Reference nutrient intake	9.0%
Average UK current intake	13.5%

Protein deficiency is common in many developing countries. This is discussed in Topic 11.

Proteins are polymers of amino acids. The different working parts of different plants and animals are made from different combinations of amino acids.

To make a 'complete set' of human proteins, a total of 20 amino acids are needed.

Essential amino acids

Twelve of the 20 amino acids can be synthesised inside our bodies from simple molecules, but eight of them cannot. These eight are the essential amino acids (EAAs). A balanced diet has to have enough of all of them.

Table 4.10 lists the amino acids – you do not have to remember their names.

Table 4.10 The amino acids

8 essential amino acids	12 other amino acids
Isoleucine	Alanine
Leucine	Arginine
Lysine	Asparagine
Methionine	Aspartic acid
Phenylalanine	Cistine
Threonine	Cysteine
Tryptophan	Glutamine
Valine	Glutamic acid
	Glycine
	Histidine
	Serine
	Tyrosine

An adult diet containing even quite modest amounts of animal protein provides more than enough of the eight EAAs. The richest sources are meat, poultry, fish, eggs, cheese and milk.

Vegetable proteins

No single vegetable source contains all eight EAAs. Additionally, **vegetable proteins** have lower EAA contents than animal products. The minimum human need can be met from a very mixed vegetarian diet, but reliance on one major starch source is unwise:

- Wheat and barley lack lysine.

- Maize lacks tryptophan.

- Soya lacks methionine.

EAA deficiency in adults causes progressively more serious disease, as the body is unable to repair and replace important proteins. Poor hair condition and hair loss are the earliest symptoms.

Very high starch diets also reduce the body's ability to absorb some essential amino acids. This makes vegan diets even more risky.

Protein and children

Previously, we have shown protein requirements as a percentage of total calorie intake. Knowing that 1 g of pure protein contains 4 kcals, we can convert calorie figures into weights of protein. Table 4.11 shows the calculations for some women.

Table 4.11 Protein requirements of women (aged 19–50) who are not pregnant or breastfeeding

	Protein as % of total calories	Total calories	Protein requirement cals/day	g/day
Estimated average requirement	7.2	1940	140	35
Reference nutrient intake	9.0	1940	175	44
Average UK current intake	13.5	1940	260	65

During all stages of pregnancy, the growing baby and associated tissues need about 6 g of protein a day for healthy development. The typical British woman eats 65 g a day of protein, so the extra needs of pregnancy do not normally involve a change in diet. However, there are potential problems if the expectant mother has a low protein diet or is vegetarian.

Nausea in pregnancy can dramatically alter the preferred diets of some women. Drastic protein reduction is inadvisable.

Children are 'selfish' from the moment of conception or perhaps the maternal instinct begins at conception – in all but the most extreme circumstances, the foetus will meet its nutrient needs, leaving whatever remains for the mother.

Women transfer about 11 g/day of protein during the first 6 months of breast-feeding. Again, human biochemistry is arranged so that the baby's needs are satisfied before those of the mother. Protein deficiency amongst breastfeeding women in the UK is rare, but not unheard of.

The total need for protein increases gradually through childhood and then reaches a plateau in the late teens (Table 4.12).

Table 4.12   Reference nutrient intakes for females

Female age	Reference nutrient intake Protein (g/day)
0–3 months	11.0
4–6 months	12.5
7–9 months	13.7
10–12 months	14.9
1–3 years	14.5
4–6 years	19.7
7–10 years	28.3
11–14 years	41.2
15–18 years	45.4
19–50 years	45.0
50 years +	45.0

These figures look straightforward, but a different picture emerges if we look at protein needs per kilogram of body weight – in proportion, infants and children need a lot more than adults (Table 4.13).

Table 4.13   Various protein needs

Female age	Average weight (kg)	RNI protein (g/day)	RNI protein (g/kg body weight/day)
0–3 months	5.9	11.0	1.9
7–9 months	8.8	13.7	1.6
1–3 years	12.5	14.5	1.2
7–10 years	28.3	28.3	1.0
15–18 years	55.5	45.4	0.8
19–50 years	60.0	45.0	0.75

Obviously, infants and children need proportionately more protein because their bodies are growing and developing; adults only need protein for maintenance and repair.

Essential amino acids and children

Per kilo of body weight, babies need 2½ times more total protein than adults. Total protein is important, but **protein quality** is vital. In proportion to their weight, babies need nine times more of the **essential amino acids** than adults (Table 4.14).

Table 4.14 Essential amino acid requirements for four age groups

Essential amino acid	3–4 months	2 years	10–12 years	Adult
Isoleucine	70	31	28	10
Leucine	161	73	44	14
Lysine	103	64	44	12
Methionine	58	27	22	13
Phenylalanine	125	69	22	14
Threonine	87	37	28	7
Tryptophan	17	12	3	3
Valine	93	38	25	10
Total mg/kg eight EAAs	714 mg	351 mg	216 mg	83 mg

Adults in developed countries are very unlikely to be short of essential amino acids. The requirement is small as a proportion of total protein and also as a proportion of total calories.

An adult woman needs 83 mg of EAAs for each kilo that she weighs. The average adult woman in the UK weighs 60 kg. This means that she needs 60 × 83 mg, equal to 5 g/day of EAAs. This 5 g is only a small part of a balanced diet:

	kcals/day	g/day
EAA	20	5
Average protein intake	260	65
Total nutrients	1,940	variable

Even in the West, it is not impossible to run the risk of EAA deficiency in some circumstances – there are several danger points.

The need for EAAs begins at conception. A healthy balanced diet is essential for pregnant women and those planning pregnancy. The foetus is totally dependent on the mother for all nutrition. If anything, the need for a balanced diet is even greater during breastfeeding.

Some toddlers and young children develop strong aversions to protein foods – preferring sugars and starches. There can be a minor risk of EAA deficiency.

Vegans and vegetarians

Vegetarianism runs in families – usually vegetarian parents arrange a proper diet for their children.

The trigger for a switch to a vegetarian diet is usually concern for animal welfare. A deep distaste for animal food and all its implications – such as slaughterhouses, live animal transport and factory farming – is more common in females and often coincides with puberty. Girls from omnivorous families who decide to 'go vegetarian' in their early teens can run serious risks of protein and/or essential amino acid deficiency. The switch to an ill-informed unbalanced diet coincides with a time when the need for high-quality protein is reaching its maximum.

Any child or teenager who decides to become vegetarian should seek medical advice. Properly managed vegetarian diets can be much healthier than the typical teenage favourites like burgers, chips and soft drinks – but only with care.

Some researchers have suggested that a badly balanced vegetarian diet, especially for young teenage girls, can increase the risks of anorexia and bulimia in later life.

Muscle is protein

Virtually every part of every kind of animal can be eaten, but strong cultural and social pressures restrict the options – especially in the West. Brains and eyeballs are valuable sources of nutrients, but they end up as dog and cat food in the UK. Hearts, liver and kidneys are far less popular than they used to be.

Most animals have three kinds of muscle:

- Cardiac or heart muscle.

- Smooth muscle – making up the structures of the alimentary canal, blood vessels and so on. Smooth muscle is not under voluntary control.

- Skeletal muscles, attached to bone, which move the limbs and body when stimulated by a motor nerve.

Nearly all the animal protein we eat is skeletal muscle. There are two kinds:

- Fast muscle fibre is used for rapid motion like running, swimming and flying. Fast muscle fibres are white or pale in colour.

- Slow muscle fibre is used for steady sustained motion. Slow muscle fibres store oxygen using a protein called myoglobin. Myoglobin is red when oxygenated, so slow muscle fibre is also red.

Fish and most birds have muscles built of fast fibres, hence their meat is white or pale coloured. Domesticated animals are the descendants of wild cattle, pigs and sheep. Originally these animals would have been active, but under intensive farming they lead sedentary lives – their meat is red and higher in fat than that of their wild ancestors.

Muscle is protein, and proteins are polymers of amino acids. With increasing age, and with greater exercise, the protein polymer chains become crosslinked. This is why the meat from older animals is tougher than from younger ones. In most societies, the meat from very young animals is the most prized – veal, lamb and suckling pig, for example.

With ordinary preparation and cooking methods it is impossible to separate completely the animal fat from an animal protein. Some industrial processes produce virtually pure animal protein, but most people find its taste unpleasant.

Different animals have different proportions of protein and fat in their muscles and surrounding tissues. Pork is the fattiest meat; white fish, shellfish and chicken have the least fat. The fat from pork, lamb, beef and poultry is mostly saturated. Fish proteins come with polyunsaturated fats.

Dairy foods

Beef, lamb, pork, chicken and fish are the main protein sources in the UK diet; dairy products and eggs provide animal proteins indirectly.

	Whole milk %	Whole egg %
Protein	3	12
Carbohydrate	5	–
Fat	4	11
Water	88	77
Fibre	–	–
Total	100	100
kcals/100 g	(68)	(147)

The starting points for virtually all processed egg and dairy foods are full cream cow's milk and whole hen's eggs:

Semi-skimmed milk has 1.6% fat; skimmed milk has virtually none. The fat removed is replaced with water.

Egg yolks have 350 kcals/100 g; egg whites have far fewer – about 40 kcals/100 g.

Dairy products are made by concentrating and processing the nutrients found in whole milk. Butter is the highest calorie dairy food – it contains about 85% fat and 15% water; most of the fat is saturated and there is little protein.

Cream is basically a mixture of fat and water with about 2% protein. Half cream is 12% fat, single cream 18% fat and double cream about 50% fat.

It is impossible to give general guidance for the protein and fat contents of manufactured yoghurts and products like fromage frais. Some are low fat, low calorie foods, others have high fat and high sugar contents. Read the label.

Cheese is often seen as a healthy alternative to animal protein; this may not always be true, because most cheeses have higher fat contents than most meats. All cheeses are richer in fat than fish and poultry. Hard cheeses like Cheddar and Cheshire make up about 85% of UK consumption. Soft cheeses like Brie and Camembert have more water and usually fewer calories per 100 g. Cottage cheese has very little fat and more water than other cheeses. Table 4.15 shows some typical calorie values.

Fat contents vary from one brand to another. Again, always read the label.

The fat in cow's milk is about two-thirds saturated and one-third monounsaturated. Most hard cheeses have fats in the same proportion. Cheese has very little carbohydrate and no fibre:

Table 4.15 Typical calorie values for cheeses

	cals/100 g
Cream cheese	440
Cheddar	410
Cheshire	390
Red Leicester	390
Danish Blue	365
Edam	315
Brie	305
Cottage cheese	105

	Cheddar cheese per 100 g
Saturated fat	24
Monounsaturated fat	9
Polyunsaturated fat	1
Total fat	34
Protein	25
Water	41
Total	100 g
kcals/100 g	410 kcals

High-protein diets

The UK average consumption of protein is higher than the recommended nutrient intake:

	Men g/day	Women g/day
Reference nutrient intake	55	44
Average UK intake	84	65

There is firm evidence that high-protein diets are dangerous for people with kidney disease or reduced kidney function, but for healthy individuals, no high-protein risk has yet been proved.

The Masai, who live in East Africa, and some Inuits, have very high-protein diets but no evidence of diet-related disease. Primitive hunter-gatherers must also have had high-protein diets.

Some research indicates a link between very high-protein diets, raised blood pressure and/or bone demineralisation. This work may not be reliable because high-protein foods are nearly always high in fat as well.

Current UK advice is to limit protein consumption to twice the recommended nutrient intake, or about 90 g/day for an adult woman. Very few people eat this much.

Amino acid supplements

Supplements containing single amino acids, mixtures of amino acids or amino acids with vitamins and minerals are widely available in pharmacies, supermarkets and health food stores.

Many of these **supplements** can be dangerous. It is very easy to overdose and the toxicity of excess consumption is poorly researched.

The authoritative 1991 UK government report gives detailed recommendations for fat and carbohydrate consumption. The guidelines for protein are less strict, because the average UK diet has more than the minimum requirement and a lot less than the recommended maximum. Put another way, protein consumption can vary widely without damaging health.

The latest dietary advice suggests that carbohydrates and fats together should contribute no more than 80% of total calories. The remaining 20%, for most adults, is supplied by protein and alcohol.

Alcohol – the fourth macronutrient?

There is no dietary need for alcohol and excessive consumption is a proven cause of disorders and disease.

Government and the medical profession are faced with a problem – they cannot be seen to encourage excessive drinking, but dietary advice cannot ignore the significant proportion of total UK calories derived from alcohol. The Royal College of Physicians has suggested safe maximum levels for alcohol intake:

	Units /week	g alcohol /day	kcals /day	% of total calories
Adult men	21	24	170	6.7
Adult women	14	16	115	5.9

Taken overall, alcohol provides about 6% of all the calories consumed in the UK. However:

- 35% of adult women and 20% of adult men don't drink alcohol at all, or drink very little.

- Very few children under the age of 15 are regular drinkers.

The population of the UK is 58.8 million. Of these, about 35 million are regular drinkers and, on average, will be getting around 9% of their total calories from alcohol.

Overall balanced diet recommendations

In summary, we can give the overall recommendations for a balanced diet (Table 4.16).

Table 4.16 A balanced diet

Macronutrient	% of total calories	
	Actual UK diet	Recommended UK diet
Extrinsic, or added, sugars	18	10 max
Intrinsic sugars and starch	24	37
Total carbohydrate	42	47
Saturated fats	18	11 max
Cis-monounsaturated fats and oils	11	13
Cis-polyunsaturated fats and oils	7	7
Trans–lipids: all types	3	2 max
Total lipids	39	33 max
Total protein	13	variable
Alcohol	6	7 max
Total calories	100%	100%

7 Dietary fibre, NSP

Words like fibre, dietary fibre and roughage are commonly used but they are imprecise terms. Biochemists and food scientists have a better definition, which is:

Plant polysaccharides that cannot be digested by the enzymes normally present in the human body.

Fibre is properly called **non-starch polysaccharides** or **NSP** – by definition it cannot be digested and therefore has no calories.

Different kinds of foods produce different kinds of NSP. Some are insoluble, others dissolve partly or completely in water.

Type of NSP	Solubility	Main sources
Cellulose	Insoluble	Very widely distributed in leafy vegetables, peas and beans
Chitin	Insoluble	Mushrooms and fungi
Pectins	Soluble	Fruit and vegetables
Glucans	Soluble	Oats, barley, rye
Inulin	Soluble	Some root vegetables
Galactans	Partly soluble	Wheat

You do not have to remember any of these names. The main point is that some NSP are soluble and some are not.

Our bodies have evolved to work best on a diet that is rich in starchy foods like fruits and vegetables.

Insoluble NSP

Insoluble NSP is essential for the proper function of the digestive system. Insoluble NSP increases stool weight, increases the frequency of defecation and reduces food transit times. There is a direct proven link between extended food transit times and a number of disorders. Some of these are inconvenient and unpleasant, others are potentially life threatening:

- Constipation
- Haemorrhoids, piles
- Gallstones
- Diverticular disease
- Bowel cancer

Soluble NSP

Soluble NSP also has a number of beneficial effects. Most of these are not immediately obvious:

- Soluble NSP lowers the digestibility of fats and proteins and therefore reduces their calorie content. Current research is trying to identify how large this calorie reduction might be.

- Soluble NSP reduces blood cholesterol. It removes low density cholesterol more rapidly than high density cholesterol. This is good news.

- Soluble NSP possibly reduces blood pressure, although the evidence is not conclusive.

Raw bran is the outer coating of cereals like wheat, rice and maize. Most of it is removed in processing. Some people add raw bran to low-fibre foods. This gives NSP, but it has an undesirable side-effect: raw bran contains a group of compounds called 'phytates'. These form strong chemical bonds with iron, zinc and calcium. Raw bran prevents the digestion of these vital minerals even if the diet contains adequate amounts.

Pregnant women should not eat raw bran. Processing removes the phytates and solves the mineral problem.

Dietary recommendations

The average UK diet contains about 10 g/day of total NSP.

Unbalanced diets have little NSP. Sugars have none, and a sugar-rich, high-fat diet may have no more than 5 g/day.

The recommended intake is 18 g/day for adults and this should be a roughly equal mix of soluble and insoluble NSP.

It is difficult to calculate the precise NSP content of any particular diet because NSP is found in many foods. A balanced diet will certainly contain more than 18 g/day of NSP. Apart from the problem with raw bran, no disease or disorder has been linked with very high-fibre diets.

The commonest fibre-rich foods are:

- breakfast cereals
- wholemeal bread
- baked beans
- boiled potatoes
- most other vegetables
- nearly all fruits, especially apples

Infants do not need NSP. There is no starch or NSP in breast milk. From about a year old, children need NSP in proportion to their body weight. For example, a 4-year-old weighing 15 kg would need about one-quarter of the NSP advised for his or her 60 kg mother. There is hardly ever any need to worry about NSP intake for children on reasonably balanced diets.

8 Water and other drinks

A previously well-nourished adult can survive for weeks without food. Fat stores are used to provide energy and many vitamins and minerals are stored in the liver and other tissues.

As a response to starvation the metabolic rate automatically slows down, thus conserving energy. Irreversible damage occurs when all the body's fat stores are exhausted – protein is then consumed, destroying nerve tissue, heart muscle and other vital organs.

There are recorded instances of individuals recovering after 65 days without food, but 40 to 50 days' starvation would kill most people.

Four days without water is thought to be the absolute human limit. Most are severely distressed after 48 hours without drinking.

All human biochemistry takes place in aqueous solution. A woman weighing 60 kg (roughly 9 st 7 lbs) contains 35 kg or 35 litres of water – equivalent to 5 st 7 lbs of water, or 7¾ gallons, or 62 pints.

Without water, all the biochemical reactions that keep us alive slow down and then stop altogether.

2.4 litres per day

The daily turnover of water in the body is about 4% of total body weight. If this is not replaced, dehydration occurs.

For a 60 kg adult woman, this 4% turnover is equivalent to 2.4 kg, or 2.4 litres, or about 4¼ pints. Water is lost as follows:

	Litres lost per day
Faeces and urine	1.5
Evaporation and sweat	0.6
Expiration (breath)	0.3
Total	2.4

This 2.4 litres per day is the irreducible minimum for non-active individuals. Prolonged exercise and higher temperatures greatly increase water loss. Long-distance runners and cyclists can lose 7 litres a day.

It is difficult for those with normal kidney and liver function to drink too much water. However, research suggests a growing trend towards Western adults drinking too little. Severe dehydration is an acute condition, but even a bit less than the recommended amount causes problems:

- Mild dehydration leads to constipation and increased food transit times. Constipation has been linked with increased risks of intestinal and bowel disease.

- Urinary tract infections are more common in people who drink too little – especially adult women.

- Skin, hair and nail condition depends on adequate fluid intake.

- Concentration, memory and coordination suffer if you do not drink enough. It is especially important that those in charge of machinery are adequately hydrated.

- Water provides bulk without calories. It can reduce the temptation to eat too much.

Mild dehydration is common amongst the elderly, in particular those with fixed and rigid lifestyles.

Water can be ingested in four ways:

- As water itself.

- By drinking liquids that are mostly water.

- By eating foods that have a significant water content.

- As a result of biochemical processes that give water as a by-product. This is called **metabolic water**.

Metabolic water

Water is made inside the body by many biochemical reactions. Most metabolic water is produced by the digestion of carbohydrates. The process is precisely the reverse of photosynthesis, and is shown in Figure 4.8.

Figure 4.8 Metabolic water through digestion of carbohydrates

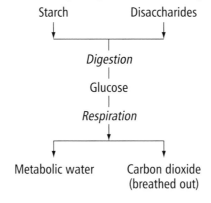

In humans and many other animals, **metabolic water** produces only a fraction of the total requirement. Animals that have evolved to live in hot, arid climates often have no need for liquid water – they live on the water content of their food plus **metabolic water**.

Water in food

Everything we eat and drink as nutrients was once alive. All living things are made up mostly of water – it follows that water is the main component of all food.

Some processed foods have low water contents, but only because water has been removed in preparation, processing and cooking.

A few unprocessed or lightly processed foods have very little water, but this is unusual. Packet sugar and some vegetable oils have only about 0.5% water.

Cooking and baking removes water. Typical oven temperatures of 140°C to 200°C are very much higher than the boiling point of water, 100°C. The more a food is cooked, the lower its water content becomes. Amongst everyday foods, biscuits have the lowest water content – ranging between 2% and 10%.

Raw fish is typically 80% water; meat and poultry before cooking ranges between 55% and 75%.

Boiling starch-based foods like potatoes, rice and pasta greatly increases their water content.

Fruits, vegetables and salads are nearly all water (Table 4.17). Their main nutrients are natural sugars, fibre, vitamins, minerals and sometimes a little starch.

Table 4.17   Average water content for some fruits, vegetables and salads

Water content (%)	Fruit or vegetable fresh uncooked
95% or more	Asparagus, broccoli, Brussels sprouts, cabbage, carrots, celery, cucumber, lettuce, mushrooms, radishes, tomatoes, watercress
90% to 95%	Beetroot, cauliflower, leeks, onions, grapefruit, apples, grapes, oranges, pears, plums
80% to 90%	Peas, beans and lentils, according to variety

Bananas are the only common fruit with any measurable starch content. Water content varies according to variety and ripeness, but averages between 75% and 80%. Bananas are still low calorie foods – about 80 kcals per banana.

Avocados and olives contain between 15% and 20% unsaturated vegetable fats, but again, these are healthy low calorie foods.

Prepared fruits and salads can include high calorie ingredients like sugars, syrups and mayonnaise. Lemon juice, vinegar, salt, pepper and most other spices have zero or very few calories.

Some foods, like milk, salad dressings and ice cream, are mixtures of oil, or fat, and water. These are **emulsions** rather than true solutions – this is why milk is white and double cream is yellowy white.

Heavily processed and high-fat foods have relatively low water contents. A diet that is also low in fruits and vegetables does not deliver anywhere near the minimum water requirement. As a general rule, the more unbalanced your food diet, the more water you need to take in as drinks.

Water in drinks

Research in the USA suggests that at least 70% of American schoolchildren never drink water. The trend towards the US pattern is accelerating in the West, in particular amongst the under-18s.

Most drinks are between 90% and 95% water. The non-water component can become a problem if water as such is an insignificant part of the diet. There are several risks:

- Sucrose, or added sugar, consumption can reach excessive levels.
- Artificial sweeteners, caffeine and some additives can become a major, but hidden part of the diet.
- Alcohol consumption can easily exceed the recommended maximum.

Most of us get our water from a variety of drinks, such as:

- beer, lager, stout
- cider
- wine
- fortified wines – sherry, port, vermouth
- spirits, liqueurs
- tea, coffee
- savoury drinks
- milk, milk-based drinks
- fruit juices
- full-sugar carbonated drinks
- low-calorie carbonated drinks

We have previously shown that the average adult woman loses at least 2.4 litres of water per day – if this is not replaced, dehydration occurs.

We can estimate very roughly the daily production of metabolic water and also the water content of a typical day's food:

	60 kg adult woman per day
Metabolic water	100 ml
Water in food	500 ml
Total	600 ml

Eight glasses a day

The amount of water that has to be taken in as drinks is simply the difference between the 2.4 litre daily requirement and the total of the 600 ml produced by metabolism together with water from food. This is 1.8 litres or 1,800 ml. For safety, we can round this up to 2 litres, or 2,000 ml per day.

The simplest way of meeting this need is to drink only water. An average glass of water is about 250 ml, so 2 litres is eight glasses a day. A recommendation to drink nothing but water is, however, unrealistic for most people and we need to look at the choices we normally make.

Alcoholic drinks

Alcoholic drinks have five possible ingredients:

- water – zero calories
- alcohol – 7 calories per gram
- sugars – 4 calories per gram
- colours and flavours – virtually zero calories
- carbon dioxide – zero calories

Pure alcohol is a deadly poison. Its manufacture and sale is very closely controlled. The strongest drinks normally available are some vodkas with between 35% and 40% alcohol by weight.

More or less any kind of fruit, vegetable or cereal can be fermented to produce alcohol. Different plants give different kinds of alcoholic drinks because each has its own 'set' of complex organic compounds giving characteristic colours, flavours and smells.

Many alcoholic drinks contain natural sugars as well as alcohol. This increases their calorie content. Most people add mixers to spirits. These can have high sugar contents and must not be ignored when counting calories.

Fizzy alcoholic drinks like champagne contain dissolved carbon dioxide – this has no calories.

The labels on the bottles show % alcohol by volume. Before we can calculate calories this has to be converted to % alcohol by weight. Table 4.18 shows average values for some common alcoholic drinks.

Most beers, wines and spirits have very little sugar. As well as alcohol, port contains about 10% sugar. Alcopops and many newer heavily advertised drinks also have high sugar contents. Some liqueurs also have very high sugar contents – these do not have to be declared.

Table 4.8 Alcohol percentage values

Drink	% alcohol by volume	% alcohol by weight
Lager, beer, stout, cider	5	4
White wine, red wine, champagne	12	10
Vermouth	15	12
Port, sherry	18	15
Spirits, liqueurs	40	34

Very few people rely totally on alcoholic drinks for their water intake. To get 2 litres a day of water, you would have to drink:

- 4 bottles of spirits
- nearly 3 bottles of wine
- 4 pints of beer

Anyone drinking 4 bottles of spirits or 3 bottles of wine a day would have much bigger problems than dehydration.

Four pints of beer a day gives 560 calories, equivalent to 21% of an adult man's total calorie requirement, or 29% of the total calorie needs for an adult woman.

Tea and coffee

Most people in the UK over the age of about 35 get most of their daily water requirement from tea and coffee. The soft drink habit is relatively new.

A mug holds about 250 ml of liquid; a dainty tea cup as little as 150 ml. Two litres a day is 8 mugs of tea or coffee.

Black unsweetened tea or coffee has no calories. Milk adds about 20 calories per mug and each spoonful of sugar is another 20 calories.

Drinking 2 litres a day of tea or coffee provides the following calories:

- Black unsweetened – zero
- White, no sugar – 160 cals/day
- White, one sugar – 320 cals/day
- White, two sugars – 480 cals/day

The healthiest option is skimmed milk and no sugar. The recommended maximum intake of added sugars is 10% of total calories, that is 195 calories a day for an adult woman – equivalent to 10 teaspoonfuls a day of sugar. Massive research effort has been aimed at the possible health risks of drinking too much tea and/or coffee. Only four consequences have been proved:

- Caffeine is a problem for some people. Individual susceptibility varies a great deal, but caffeine induces hyperactivity and insomnia. Tea generally has more caffeine than coffee.

- Tea is very probably an antioxidant offering some protection against some cancers for some people.

- Excessive tea consumption reduces iron absorption.

- Teeth are stained, but not damaged, by tea and coffee.

Milk

The calorie and nutrient content of milk varies according to its fat content:

	Whole milk %	Semi-skimmed %	Skimmed %
Protein	3	3	3
Carbohydrate	5	5	5
Fat	4	1.5	trace
Water	88	90.5	92
Total	100%	100%	100%
Calories/100 ml	70	45	35

The carbohydrate in cow's milk is lactose, a disaccharide sugar. The fat is about two-thirds saturated and one-third polyunsaturated.

Drinking 2.2 litres a day of milk would provide 2 litres of water, but also a great many calories – between 770 and 1,550 calories a day, depending on type. Milk is best regarded as a food rather than a drink.

Flavoured milks and milk shakes often have high added sugar contents – check the label.

Fruit juices

Pure fruit juices contain about 10% natural sugars, like glucose and fructose, and 90% water. Most have about 40 kcals/100 ml – that is about 80–100 kcals for a typical glass.

Some fruit juices have added sugars. It is not always easy to tell this from the label, but anything with more than about 50 kcals per 100 ml has to contain added sugar.

Aside from water, natural fruit juices are the best way of providing the minimum daily fluid requirement.

Soft drinks

The UK consumption of carbonated soft drinks has increased dramatically over the last 30 years, in particular amongst younger people. This has not happened by accident and the reasons have nothing to do with nutrition or a balanced diet.

Most full sugar soft drinks have similar formulations – they are about 10% sucrose and 90% water. Carbon dioxide is dissolved in the water under pressure. This gives a mildly acid solution and a sharp, pleasant taste. Flavours and colours are added to produce different kinds of drinks – some are natural, others are not.

Soft drinks are pleasurable, but also exceedingly profitable for large manufacturers. Table 4.19 gives an approximate product costing for a full sugar canned carbonated soft drink.

Table 4.19   Sugar content of a carbonated soft drink

	Cost (pence per 330 ml can)
89% water, 294 ml	virtually free
11% sucrose, 36 g	1.25
Carbon dioxide, flavours and colour	0.25
Packaging – 330 ml can	0.50
Total	2.0

The selling price of a 330 ml can varies widely, but the UK average is about 50 p.

The ingredient and pack costs are about 4% of the retail selling price. Put another way, the gross profit margin is around 96%. This margin has to cover very many other costs, but there are two important implications:

- Soft drink manufacturers can afford to pay retailers very large margins. Retailers always give shelf space to the most profitable products.

- The gross profit margin on soft drinks funds massive and sustained advertising. This advertising is targeted at younger people and at developing countries.

Diet soft drinks

Manufacturers have responded to public doubts about their traditional products by introducing variants – which are also heavily advertised:

- The 'diet' variants, in which sugar is replaced with aspartame or other artificial sweeteners.

- Caffeine-free variants – from which caffeine has been removed.

- Flavour variants.

Full sugar soft drinks contain around 8 to 11.5% added sucrose. Some products, which are not sold as diet drinks, contain mixtures of sugar and artificial sweetener to reduce production costs.

Tonic water and glucose drinks are exceptions to the general rule:

- Full sugar tonic waters have around 6% sugar.

- Typical glucose drinks have 18% sugar as glucose. Glucose and sucrose both have 4 calories per gram.

Six cans a day!

Many teenagers and younger people take all or most of their water requirement as soft drinks. Two litres a day is roughly equivalent to six 330 ml cans.

Replacing tea, coffee or water with full-sugar soft drinks can easily lead to very high levels of hidden or accidental sugar consumption. Table 4.20 shows what can happen, based on the following:

- One can of soft drink is 330 ml.

- The product is 11% sugar.

- One can contains 0.11 × 330 equivalent to 36 g of sugar.

- 36 g of sugar have 145 calories.

Table 4.20   Percentage of total daily calories provided by soft drinks

Cans per day	Teenage boy	Adult man	Teenage girl	Adult woman
1	5	6	7	8
2	10	11	14	16
3	16	17	21	23
4	21	23	27	30
5	27	29	34	37
6	32	34	41	45

These figures are astonishing but for many groups of people not unrealistic. The recommendations are that no more than 10% of total daily calories should come from added sugars. Some teenagers are eating two or three times the recommended maximum.

To encourage consumption, many suppliers have increased the mainstream pack size over the years:

Period	Best selling bottle/can size
UK before 1960	150 ml
UK 1960–80	250 ml
UK 1980–present	330 ml
USA present	570 ml

A 570 ml serving of a carbonated full-sugar soft drink is roughly a pint, and contains around 250 calories.

Artificial sweeteners

Sugar can be fully or partly replaced with artificial sweeteners. These drinks are sold as 'diet', 'light', 'reduced calorie', 'no calorie' or under a variety of trade names.

Artificial sweeteners are intensely sweet. Weight for weight they are about 200 times sweeter than sucrose. This means that they are present as tiny amounts per can or per bottle. Artificial sweeteners have no calories or very few calories.

Three kinds of artificial sweeteners are widely used in the UK: saccharin, acesulfame and aspartame.

Saccharin was discovered in the 19th century. It is very cheap to make but many consumers find its taste unpleasant.

Two new sweeteners were licensed for UK sale in the 1980s – acesulfame and aspartame. Few people can taste the difference between aspartame and sugar.

These newer sweeteners have given a huge boost to the diet soft drinks market. About 40% of the soft drinks sold in the UK now contain aspartame instead of sugar.

Aspartame diet soft drinks are 99.5% water. They have no sugar and no calories.

High consumption of aspartame is alleged to cause headaches, dizziness and migraine in some people – but no health risk has been proved.

Diet soft drinks often contain high levels of caffeine.

Dietary recommendations

In conclusion, water and fruit juices can be drunk almost without limit – these are by far the best drinks for young people.

Tea and/or coffee are the next best choice, if too much added sugar is avoided.

Milk is a healthy food. Too much can add unwanted calories. Skimmed or semi-skimmed milk are better than full fat.

It is impossible to rely on alcoholic drinks for liquid intake without danger-ously exceeding the safe alcohol limits.

It is best to avoid full-sugar soft drinks.

Diet soft drinks are a good alternative but beware of individual susceptibility to aspartame and caffeine.

9 Vitamins

Carbohydrates, fats and proteins are macronutrients – a balanced diet has to include relatively large amounts. Macronutrients can be weighed on kitchen scales.

Water and fibre are also needed in relatively large, easily measured quantities.

Vitamins and minerals are essential for life, but only in very small amounts – these are micronutrients.

Table 4.21 shows a rough estimate of the weight of one year's balanced diet for an adult woman.

Table 4.21 Balanced diet for an adult woman

Macronutrients, water and fibre		Micronutrients	
	kg		g
Water	730	Minerals	600
Food	325	Vitamins	20
Fibre	6.5		

The average woman needs about 1 tonne of food and drink in a year. A year's supply of all the essential vitamins would almost fit into 1 tablespoon.

Just as a reminder:

- 1,000 grams = 1 kilogram

- 1,000 milligrams = 1 gram

- 1,000,000 micrograms = 1 gram

Some of these small weight units are used to describe the daily requirements of micronutrients.

Names, letters and numbers

The naming of vitamins can be confusing, even for professional biochemists and food scientists.

Vitamins are a varied group of organic compounds. Most were isolated before their chemical structures were worked out.

Originally, vitamins were named after letters of the alphabet, but it was then discovered that some are mixtures of two or more different compounds.

Most vitamins are named using a letter, a number and a chemical description. For example, vitamin B_1 is one of many B vitamins. It is also called thiamin.

Vitamin C and the B vitamins are soluble in water. Vitamins A, D, E and K do not dissolve in water but they are soluble in fats. This is an important difference because it determines which kinds of foods are the best source of each.

Fat-soluble vitamins can be stored in the body. Water-soluble vitamins are usually excreted quite rapidly.

Table 4.22 shows the most important vitamins and their alternative chemical names. You do not have to learn these.

Table 4.22 The most important vitamins

Fat-soluble vitamins	Alternative names
Vitamin A	Retinol, β-carotene
Vitamin D	$D_1, D_2, D_3,$ cholecalciferol
Vitamin E	α-tocopherol
Vitamin K	K_1, K_2

Water-soluble vitamins	Alternative names
Vitamin B_1	Thiamin
Vitamin B_2	Riboflavin
Vitamin B_6	Niacin, nicotinic acid
Vitamin B_{12}	Biotin
Folates	Folic acid
Vitamin C	Ascorbic acid

Vitamin A

Vitamin A is required for the normal growth and development of many tissues. Prolonged deprivation is fatal.

One of the earliest signs of vitamin A deficiency is inflammation of the eyes, leading to dryness, scarring of the cornea, night blindness and eventually loss of sight. Vitamin A deficiency is a major health problem for children in the developing world.

Vitamin A deficiency also damages the immune system – vitamin A deficient children are vulnerable to measles and intestinal infections.

Vitamin A is not widely distributed in food. There is some in milk, eggs and fish oils but the main source is liver.

Another substance, β-carotene, beta-carotene, is found in a variety of vegetables, in particular cabbage, carrots and spinach. The body converts β-carotene into vitamin A.

The vitamin A recommended intake is 600 μg/day for adult women or 950 μg/day for women who are breastfeeding. (μg is the symbol for microgram.)

All mammals store vitamin A in the liver. Well-fed individuals may have 18 months' supply.

High doses of vitamin A are toxic. Most important of all, very high intakes are a proven cause of damage to unborn children.

Pregnant women, or women who have any chance of becoming pregnant, must never take vitamin A supplements without medical advice. Animal livers contain between 15,000 and 40,000 µg of vitamin A per 100 g. Pregnant women and those planning to become pregnant should not eat liver.

β-carotene is non-toxic and a safe source of vitamin A in pregnancy.

Vitamin D

The main role of vitamin D is to control the conversion of dietary calcium into bone cells. Deficiency in children causes rickets – a disease where the long bones of the arms and legs become deformed. Vitamin D deficiency in adults causes osteomalacia – a painful, progressive softening of the bones leading eventually to fracture.

Vitamin D is formed by the action of sunlight on exposed skin. Most people do not need vitamin D as part of their diet.

In the UK, there is not enough sunlight between October and March to make vitamin D, but it can be stored and summer exposure produces enough to last until the following spring.

Some groups are at risk of vitamin D deficiency:

- Africans, Asians and dark-skinned people living in temperate climates.
- Miners and others who work underground or in artificial light.
- Those living in institutions like hospitals and prisons.
- Women who, for cultural or religious reasons, do not expose their skin.
- Infants and babies who need vitamin D for bone formation but spend little time outdoors.

Eggs and fatty fish are the main dietary sources of vitamin D. Supplements are sometimes advised for vulnerable groups.

Vitamin E

The role of vitamin E is not fully understood. It is known to be involved in muscle development and fertility but it may have other functions.

Vitamin E is an antioxidant and part of the body's natural defences against some forms of cancer.

Vitamin E deficiency is virtually unknown.

Vitamin K

Vitamin K has an essential role in the processes that allow normal blood clotting.

Vitamin K deficiency is hardly ever reported in humans older than about 3 months.

Some babies are born with severe vitamin K deficiency. This increases to normal levels by the age of 3 months, but in the meantime, these infants are vulnerable to haemorrhagic disease – uncontrolled bleeding.

The biggest danger is intracranial bleeding occurring between the 3rd and 8th weeks of life. Death is common; brain damage is probable for survivors.

The condition is rare but has catastrophic consequences for the few sufferers. Even very high doses of vitamin K are not toxic, so as a precaution, all babies are given a vitamin K supplement at birth.

The B vitamins

The biochemistry of the B vitamins is complicated. Some exist in several different forms and their precise biological function is still being researched. Three generalisations can be made:

- The B vitamins are widely distributed in common foods. Meat, milk, yeast and wholemeal bread are the richest sources.

- Vitamin B deficiencies are very rare in the West, but often occur in the developing world.

- The B vitamins are essential for many of the body's most basic biochemistry – in particular the digestion of fats and carbohydrates and the synthesis of proteins from amino acids.

By law in the UK, B vitamin supplements have to be added to white flour.

Table 4.23 shows recommended intakes per day for adult women.

Table 4.23   Recommended daily intakes of the B vitamins for an adult woman

B vitamin	Adult woman	Pregnancy	Lactation
B_1 thiamin	0.8 mg	+ 0.1 mg	+ 0.2 mg
B_2 riboflavin	1.1 mg	+ 0.3 mg	+ 0.5 mg
Niacin	13 mg	–	+ 2 mg
B_6	1.2 µg	–	–
B_{12}	1.5 µg	–	+ 0.5 µg
Folates, folic acid	200 µg	+ 100 µg	+60 µg

Thiamin deficiency causes beri beri. Niacin deficiency causes pellagra. Both diseases are unknown in the West.

Folates and folic acids are a related group of vitamins that deserve special mention. Women who are deficient in folates run an increased risk of giving birth to children with cleft palate and/or spina bifida. Pregnant women and those planning pregnancy are usually advised to take folic acids supplements.

Vitamin C

Most animals make vitamin C and therefore do not need the vitamin as part of their diet. Humans and some of the great apes are unusual in that they cannot synthesise vitamin C. This oddity can be taken as proof that our natural diet should always include a variety of fruits and vegetables.

Vitamin C is the least stable of all nutrients – it is easily destroyed by oxidation, metal ions, high pH, heat and light. Vitamin C cannot be stored in the body and is rapidly excreted. Fruits and vegetables should be eaten every day.

The richest sources of vitamin C are citrus fruits, soft fruits and the growing points of vegetables and salads. Cereals and starches do not contain vitamin C.

Cooking destroys vitamin C rapidly. Boiling vegetables in an open saucepan for about 10 minutes removes nearly all of the vitamin content of the fresh product. Vitamin C dissolves in steam.

Vitamin C deficiency causes scurvy. The first symptoms are hair loss, bleeding gums and slow wound healing. Untreated scurvy is eventually fatal.

The recommended daily intake is 40 mg/day, 50 mg/day during pregnancy and 70 mg/day when breastfeeding.

Smokers are advised to triple their vitamin C consumption to 120 mg/day.

10 Minerals

Vitamins are large complicated organic compounds. Minerals are chemically much simpler – usually just the cation of a metallic element. Table 4.24 shows the recommended daily intakes of the most important minerals. We will look at calcium and iron in detail and the others in outline.

Table 4.24　Recommended daily intakes of the most important minerals

Mineral		Recommended daily intake for an adult woman
Potassium	K	3500 mg
Sodium	Na	1600 mg
Calcium	Ca	700 mg
Phosphorus	P	550 mg
Magnesium	Mg	270 mg
Iron	Fe	15 mg
Zinc	Zn	7 mg
Copper	Cu	1 mg
Iodine	I	140 µg
Selenium	Se	60 µg
Boron	B	uncertain
Cobalt	Co	uncertain
Nickel	Ni	uncertain

Potassium, sodium and magnesium

Potassium is essential for nerve and muscle function and pH regulation. With sodium it controls fluid balances around the body. Deficiency is very rare.

Sodium's function is similar to that of potassium. Its major role is in controlling fluid balance. High-sodium diets have been linked to hypertension (high blood pressure), especially in older men. The evidence is very strong but not totally conclusive. Salt reduction can do no harm and is generally recommended; children accustomed to a high salt diet may find it difficult to reduce in later life. Many packaged foods have very high salt contents.

Unaccustomed hard exercise and/or high temperatures can cause major salt losses through sweat. The body rapidly adjusts to produce more dilute sweat if exercise at high temperatures continues for more than two or three days.

Magnesium is involved in bone formation, muscle activity and nerve impulse transmission. Deficiency is one of the first signs of starvation. Acute alcoholics are often magnesium-deficient, as are those suffering from persistent diarrhoea.

Zinc, iodine and selenium

Zinc is present in all tissues and it is an essential component of many enzymes. It is also likely that zinc is involved in fertility. The best dietary sources are red meats.

Iodine is an essential part of thyroxine, a hormone that controls the metabolic rate. Iodine is vital in the first 3 months of pregnancy; severely iodine-deficient mothers can have children suffering from major mental and physical disabilities. There have been many instances of iodine-deficient communities – usually isolated inland villages. Milk and seafood are the richest sources of iodine.

Selenium is part of an enzyme that protects tissues against oxidation, cereals are the main source of selenium in the UK.

Bones, teeth and calcium

The average adult woman contains a bit more than 1 kg of calcium – almost all of this is in the bones and teeth. The need for calcium varies with age; the peaks coincide with periods of maximum skeletal growth (Table 4.25).

Table 4.25   Calcium needs vary with age

Age	Females mg/day
0–12 months	525
1–3 years	350
4–6 years	450
7–10 years	550
11–14 years	800
15–18 years	800
19–50 years	700
50+ years	700
Lactation	+550

Peak bone mass is reached at about 35, thereafter there is a gradual decline. Bone mass loss accelerates after the menopause, but the process is complex and not correctable just by increasing calcium intake. Hormone replacement therapy slows the rate of loss, as the hormone oestrogen is involved in calcium absorption and deposition.

Typically the body only absorbs about 35% of the calcium taken in as food. Absorption rates vary with the type of food, hormone levels and vitamin intake. The precise mechanisms are not fully understood.

During pregnancy the foetus is supplied with calcium from the mother's stores; these are normally replaced after breastfeeding stops. Pregnant and breastfeeding teenagers run considerable risks of calcium deficiency; a breastfeeding 18-year-old needs to eat 1,350 mg/day to prevent problems in later life.

Calcium source	% of average UK intake
Milk and dairy products	63
Bread and cereals	22
Vegetables and other foods	15
Total	100%
Average UK intake	1,060 mg/day

The average UK diet contains more than the minimum calcium need for most people. There is a legal requirement to add calcium supplements to white flour.

Hard water contains dissolved calcium salts; this adds another 200 mg/day to the average UK diet.

Blood and iron

Each haemoglobin molecule contains four iron atoms. Iron is also an essential part of many enzymes. Severe deficiency causes anaemia and is fatal if not treated. Moderate iron deficiency causes tiredness, loss of concentration and an inability to keep warm even on mild days.

Moderate iron deficiency is quite widespread in the UK – it is the only micronutrient deficiency that the average person needs to worry about. There are several vulnerable groups:

- Infants, toddlers and teenage girls.
- Pregnant women and menstruating women.
- The elderly and those who drink a great deal of tea.

The main sources of iron in the UK diet are wholemeal bread, pasta, brown rice, eggs, nuts, dried fruits and dark green leafy vegetables.

Only about 15% of iron in the diet is absorbed; some foods increase absorption, others reduce it:

Iron enhancers	Iron inhibitors
Vitamin C	Tea (tannin)
Fructose	Raw bran
Alcohol	Eggs

The recommended intake of iron is 15 mg/day for women who menstruate and 9 mg/day for those that do not. The average iron loss per period is about 20 mg, but for some women this can be as high as 50 mg per month.

The recommended 15 mg/day is not enough for between 10% and 20% of menstruating women – these should take iron tablets after medical advice.

Keep away from children!

Women taking iron supplements, almost by definition, will be living with young children. Iron tablets are easily mistaken for sweets and fatal iron poisoning, usually of a toddler, happens several times a year in the UK – 300 mg of iron will make a 3-year-old very ill; the lethal dose is about 2,000 mg. Always keep iron tablets away from young children.

In the UK you are not allowed to donate blood more than once every 4 months, or if you are underweight – usually 8 stones. These rules are designed to prevent iron deficiency.

Vitamin and mineral supplements

Most people know that vitamins and minerals are vital for health, but they have little idea of what foods contain which micronutrients – and what is needed for a healthy diet. This conflict sets up anxiety, especially in younger parents trying to do the best for their families.

Most people, nearly all of the time, have no need to worry about vitamins and minerals. A balanced diet automatically delivers all of everything that is needed.

The best advice is:

- Spend the money you would have used on supplements to buy fresh fruit and vegetables instead.

- If you think you need a supplement, see your GP. He or she will give you a prescription for anything essential – this is what the NHS is for. Never exceed the stated doses.

- Keep all supplements away from children – vitamin A and iron are especially dangerous.

- See your doctor if you are pregnant or planning to become pregnant. Pregnant women should not take any kind of supplement without medical advice.

11 Malnutrition

Malnutrition means bad nutrition. It is a wide and general term describing any sustained departure from a balanced diet. Malnutrition usually takes two very different forms:

- Western or first world malnutrition.

- Developing, second or third world malnutrition.

We have discussed the major differences between the typical UK diet and the ideal. In summary, the UK diet contains:

- too many calories

- too much sucrose

- too much fat

- too many saturated fats

- too many trans-fats

- not enough NSP

- too little iron for vulnerable groups

Generalisations are difficult, but in many third world countries, the food supply is insecure and body reserves of essential nutrients are low. Third world malnutrition may include:

- inadequate water supply

- polluted or contaminated water

- poor food hygiene

- too few calories

- too little protein

- too little high-quality protein

- vitamin A, B_1 and niacin deficiency

- calcium deficiency

- iron deficiency

- trace mineral deficiency

Three worlds

In the middle of the year 2000, the world's population was 6,055 million. According to their wealth and level of development, countries can be allocated to one of three categories:

- Developed or first world.
- Developing or second world.
- Least developed or third world.

Table 4.26 shows the main characteristics of the three groups.

Table 4.26 Three worlds, year 2000

	First world	Second world	Third world
Access to clean running water	Universal household supply	Central community supply	Distant and unreliable
Healthcare	Sophisticated and generally affordable	Available to the wealthy	None
Education	Compulsory to 16+	Elites are well educated	Very limited, especially for girls
Political stability	Stable, mostly democratic	Variable, often autocratic	Despotic and violent
Demography	Low population increase Low infant mortality High life expectancy	High population increase Moderate infant mortality Variable life expectancy	High population increase High infant mortality Low life expectancy
Infrastructure	Efficient national food distribution	Local distribution systems	Non-existent or unreliable food distribution
Food trade	Much imported food	Often self-sufficient or food exporters	Often food aid dependent

One in five

Only about one person in five has guaranteed access to a safe, affordable, fully balanced diet. The great majority of these live in Europe, North America and Japan (Table 4.27).

Table 4.27 First world populations for the year 2000

	First world population 2000 (millions)
All of north-west and southern Europe	422
Most of Eastern Europe and Russia	260
USA	279
Canada	31
Japan	127
South Korea	48
Australia	19
New Zealand	4
Rich minorities elsewhere	~110
Total	1,300 (21.5%)

Most of the world's population live in developing countries. Six of these account for 49% of all the people in the world:

Table 4.28 Six developing countries

	Population 2000 (millions)
China	1,278
India	1,015
Indonesia	212
Brazil	170
Pakistan	156
Bangladesh	129
Total	2,960 (49%)

The UN estimates that about 19 million children a year die directly from starvation or from diseases caused entirely by malnutrition. To put this number in context, the total population of Australia is 18.9 million, the total population of London plus all of South-East England is 17.8 million.

The population of the least developed, or third world, is around 800 million. Most of these live in Africa, as shown in Table 4.29.

Table 4.29 The first, second and third world populations for the year 2000

Continent	First world (millions)	Second world (millions)	Third world (millions)	Total (millions)
Asia	245	3,278	160	3,683
Africa	15	169	600	784
Europe	682	47	–	729
South America	25	454	40	519
North America	310	–	–	310
Oceania	23	7	–	30
World	1,300	3,955	800	6,055
World %	21%	66%	13%	100%

Comparing diets

The diagram below compares the macronutrient balance of the UK, the ideal and a typical third world diet.

- The UK figures are from a recent survey. They may differ slightly from percentages shown previously.

- Obviously, not all third world diets are the same. The diagram is an illustration. The defining feature is a very high calorie contribution from starch-based foods.

- Third world diets usually have adequate fibre and vitamin C, but there are deficiency risks for other micronutrients.

Nutrient % of calories	UK % of calories	Balanced % of calories	Third world % of calories
Added sugars	19.4	10	3
Starches	25.2	37	80
Total carbohydrate	**44.6**	**47**	**83**
Saturated fats	17.4	11	3
Cis-mono fats	12.5	13	6
Cis-poly fats	6.2	7	2
Trans fats	2.2	2	–
Total fats	**38.3**	**33**	**11**
Protein	**10.6**	**13**	**6**
Alcohol	**6.5**	**7 max**	**–**
Total macronutrients	**100.0%**	**100%**	**100%**
NSP g/day	12 g	18 g	25 g
Total calories {	More than enough	Adequate	Unpredictable

Marasmus and kwashiorkor

A shortage or complete lack of food leads to starvation. Energy and/or nutrient intakes are inadequate.

People who are well fed before a food shortage do not suffer from immediate micronutrient deficiency because their bodies have adequate stores. Those who were previously underfed will rapidly display the symptoms of vitamin A deficiency.

Two severe malnutrition conditions are recognised: **marasmus** occurs when virtually all nutrients are absent; **kwashiorkor** happens when protein is absent and energy intake is very low.

In kwashiorkor, body proteins are broken down to give energy. These include the proteins that make up muscle tissue and blood plasma. Reduction in blood plasma concentration causes oedema – bloating of the abdomen and enlargement of the liver.

Both kwashiorkor and marasmus produce muscle wasting and stunting. Protein deficiency reduces the body's ability to reach its full potential height. After prolonged protein deficiency, stunting is not reversible.

Typical symptoms shown by sufferers of kwashiorkor and marasmus are:

Kwashiorkor	Marasmus
underweight	very underweight
oedema	no oedema
moon face	'old man's face'
muscle wasting	muscle wasting
dry brittle hair	no hair change
fatty, enlarged liver	little fat
bloated appearance	wrinkled skin
listless, apathetic	mentally alert
loss of appetite	eager to eat

Foods given as emergency aid during famine relief have to be carefully formulated not to include too much protein. A rapid switch to a high-protein diet is dangerous. Emergency food always includes added vitamins A, B_1 and B_2, calcium and iron.

Third world type malnutrition can happen anywhere. Famine often follows war or major civil disruption. Millions of Russians and Ukrainians starved to death during the 1930s and there were widespread food shortages across Europe after the end of World War Two. There was a major famine in North Korea during 1997 and 1998.

Self-inflicted malnutrition

Sufferers from third world malnutrition are usually the victims of others. However, it can be argued that most first world malnutrition is self-inflicted, although it is true that significant minorities in the West struggle to afford a balanced diet. Western malnourishment runs in families – badly fed parents have badly fed children.

The UK advertising expenditure of the big food and drink companies is very roughly about 200 times the government's spending on healthy eating campaigns. The most heavily advertised products are alcohol, confectionery, crisps, soft drinks, margarine and fast foods.

It can be virtually impossible to persuade some children to eat a balanced diet. Nutrition, food preparation and food hygiene is a small part of the school curriculum, although food education is improving.

Life patterns are moving away from fixed meals and towards informal eating, snacking and grazing.

Alcohol has been part of the human diet for thousands of years, but alcohol abuse is largely a first and second world disease. Very few heavy drinkers have a balanced diet:

- Most regular drinkers exceed the 7% of total calories safe limit.

- Heavy drinkers can easily take in 500 to 1000 calories/day as alcohol. This either adds to total calories or replaces essential nutrients.

- Vitamin and protein deficiency are common consequences of acute alcoholism.

- Heavy drinkers often eat irregularly and rely on high-fat fast foods.

- Heavy drinkers are also mostly heavy smokers, with an aversion to exercise.

- UK alcohol consumption is not high by Western standards, but binge drinking is a British disease. Teenage girls are the most vulnerable group.

Anorexia and bulimia

Anorexia nervosa is 20 times more common in females than males. It is thought to affect about 2% of teenage girls in the UK – mostly from well-educated families.

The physical symptoms include a body weight loss of 25% or more, and cessation of menstruation.

There is probably no single cause of anorexia, but factors include distorted body image, social pressure to be thin, fear of adulthood and fear of parental rejection.

Symptoms result from:

- self-starvation
- excessive exercise
- self-induced vomiting
- abuse of laxatives and diuretics

Secretive and obsessive behaviour is universal. Commonly, sufferers wear many layers of loose clothing to disguise weight loss and lie about what they have eaten and when they last ate.

Anorexics suffer from anaemia, low blood pressure, slow heart rate, swollen ankles and osteoporosis. Sudden death from heart failure is the major risk. Starvation leads to heart muscle wastage and abuse of diuretics causes potassium deficiency. Potassium helps control heart function.

Early diagnosis and treatment is vital. The figures for the UK are alarming:

- 50% of anorexics recover within 4 years.
- 25% improve but remain severely underweight and infertile.
- Recovery after 10 years is unusual. About 3% of long-term anorexics die of the disease – of these, about 1% commit suicide.

Bulimia and anorexia are related conditions, but bulimia is more common in older women. The classic pattern is binge eating followed by self-induced vomiting and laxative misuse. Bulimia is not life-threatening, but repeated vomiting can cause salivary gland infections, dehydration and tooth damage.

The incidence of anorexia and bulimia has increased over the last 30 years but there are some indications that the rate of increase may be declining. There is a greater awareness of the disease but, more importantly, the 'ideal female body image' may be changing. More young women want to look fit and toned rather than thin and fragile.

Chapter 5

Cell structures

National unit specification.
These are the topics you will be studying for
this unit:

1 Evolution, diversity and complexity
2 Microscopes and microscopic measurements
3 Prokaryotic and eukaryotic cells
4 Cell organelles
5 Cell division
6 Mitosis
7 Meiosis and human variety
8 Meiosis – the mechanisms
9 Genetics

Additionally you will be asked to carry out a cell biology experiment. It will help to read or reread Chapter 1, Scientific Communication and Method, before you begin to plan your laboratory work.

1 Evolution, diversity and complexity

Although this unit has a very specific title, cell structures, it is essentially an introduction to biology. Biology and chemistry are the two major sciences that underpin all medicine and healthcare. Biology is easily defined as the study of living things, but 'what is living?' and 'what is life?' need not be straightforward questions. Happily, most biologists agree on the general characteristics of living organisms:

- They are highly organised and their body functions are interlinked. This is another way of saying that living things are complex.

- They are chemically different from their surroundings.

- They take in energy from the environment and use it for their own purposes.

- They can produce offspring that resemble themselves.

- They can respond to stimuli.

- They are suited to their environment and can usually adapt if this environment changes.

A species is a group of similar but not identical organisms that interbreed or have the potential to interbreed. Nobody knows how many different species are living today – there are certainly 5 million, there may be as many as 30 million. We and every other species are just the survivors. At least another 500 million species have evolved and become extinct since life began. Some estimates put the number of extinct species as high as 2 billion.

3.5 billion years ago

Our planet is thought to be about 5 billion years old. Fossil evidence proves that living organisms existed at least 3.5 billion years ago.

Biology can be better defined as the study of the complexity and diversity of life. You will not be assessed or examined on the details of evolution or the classification of living things described in this first topic – however, it is essential background if you want properly to understand how cells work and how they differ.

Biological complexity can be examined at several different levels. Molecular biology is concerned with the atoms and molecules that make up living things. This branch of biology overlaps significantly with biochemistry. Molecules combine together to form cells – all living things are composed of one or more cells. Cells may combine to form tissues and tissues can come together to form organs. Some cells have specialist functions; all tissues and organs are specialist. Organ systems can combine to form an individual. Individuals usually live together in groups and colonies. Literally, and in other ways, biology can be studied at different levels of magnification.

Clearly, some living things are far more complicated than others. A bacterium is a living thing made of one simple all-purpose cell. A mammal has billions of cells, most of which are specialist.

Charles Darwin

The first origins of life are uncertain. However, all serious scientists now agree that the diversity of living things is explained by the theory of evolution first proposed by Charles Darwin in 1859.

Biologists are still arguing about the pace of evolution. Some think it has been a gradual process, others believe that long periods with little change have been punctuated by relatively short periods of rapid and dramatic expansions in diversity. We know for sure that several mass extinction events have occurred in the history of the planet. We do not yet know, and we may never know, if any of these have been total extinction events. Put differently, life on Earth may have started from scratch many times – not just once.

The possibility that the first living things arrived on Earth from elsewhere in the universe does not damage the theory of evolution. Wherever the first living things came from, evolution still explains the diversity we see today.

Like most fundamentally important theories, Darwin's is delightfully simple.

Living things reproduce. The next generation is very similar to the previous one, but not identical. The instructions for making a new individual are passed from parent to offspring via DNA, a very large, complicated molecule. The reproductive process involves many consecutive copyings of DNA. Sometimes this copying goes wrong and 'mistakes' are passed down the generations. This is mutation.

Additionally, sexual reproduction introduces variety. In very general terms, males and females each contribute half of their genetic code to their offspring.

Sexual reproduction causes a continual shuffling of the genetic pack.

Survival of the fittest

The world that living things inhabit is constantly changing. Some organisms are better able to survive and reproduce in the new environment than others. Those inheriting favourable or useful mutations will have more offspring than those who are badly adapted to the changed conditions. Eventually, the least well adapted will die out and the better adapted will prosper and multiply. Different species evolve when groups become geographically isolated – often adapting to slightly different conditions. After enough time has passed, the differences in the DNA of the two groups become too large to allow inter-breeding and the production of fertile offspring. Darwin's original research paper was called *On the Origin of Species by Natural Selection or the Preservation of Favoured Races in the Struggle for Life*.

This was published in 1859. We did not prove that DNA was the carrier of the genetic code until 1953.

When Darwin first wrote his theory, we had little idea how old the world was, or when life first began. Some estimates said that the universe was no more than a few thousand years old. Evolution produces astonishing diversity only because the selection of the fittest has been going on for an almost unimaginably long period of time. We need to count generations rather than years.

Counting generations

All of mankind's direct ancestor species are extinct. We first emerged as a separate species about 150,000 years ago. In modern developed societies, female humans can give birth from the age of about 12 or 13, however cultural and social pressures usually delay the age of first reproduction to the 20s or thereabouts. Averaged across our history, a human generation is something like 15 years – so we have been around for 10,000 generations.

Many of us can trace bits of our family tree back about five or six generations. The royal families of Europe and Japan have partial records going back around 1,000 years, but the greater part of our 10,000-generation history is lost.

A bacterial generation can be as short as 20 minutes and some can lay dormant for years. If you assume that the average bacterium produces a new generation every 24 hours, about 1,400 billion bacterial generations have lived since life began.

Without knowing our precise evolutionary path, it is impossible to calculate how many generations it has taken for primitive bacteria to evolve into human beings – it is certainly a huge number.

Evolution has many implications. All life must have originated from a common ancestor – one species – or perhaps a very small group of common ancestors.

Early evolving life forms must have been simpler than those that came later.

Very different species must have taken very different evolutionary paths much earlier than very similar ones. Bacteria, yeast, cabbages, ants, dogs, chimpanzees and man all evolved from the same organism. Because men and chimpanzees are much more alike than men and bacteria, the common ancestor of men and chimps must have been living a few million years ago. However, the common ancestor that man shares with bacteria probably became extinct billions of years ago.

Because all living things are made of cells, these must also have become more complex with the passing of time.

Classes and categories

Man has always been fascinated by the diversity of life, and countless attempts have been made to classify living things into groups or categories. Until about 200 years ago, it was thought that organisms could be subdivided into just three groups – plants, animals and men.

In 1683, Anton van Leeuenhoek, the inventor of the first relatively sophisticated microscope, discovered that most samples of water were swarming with tiny things that we now know were bacteria. His discoveries were forgotten for nearly 70 years, and it was not until about 1750 that another category of microscopic living organisms was recognised.

In 1735, a Swedish botanist, Carolus Linnaeus, proposed a general system for naming and classifying all living things. With modification, his system is still used today.

Originally, plants and animals were put into different categories, based on simple observation. The more one species resembled another, the more closely related they were assumed to be. This is still the way we classify life into categories, but 'resemblance' has taken on new meaning as technology has advanced. It would, for example, seem sensible to put all flying things into one group. However, the ability to fly has evolved separately in insects, birds and mammals like bats. We also know that some dinosaurs, extinct reptiles, could fly. In reality, this similarity is superficial and results from parallel evolution – very different organisms have evolved to solve the same problem in the same way.

Anatomy is the branch of biology concerned with how a living organism is constructed. As a generalisation, organs and organ systems become more sophisticated and/or more specialist as evolutionary time passes. Plants do not have a central nervous system, insects do not have lungs and reptiles cannot control their body temperature.

Many of the earliest classifications of higher animals were based on the way tooth arrangement differs from one species to another.

Biochemistry is the study of the chemical reactions that sustain life. The biochemistry of most organisms is remarkably similar – this alone is very strong evidence for a common ancestor. Some organisms, in particular the simpler ones, have different biochemistries. The greater these differences, the more distant the relationship between the species concerned.

The stages in the development of an embryo sometimes mimic evolution. In early pregnancy, human embryos have gill slits around the throat – these are absorbed well before birth. It is virtually impossible to deny that some of our ancestors must have lived in water.

Recent advances in our understanding of the genetic code have started to solve many of the mysteries of evolution. Detailed DNA studies can give direct clues to the relationship between species.

It is very unlikely that we will ever have a complete picture of evolution, simply because most of the pieces of the puzzle are lost and gone forever. Almost all of the species that have ever evolved are now extinct. Fossil evidence is invaluable, but it only explains a tiny fraction of the past.

Carolus Linnaeus, genus and species

Linnaeus was the first scientist to propose an ordered system for describing and classifying living things. He suggested that names should identify closely related species and that they should avoid confusion between language, countries and regions. The bird we call a robin is a totally different species from the bird called a robin in the USA, for instance. Linnaeus used Latin as a common language and gave each living thing two names – its **genus** and its **species**.

A genus name always starts with a capital letter, a species name always with a lower case letter – both are written in italics. The plural of genus is genera. The plural of species is species. Table 5.1 gives a number of examples.

Table 5.1 Examples of common genera and species

Genus	Species	Common name
Homo	sapiens	mankind
Homo	habilis	none
Pan	troglodytes	chimpanzee
Tyto	alba	barn owl
Strix	aluco	tawny owl
Apis	mellifera	honey bee
Taxus	baccata	yew tree
Allium	sativum	garlic
Escherichia	coli	none

Homo habilis was one of mankind's direct ancestors. This species became extinct about 1.5 million years ago. Superficial similarity does not prove a very close relationship – barn owls and tawny owls belong to different genera.

The genus is often abbreviated to a single capital letter, as in *E. coli*.

Different species of the same genus have a relatively recent common ancestor (Table 5.2).

Sometimes, different species can mate and produce offspring, but these are infertile. For example, horses and donkeys produce sterile mules.

Table 5.2 Common ancestors

Genus	Species	Common name
Acer	saccharum	sugar maple tree
Acer	nigrum	black maple tree
Acer	rubrum	red maple tree
Mustela	erminea	stoat
Mustela	nivalis	weasel
Mustela	putorius	polecat
Parus	caeruleus	blue tit
Parus	major	great tit
Parus	alter	coal tit

Evolution never stops. A third or subspecies name is used to distinguish groups of the same species that have become geographically isolated. Where their ranges overlap, subspecies can breed and produce fertile offspring. Continued isolation would eventually produce two different species that cannot interbreed. For instance:

Genus	Species	Subspecies	Common name
Corvus	*corone*	*corone*	carrion crow
Corvus	*corone*	*cornix*	hooded crow

Carrion crows live in Wales and southern England. Hooded crows live in northern England, Scotland and Ireland.

Modern man has no subspecies. Neanderthals were very probably a subspecies – they died out about 40,000 years ago.

Five kingdoms

Since Linnaeus, we have learned a great deal more about the differences between species. The ancient subdivision of all living things into three groups – men, animals and plants – has been proved wrong. Most biologists now agree that there are five fundamentally different life forms on Earth. These are the five **kingdoms** shown in Figure 5.1.

Figure 5.1   The five kingdoms

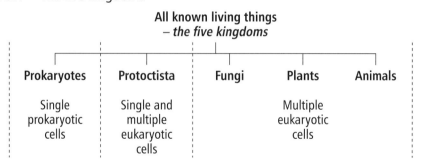

Prokaryotes – pronounced 'pro-carry-oats' – are the simplest living things. They are almost all single-celled organisms. A prokaryotic cell is relatively uncomplicated. In particular, it lacks a nucleus. Pro- means before and karyon, in Greek, means nut, seed or kernel. Therefore, prokaryote means 'before the nucleus evolved'.

Most prokaryotes are bacteria. Some, called **cyanobacteria**, resemble higher plants, in that they can photosynthesise. **Cyanobacteria** used to be called blue-green algae.

Protoctista were called protista in earlier classifications. Most protoctista are microscopic and all are made from more advanced structures called eukaryotic cells – pronounced 'you-carry-otick'. Eu- means true, so a eukaryote is made from a more highly evolved type of cell with a true or clearly defined nucleus.

Protoctista do not have to be tiny or unicellular. Seaweeds and kelps are protoctista.

The other three kingdoms – fungi, plants and animals – are all multicellular eukaryotic organisms.

Later in this chapter, we look at the differences between prokaryotic and eukaryotic cells in greater detail.

Viruses

The five kingdom classification excludes viruses, because these exist on the blurred borderline between very complex chemical structures and the simplest life forms. Viruses are incapable of independent existence outside the bodies of organisms from one of the five kingdoms. Viruses are the ultimate parasite – without a host, they cannot grow and they cannot reproduce. Many viruses can be crystallised in the same way as non-living chemical compounds.

Some recent theories suggest that viruses may be genetic material that has escaped in the past from the body of the host organism. Polio viruses cause disease in man and some of the great apes; the tobacco mosaic **virus** damages tobacco plants. Polio viruses may be more closely related to man than to the tobacco mosaic virus. Similarly, the living organism that most closely resembles the tobacco mosaic virus is probably the tobacco plant.

Describing the red fox

Many biologists spend their working lives trying to understand the precise relationships between living things. All scientists agree on the principles of classification. However, there are never-ending arguments over detail. Some researchers use a six kingdom classification because they divide the prokaryotes into two different kinds of organism.

We have described the fundamental grouping of living things into kingdoms. Linnaeus used only two categories – genera and species. The full modern classification has four extra groupings to fill the gap between kingdoms and genera. As an example, the box shows the full biological classification for the common or red fox:

The Red Fox *Vulpes vulpes*

Kingdom – animals

All animals develop from an embryonic stage called a bastula – this is a hollow ball of cells.

Phylum – chordates

There are about 35 very different groups of animals. Each of these is called a phylum. The plural of phylum is phyla. Most animal phyla are small worm-like creatures. The two most familiar phyla are the arthropods – crabs, spiders, insects, centipedes and millipedes – and the chordates. The red fox is a chordate, as are all fish, amphibians, reptiles, birds and mammals.

All chordates have a central nerve or cord that extends along the back of the animal.

Class – mammals

Mammals can control their body temperature. Between conception and birth, the offspring develop inside the body of the female. After birth, the offspring are suckled. Mammals have a highly developed four-chambered heart. All the common large land animals are mammals, as are whales and dolphins. So, of course, are we.

Order – carnivores

All carnivores have a set of scissor-like teeth, although not all are exclusively meat eaters. All dog- and cat-like animals are grouped in this order, as are bears and smaller animals like weasels, badgers, racoons, hyenas and mongooses.

Family – canids

Canids are dog-like animals distinguished from other carnivores by the special bone structure of their front legs. The canid family is further subdivided into 11 genera. These include arctic foxes, jackals, dingos, coyotes, wolves, fennec foxes and domestic dogs.

Genus – *Vulpes* Species – *vulpes*

The common red fox, *Vulpes vulpes,* is widely spread across North America, Europe and Asia. There are nine closely related species in the *Vulpes* genus. Each has evolved from a relatively recent common ancestor:

Vulpes ancestor
— *Vulpes bengalensis*   Indian fox
— *Vulpes cana*   Afghan fox
— *Vulpes chama*   South African cape fox
— *Vulpes corsac*   Russian steppe fox
— *Vulpes ferrilata*   Tibetan fox
— *Vulpes pallida*   African pale fox
— *Vulpes rueppelli*   North African sand fox
— *Vulpes velox*   American swift fox
— *Vulpes vulpes*   Common red fox

For the red fox, the species and the genus names are the same. This usually shows that this was the first species in the genus to be studied and classified. Sometimes this naming system is used for genera with only one species.

Subspecies – *Vulpes vulpes vulpes*

Evolution is a never-ending process and widely spread species begin to differ as they carry on adapting to changing conditions. The red fox has over 40 subspecies. *Vulpes vulpes vulpes* is the commonest. *Vulpes vulpes japonica*, for example, lives in Japan.

In summary:

Kingdom	animals
Phylum	chordates
Class	mammals
Order	carnivores
Family	canids
Genus	*Vulpes*
Species	*vulpes*
Subspecies	*vulpes*

2 Microscopes and microscopic measurements

Most of the world and the universe around us is invisible to the naked eye. This may seem obvious, but it is worth thinking about in more detail.

We only see the surface of structures because our eyesight cannot penetrate most substances. We use words like 'opaque', 'translucent' and 'transparent' to describe what we cannot and can see through.

We cannot see in the dark. At the other end of the scale, very bright light sources make us uncomfortable and may even damage our eyesight.

We have colour vision and we have words for basic ideas like black, white, red, blue and yellow. We can also recognise very slight colour differences. Our colour vision is much better than our ability to describe these differences – for example, we do not have enough language to describe a thousand shades of green.

We cannot see far. The Sun, the Moon and the stars are visible only because they are huge and brilliant.

We cannot see small things. Size is a relative idea. The word 'small' is defined by reference to human body size and the limits of human vision.

All living things respond to stimuli. These stimuli have to be sensed before any reaction can occur. All living things have evolved senses – their efficiency and the combinations in which they are used vary enormously from one group of organisms to another.

Most organisms respond to light, which means they must be able to detect it, but vision, as we understand it, has only evolved in the animal kingdom. Different animals have evolved sensitivities to different kinds of light and different levels of light. We are just another kind of animal.

We tend to think that vision only involves the structures of the eye itself. This is not so. Light is sensed and then the information it provides has to be processed. The eye and the optic nerve are best described as extensions of the brain.

Units of length

Length can be measured in dozens of different units like inches, feet, yards, kilometres and miles. Science works with an internationally recognised system of metric units and the fundamental unit of length is the metre.

Very few adult humans are shorter than 1 metre or taller than 2 metres, so we have no trouble understanding how long 'about a metre' is. Our species evolved 150,000 years ago, but the scale of the universe was determined many billions of years ago. It follows that some measurements will be alien to our everyday experience. The size of anything could be expressed in metres, but the multiples and fractions involved soon become clumsy and difficult to understand.

The international system uses prefixes to indicate smaller and smaller sub-divisions of a metre. You need to learn the names and meanings of six of these (Table 5.3).

Table 5.3 Six important subdivisions of a metre

Unit of length	Abbreviation	Number of units in one metre	Scientific notation
metre	m	1	1
centimetre	cm	100	10^{-2} m
millimetre	mm	1,000	10^{-3} m
micrometre	μm	1,000,000	10^{-6} m
nanometre	nm	1,000,000,000	10^{-9} m
picometre	pm	1,000,000,000,000	10^{-12} m

The abbreviation for micrometre uses the Greek letter μ (pronounced mew). This avoids confusion between millimetres and micrometres.

Scientific notation is a shorthand used to save the bother of writing out long strings of zeroes. For instance:

$$\text{One micrometre} = \frac{1}{1,000,000} \text{ of a metre} = 10^{-6} \text{ of a metre}$$

The power number $^{-6}$ says divide 1 by 1,000,000, which is one followed by six zeroes. In the same way, 10^{-3} is $\frac{1}{1,000}$ and so on.

Table 5.4 shows the relative scale of living things and the cells, molecules and atoms they are made from. Starting from the top:

- The blue whale is the largest living animal.

- We think of ourselves as an average-sized animal – in fact we are also one of the largest that has ever existed.

- Small animals like mice and insects are still huge compared with simpler living things like bacteria.

- As a generalisation, plant cells are bigger than animal cells and primitive prokaryotic cells are nearly always smaller than the more advanced eukaryotic cell. Birds' eggs are a dramatic exception – before fertilisation, an egg is a single cell. The largest cell of all is an ostrich egg.

- The smallest bacterium, which is a single prokaryotic or primitive cell, is about 1 μm in diameter.

- Viruses vary in size from about 20 to 400 nm. Again as a generalisation, viruses are very much smaller than bacteria. The smallest viruses are 20 nm long or 20,000 pm.

Table 5.4   The relative scale of living things

	Metres	Centimetres	Millimetres	Micrometres	Nanometres	Picometres
	m	cm	mm	μm	nm	pm
Blue whale – length	30	3,000	30,000	30 million		
Man – height	1.7	170	1,700	1.7 million		
House mouse – length		10	100	100,000	100 million	
Black ant – length			5	5,000	5 million	
Plant leaf – thickness			0.5	500	500,000	500 million
Typical plant cell – length				50	50,000	50 million
Human ovum – diameter				35	35,000	35 million
Human sperm – length				4	4,000	4 million
Bacterium				1	1,000	1 million
Virus					100	100,000
Sugar molecule					1	1,000
Water molecule						200
Hydrogen atom						60

Everything in the universe is made ultimately from atoms. A molecule is two or more atoms joined together by chemical bonds. At this level of magnification, we have to make comparisons in picometres. There are a million million picometres in a metre. Most living things are made mainly from carbon, hydrogen, oxygen and nitrogen atoms. Some relative sizes are given in Table 5.5.

Table 5.5   Relative sizes

	Size in picometres 10^{-12} m
Typical bacterium diameter	1,000,000
Typical virus length	100,000
Medium sized molecule – sugar – length	1,000
Small molecule – water – length	200
Carbon atom diameter	150
Nitrogen atom diameter	140
Oxygen atom diameter	130
Hydrogen atom diameter	60

Again this table generalises, however it should be clear that all living things are made from almost unimaginable numbers of cells, molecules and atoms.

Wavelength and colour

In strong light, somebody with excellent vision can detect objects as small as 100 μm. Between 150 and 300 μm is the lower limit for most of us. Nearly all cells are invisible to the naked eye.

We have all seen rainbows or light separated into a range of colours by a prism or a thin film of oil on water. Hot objects like the Sun, a flame or the filament of a light bulb emit light that is a mixture of wavelengths. Our eyes can distinguish very small differences in wavelengths and the brain translates these into a concept we call colour.

Figure 5.2 Visible wavelengths

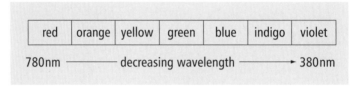

Remember that there are a billion nanometres in one metre. The wavelength is the distance between crests of successive waves:

Figure 5.3 A wavelength

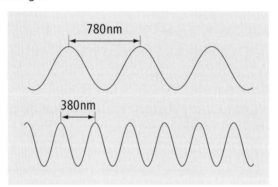

The electromagnetic spectrum

Some organisms have evolved to see wavelengths invisible to humans. Many birds and butterflies can see wavelengths shorter than the colour we call violet. Reptiles can see wavelengths longer than the colour we call red.

Figure 5.4 The electromagnetic spectrum

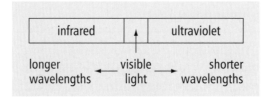

Infrared means 'below the red'; **ultraviolet** means 'above the violet'.

Shorter wavelengths carry more energy than longer ones. Again, this is a familiar idea. Midday summer sunshine has a higher proportion of ultraviolet wavelengths, causing sunburn and potentially dangerous skin damage.

In theory, there is no upper or lower limit to wavelength. Visible light is only a tiny part of what is called the **electromagnetic spectrum**.

Longer wavelengths

Longer wavelength electromagnetic radiation is used in radio, TV and mobile phone communications:

System	Wavelength range
Visible light	380 nm to 780 nm
Infrared	780 nm to 0.1 mm
Microwaves	0.1 mm to 1 mm
TV	1 mm to 1 m
FM and short-wave radio	1 m to 100 m
Medium-wave radio	100 m to 1000 m
Long-wave radio	1 km to 100 km

TV and audio system remote controls use infrared. Mobile phones and radar work with microwaves. Microwave ovens use highly focused microwave radiation.

There is a fixed relationship between wavelength and frequency. Radio station identifications are often given as frequencies rather than wavelengths.

Longer wavelengths carry very little energy. As you are reading this page, hundreds of different radio and TV signals are passing harmlessly through your body.

All electromagnetic radiation travels at the same speed. The speed of radio waves, for example, is identical to the speed of light.

Shorter wavelengths

The shorter the wavelength the more energy it carries. Very short wavelength radiation is lethal to virtually all living organisms. Life on Earth is only possible because the atmosphere absorbs most of the Sun's highest energy radiation before it reaches sea level.

Electromagnetic radiation	Wavelength range
Visible light	780 nm to 380 nm
Ultraviolet	380 nm to 13 nm
Gamma rays and X-rays	13 nm to 10^{-6} nm

Light microscopes

There are three kinds of microscope. Traditional instruments work with visible light, others use ultraviolet light or high energy electrons.

The shortest wavelength we can see is blue light, with a wavelength of about 400 nm. Any object much smaller than this cannot be seen using a conventional light microscope. An object has to interact with a visible light wave before our eyes can send a signal to the brain to tell us it exists.

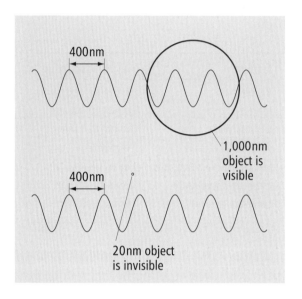

Even the best light microscopes cannot see objects smaller than around half a visible wavelength – somewhere between 200 nm and 300 nm. This corresponds to a maximum possible magnification of about 1500 times.

Some microscopes use ultraviolet light with a wavelength of 275 nm. These give magnifications of up to 3600 times and reveal objects as small as 130 nm. Cells are visible in outline, but none of their detailed structure can be investigated.

Magnification and resolution

Magnification is a simple idea. It can be defined as the size of the image of an object divided by the real size of the object. For example, a structure might appear to be 5 millimetres long when it is in fact 60 micrometres in length.

$$\text{Magnification} = \frac{5\,\text{mm}}{60\,\mu\text{m}} = \frac{5,000\,\mu\text{m}}{60\,\mu\text{m}} = 83$$

Hence a magnification of about 80 times or 80 diameters.

Resolution and magnification are different concepts. **Resolution** is the ability of a microscope to produce separate images of two adjacent points.

Light microscopes cannot achieve resolutions better than 200 nm. Points or objects closer together than this produce a single image – the light microscope cannot tell them apart.

In theory, there is no limit to magnification – a photograph taken through a microscope could be enlarged to any size, for instance. At magnifications beyond the highest resolution, point images become increasingly blurred and indistinct.

Electron microscopes

The shorter the wavelength used, the greater the resolving power of a microscope becomes. X-ray instruments have been built, but X-rays are difficult to focus. Heated metal filaments emit high-energy, rapidly moving electrons. These behave in a way that closely resembles X-rays. An **electron microscope** focuses beams of electrons using magnets and electric fields. Visible images are produced with computer technology.

Transmission electron microscopes give very high magnification two-dimensional images. Scanning electron microscopes give excellent three-dimensional pictures, but at lower magnifications.

Colour has no meaning for things smaller than the shortest visible wavelength of about 400 nm. Pictures produced by electron microscopes are given false colours using specialist computer software.

Some larger organisms are stained or coloured before examination with light microscopes. This often reveals details that would not otherwise be obvious.

System	Maximum magnification (times)	Smallest visible object		
		μm micrometres	nm nanometres	pm picometres
Naked eye	–	150 to 300	150,000 to 300,000	
Light microscope	1,500		200 to 300	
UV microscope	3,600		100 to 150	
Scanning electron microscope	~100,000		10 to 20	10,000 to 20,000
Transmission electron microscope	~1,000,000		0.2 to 0.5	200 to 500

Few commercially produced light microscopes give magnifications much greater than 500 times.

Hydrogen is the smallest atom, with a diameter of 60 picometres. It is therefore invisible, even with the most powerful electron microscopes.

3 Prokaryotic and eukaryotic cells

Single magnifying lenses were first used in the 13th century. Their quality was generally poor and they produced distorted images at low magnifications.

In 1590, Dutch instrument makers invented the first compound microscope, two lenses separated by a tube. These gave clearer images at much higher magnifications. During the 1600s, for the first time, much of the smaller detail of living organisms was revealed.

In 1665, Robert Hooke, an English scientist, examined thin slices of cork under a microscope. Cork is the bark of the cork oak and what Hooke saw was a network of dead plant cells. Hooke was the first to use the word 'cell'.

The cell theory

Three German researchers developed the **cell theory** and this has become the foundation of biology and medical science.

In 1830, Matthias Schleiden suggested that all plants were made of cells. A year later, Theodor Schwann proposed that animals were also cellular. In 1855, Rudolph Virchow realised that all cells are derived from other cells.

We now know that the cell theory applies to every species and all five kingdoms.

Viruses are an exception. They are sometimes called akaryotes, meaning 'without cells or nuclei'. They have a central core of DNA or RNA, surrounded by a protein coat. Viruses cause disease by disrupting normal cell processes.

The development of the light microscope and then the electron microscope has shown that cells have an internal structure. These structures, in particular the more complicated ones, are called organelles – meaning 'little organs'.

Previously, we have described the subdivision of all living things into five kingdoms. Cell evolution and specialisation is the driving force behind biological diversity. We can redraw the five kingdom family tree to show cell differences. This is shown in Figure 5.5.

Figure 5.5   Cells and the five kingdoms

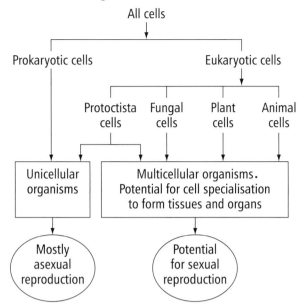

The first cells were prokaryotic

The first life forms were single prokaryotic cells. These have simple internal structure without larger or complex organelles. The evolutionary leap that produced the first eukaryotic cells, about 1.2 billion years ago, explains the existence of all higher organisms, including us. Eukaryotic cells have the potential for specialisation – prokaryotic cells do not. All mammals, for example, are made from thousands of different specialist cells that combine together to form tissues and organs. Nerve, liver and red blood cells are all eukaryotic, each with a different function.

Prokaryotic organisms usually reproduce by simple cell division, although some bacteria have a donor receptor system, where one organism passes variable amounts of DNA to another.

The eukaryotic cell – an evolutionary leap

Sex and sexual reproduction were invented by the eukaryotic cell. The constant shuffling and reshuffling of genes is only possible because some eukaryotic cells evolved into specialist female or egg cells, and others became sperm or male cells.

The invention of sex greatly accelerated the pace of evolution. The more one generation differs from the next, the more rapidly one ancestor species can fragment into a number of descendant species, each adapted to small environmental differences.

Four essential structures

All cells have at least four structures in common – a cell membrane, cytoplasm, ribosomes and DNA.

A thin surface membrane, sometimes called a plasma membrane, completely surrounds all cells. Its detailed structure is only revealed under very high magnification. The membrane is partially permeable – it allows molecules of a particular size to enter and leave the cell. In this way, the cell can take in substances from its surroundings and excrete waste products. Life would be impossible if **cell membranes** were impermeable or freely permeable. Their development must have been an essential stage in the first emergence of life.

All cells contain **cytoplasm**. Early researchers thought cytoplasm was just a simple watery solution – we have since discovered it is an exceedingly complicated mixture of water, salts and other organic compounds.

Living things and their food, because all living things eat other living things, are largely water, but three kinds of molecules account for most of the rest of their weight. These are carbohydrates, fats and proteins. Fats and oils together are properly called lipids.

Carbohydrates and lipids are mostly used as food stores. Proteins can be seen as the working parts of organisms. Life forms differ because they are made from different combinations of proteins assembled in a huge variety of shapes and sizes.

The instructions that tell a cell which proteins to make are the genetic code. There are a theoretically limitless number of proteins that could be constructed. The genetic code is carried by DNA. All cells contain DNA in one form or another.

All cells also contain very small organelles called **ribosomes**. These are essentially protein factories assembling proteins based on the instructions carried by the DNA molecule.

All cells have to have a cell membrane, cytoplasm, DNA and ribosomes. The simplest prokaryotic cells also have a fifth essential feature – a rigid cell wall that surrounds the membrane to protect the cell's contents. This cell wall has small pores to allow molecular exchange between the cell and its surroundings.

Prokaryotic cells may also have:

A flagellum – a simple whip-like tail that allows the cell to move through water or a watery solution.

Pili – hair-like extensions used for attaching the cell to surfaces or to other cells.

The cell membrane may also be folded in on itself, creating tubes and tunnels that act as sites for photosynthesis in cyanobacteria or blue-green algae. Infoldings may also contain DNA. At some stage in the cell's life cycle, this arrangement is part of the cell division process.

Figures 5.6 and 5.7 show prokaryotic cells. Figure 5.6 shows the essential features, present in all prokaryotic cells. Figure 5.7 shows the additional features that some prokaryotic cells can have.

Figure 5.6   Features of all prokaryotic cells

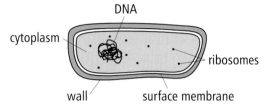

Figure 5.7   Features seen in some prokaryotic cells

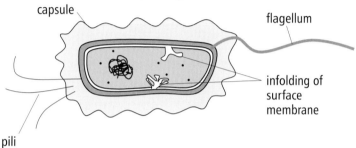

Comparing prokaryotic and eukaryotic cells

The defining difference between **prokaryotic** and **eukaryotic** cells is that the more advanced eukaryotic cell has a distinct nucleus. Prokaryotic cells do not. There are other distinguishing features. These are summarised in Table 5.6.

Table 5.6   Comparing prokaryotic and eukaryotic cells

Prokaryotic cells	Eukaryotic cells
Cell diameters usually 1 to 10 μm	Cell diameters usually 10 to 100 μm
DNA formed into a closed loop, floating freely in the cytoplasm	DNA is not circular and it is contained within a nucleus. The nucleus is enclosed by two membranes
DNA is not combined with proteins	DNA is combined with proteins and assembled into packages called **chromosomes**
Simple cytoplasm	Complex cytoplasm
Few organelles, none surrounded by double membranes	According to kingdom and degree of cell specialisation, many different kinds of organelle. Some unbounded, some bounded by single and some by double membranes
Smaller ribosomes, typically 18 nm diameter	Larger ribosomes, usually about 22 nm diameter
Cell wall always present	Cell walls sometimes present, most commonly in plants and fungi

Bigger is better

It should be remembered that a difference in the length or diameter of a cell translates into a much bigger difference in volume. For example, comparing two spherical cells:

	Prokaryotic cell		Eukaryotic cell
Diameter – micrometres (μm)	2		40
Volume – cubic micrometres (μm^3)	4.2		33,500
Volume ratio	one	to	8,000

Clearly, eukaryotic cells have a much greater capacity to accommodate a range of different organelles and other structures.

In the next topic, we look at organelles in more detail and consider the typical differences between plant and animal cells.

4 Cell organelles

Figure 5.8 shows the **organelles** and structures that are always or sometimes present in the cells of the five kingdoms. Yet again, this mimics the evolutionary family tree.

We show the four structures that all cells – prokaryotic and eukaryotic – must contain. No cell can function without a partially permeable outer membrane, ribosomes to make proteins, cytoplasm, or its genetic code contained in molecules of DNA.

The diagram also shows the organelles and structures that all eukaryotic cells contain, plus the three specialist structures only found in plant cells, and another specialist organelle that only animal cells have.

Finally, the diagram shows there are two kinds of ER – endoplasmic reticulum – and that the nucleus has important substructures.

Cell biology is a highly specialised science. Research teams spend many years investigating the detailed structure and precise functions of just one organelle, or even a subunit of an organelle. You will only be assessed on a general understanding. These notes summarise what you need to know.

Figures 5.9 and 5.10 show a typical animal cell and a typical plant cell.

Mitochondria

The singular of **mitochondria** is mitochondrion.

Mitochondria are just about visible under a light microscope. At higher magnification they are seen to be rod-shaped; around 8 μm long and roughly 1 μm wide.

All organisms need to take in energy from the environment. Some organisms produce energy by oxidising food, others trap light energy by photosynthesis.

The reaction between food and oxygen from the air takes place inside mitochondria and these organelles provide the energy that sustains the whole organism.

Plant cells contain mitochondria but, generally, these are only active at night.

It is thought that mitochondria were originally free-living bacteria that became incorporated into the first eukaryotic cells more than a billion years ago. Mitochondria multiply by simple cell division – just like bacteria.

All eukaryotic cells have at least one mitochondrion – some have several thousand.

Figure 5.8 Cell organelles and structures

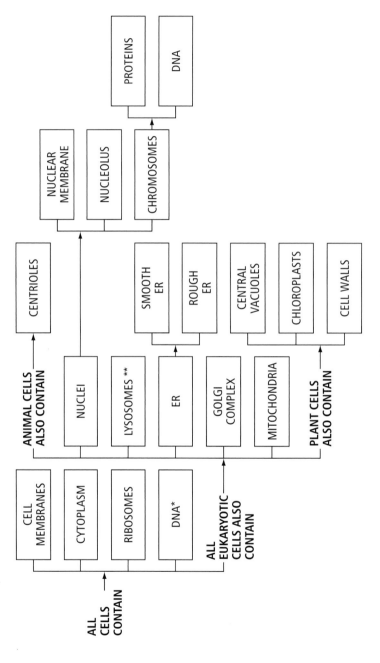

Mitochondria have a complex inner structure including a kind of DNA that differs from that of the cell nucleus. Human mitochondrial DNA mutates about ten times more rapidly than nuclear DNA, and it is inherited by sons and daughters from their mothers without any male involvement.

Mitochondrial DNA investigations are revealing a great deal about human evolution and diversity.

Lysosomes

Lysosomes are small spherical organelles whose major component is a range of digestive enzymes. Their main function is to get rid of old, worn out or unwanted organelles or structures. Lysosomes play a vital role in the immune system and in sexual reproduction. Sperm cells contain a lysosome that can digest part of the membrane of an egg cell, making a hole for the entry of the sperm and hence fertilisation.

Endoplasmic reticulum

Scientists in general, and biologists in particular, can often be accused of using difficult technical words when simpler ones would do just as well. Endo means 'inside' and reticulum means 'a net or a network'. Therefore, endoplasmic reticulum just means 'a network inside the cell'. It is usually abbreviated to **ER**.

The ER is a network of interconnected tubes and sacs called cisternae. The ER generally can be regarded as the transport and packaging system of the cell.

Rough ER has many ribosomes embedded in its surface. Ribosomes are very small spherical organelles whose job is to manufacture proteins. Proteins are distributed around the cell through the rough ER.

The smooth ER is more tubular than rough ER. Smooth ER is involved, amongst other things, in the manufacture and transfer of lipids.

The Golgi complex

The **Golgi complex** is named after its discoverer, Doctor Camillo Golgi, an Italian biomedical scientist. It is often also called the Golgi body or the Golgi apparatus.

The complex is a system of stacked interconnected flattened sacs sandwiched between two networks of tubes. Its structure is similar to the ER.

The Golgi complex is involved in the manufacture of various cell components using the proteins transferred to it via the rough ER as starting materials. In general terms, the Golgi complex is an essential intermediate in the production of lysosomes, cell surface membranes and rigid cell walls in plants. The complex also packages materials to be pumped out of or secreted from the cell.

The nucleus

The nucleus is roughly spherical and is the largest organelle in most cells. Typically, it is around 15 μm in diameter, making it easily visible with a light microscope.

The nucleus controls all the cell's activities and it also houses the genetic material. Nuclear division is the first stage in cell division and multiplication.

The nucleus is surrounded by a double skin or membrane. The gap between the two is very small, usually about 30 nm. Only electron microscopes show this detail – it looks like a single layer under a light microscope.

The outer membrane has ribosomes embedded in its surface and is joined directly to the ER. At intervals around the surface of the nucleus, the inner and outer membranes fuse together to form holes – nuclear pores.

The nucleus is filled with a jelly-like fluid called nucleoplasm.

Smaller spherical organelles called nucleoli float freely in the nucleoplasm. Their job is to make ribosomes. All cells have at least one nucleolus, some have many.

In a nucleus that is not undergoing division, the chromosomes form a loose network called **chromatin**.

The chromosomes themselves are only clearly visible when the nucleus is dividing. Chromosomes are packages of DNA combined with proteins.

Chromo- means 'coloured' and -some means 'body or object'. Chromosomes are readily stained with dyes, making them more visible under a microscope – hence the terms chromosome and chromatin.

Figure 5.9 A typical animal cell

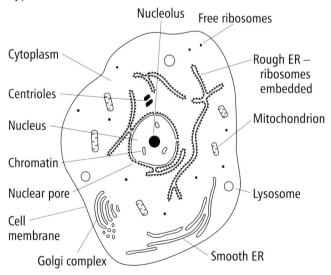

This diagram is simplified. A real animal cell viewed through an electron microscope would show many more unattached ribosomes and mitochondria. Additionally, the smooth and rough ER extends throughout most of the cell.

Cell walls

Animal cells do not have rigid cell walls. Structures like teeth and bone are living tissues supplied with nerves and blood vessels. A matrix of cells interlaced with cavities containing calcium salts accounts for their strength and rigidity.

Plants, fungi, some prokaryotes and some protoctista have cell walls protecting the membrane and the cell's contents. The material to make the cell walls is secreted from the cell, but the wall itself is non-living.

Green plants have a primary cell wall composed mainly of cellulose. Soft plant tissues like leaves and flowers are made of cells with primary cell walls. A secondary cell wall is found in cells that make up the stronger more rigid structures of larger plants and trees. The secondary structure is essentially a criss-cross lattice of cellulose fibres.

The cell walls of adjacent plant cells are held together by a sticky jelly called the middle lamella.

Each cell wall has one or more narrow pores that allow material to pass from one cell to the next.

The chemical composition of cell walls differs from one kingdom to another.

Chloroplasts

Chloro- means 'green'. **Chlorophyll** is the substance that makes plants green.

The prokaryotes were originally divided into two kingdoms or subkingdoms: bacteria, which take in food from their environment to produce energy, like animals; and blue-green algae, which make energy from sunlight, like plants. Blue-green algae are now recognised as a kind of bacteria and have been renamed cyanobacteria, cyano- meaning 'blue'. Cyanobacteria contain chlorophyll loosely associated with the cell membrane – remember these are primitive prokaryotic cells.

All plants contain chlorophyll in more highly evolved organelles called **chloroplasts**.

Some plant cells do not contain chlorophyll, in particular those not exposed to light, like root cells. No animal cells have chlorophyll or chloroplasts.

Photosynthesis and evolution

Photosynthesis is the most important of all chemical reactions and the one on which all life depends. Using chlorophyll as a **catalyst**, plants take in water and carbon dioxide and produce sugars and oxygen:

$$\text{carbon dioxide} + \text{water} \xrightarrow[\text{sunlight}]{\text{chlorophyll}} \text{sugars} + \text{oxygen}$$

The Sun's energy is trapped inside the chemical bonds of the sugars and this energy is released when animals eat plants. Some animals eat other animals and the energy originally obtained from the Sun is passed along the food chain. The most basic foodstuff is glucose, a simple sugar.

Today's atmosphere is roughly 20% oxygen. Before life evolved, the atmosphere contained little or no oxygen. The modern atmosphere was created in the beginning by cyanobacteria, with later contributions from higher plants. If chlorophyll-containing cells had not been adding oxygen to the atmosphere for billions of years, animals, including us, could not have evolved.

The earliest members of the plant kingdom were mosses, ferns and conifers. Flowering plants came relatively late in evolutionary history. Most animals depend directly or indirectly on the seeds of flowering plants. Wheat, barley, oats, maize, millet, sorghum and rice provide at least 70% of the calories consumed by the human population. We eat seeds and so do most of the domestic animals that provide us with fats and proteins.

Chloroplasts show up as green flattened discs under a light microscope. Typically, a chloroplast is around 3 or 4 μm in diameter. Chloroplasts themselves have a complicated inner structure. Some plant cells – leaf cells in particular – have very many chloroplasts.

Figure 5.10   A typical plant cell

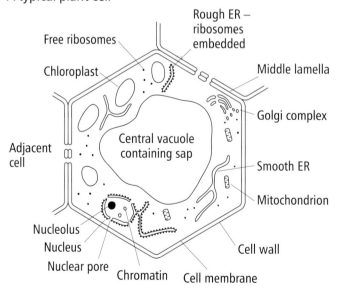

A real plant cell would usually have many more chloroplasts and unatttached ribosomes than we have shown, and a more extensive network of smooth and rough ER. The size of the central vacuole varies from one kind of plant cell to another.

Central vacuoles

A **vacuole** is a hole, so a central vacuole is a hole in the centre of a cell.

Some animal cells have small vacuoles. These are usually temporary and often formed when the cell's defence mechanisms engulf or surround and then digest a foreign body.

Most plant cells have large central vacuoles. Typically, an immature cell has many smaller vacuoles and these fuse together as the cell grows.

The central vacuole occupies up to 90% of the volume of some plant cells – forcing the cytoplasm and the other organelles into a thin layer trapped between the vacuole and the cell membrane.

The vacuole is surrounded by a membrane and contains sap. Sap is a solution of salts, sugars and sometimes dissolved proteins. Sap is slightly acidic in most plant species and very acidic in some, like citrus fruits.

The central vacuole exerts pressure on the rigid cell walls, adding rigidity to the plant's overall structure. Plants wilt if they lose more water than they absorb – this is because the fluid pressure in the vacuole has reduced.

Centrioles

Most animal cells contain pairs of small organelles called **centrioles**. Under high magnification, these look like hollow cylinders about 500 nm long. The precise functions of centrioles are still being investigated – they are certainly involved in nuclear division and cell multiplication.

Plant cells do not have centrioles.

5 Cell division

The cell theory is the foundation of biology. It says that all living things are composed of one or more cells and that all cells originate from other cells. We do not need microscopes or advanced science to notice many of the characteristics of living organisms. These ideas are so familiar that we do not see them as remarkable.

All living things grow. Very large organisms develop from small beginnings. An acorn weighs a few grams, a fully grown oak tree weighs many hundred of tonnes. Immature organisms differ from mature adults.

Organisms can repair themselves if their structures are damaged or interfered with. This ability varies from one species to another and some damage cannot be repaired. Hair and nails regrow if they are cut, wounds heal, but severed limbs do not usually regenerate. Plants seem to repair themselves more effectively than animals. A tree will often regrow even if everything apart from its root structure is removed.

All living things die. Different species have different lifespans.

The life cycle of animals and many plants can be divided into three phases: an immature stage, when the organism cannot reproduce; a fertile phase; and often an older post-fertile period.

Offspring resemble their parents, but there are two kinds of reproduction. New plants can be made by taking cuttings; animal reproduction usually seems to involve two parents.

Both males and females pass characteristics to their offspring. However, by simple observation, it is not usually possible to decide if males and females make equal contributions to the next generation.

Some characteristics skip one or more generations. There are often stronger resemblances between grandparents and grandchildren than between parents and children, for example.

It is obvious that the females of animals like birds, reptiles and amphibians produce eggs. It is also obvious that the males of many animals produce semen. By extension, it seems reasonable to assume that all sexual reproduction involves the combination of eggs and sperm.

Male and female structures are often clearly observable in plants as well as animals.

The cell theory must be able to explain all these familiar processes of growth, repair and reproduction. Clearly none of these could happen unless some physical object or objects are passed from one generation to the next in reproduction, or from one part of an organism to another in growth and repair.

Dyes and microscopes

During the 19th century, German chemists invented a number of permanent dyes and German instrument-makers produced greatly improved microscopes. It was found that:

- Cells divide to give two new cells. These cells grow and then divide again. Repeated division is the growth mechanism.

- Under a good light microscope, eukaryotic cells have a clearly visible nucleus. The first stage in cell division is a separation of the nucleus into two new nuclei.

- Some substructures inside the nucleus absorb chemical dyes more readily than others. The nucleus contains minute threads that stain easily, revealing much about their makeup and behaviour. At times, these threads split and separate. This process is very precise and it comes before nuclear division and before cell division.

We know now that these easily dyed threads are chromosomes and that each chromosome contains a single very long DNA molecule. We also know that different arrangements of atoms in sequence along the DNA strand are genes, and that one chromosome carries many genes.

Improved microscopes allowed detailed examination of egg and sperm cells. Although egg cells are nearly always much larger than sperm cells, it could be seen that their nuclei were very similar in size and indistinguishable from each other. This suggested, but did not prove, that males and females made equal genetic contributions to the next generation.

Lamarck versus Darwin

Darwin was not the first to suggest a theory of evolution. A French scientist, Jean Baptiste de Lamarck, thought that characteristics acquired during the lifetime of an individual could then be passed on to that individual's offspring. Lamarck died in 1829, 30 years before Darwin published *The Origin of the Species*. Lamarckism has been totally discredited, but confusion between inherited characteristics and acquired characteristics is still widespread.

Lamarckism was initially disproved by an experiment with rats. A litter of baby rats from normal parents had their tails removed before they became sexually mature. These 'amputated' rats were then bred again and the process repeated for 20 generations – at no stage was a baby rat born without a tail or with any kind of shortened tail.

In evolutionary terms, we are closely related to rats. Two human examples further illustrate the difference between acquired and inherited characteristics:

- In many societies, ear-piercing is traditional. A child descended from a long line of parents with pierced ears is never born with ear piercings, although piercing must alter or destroy ear cells.

Some forms of deafness are, however, passed from one generation to the next. In this case, a particular combination of ear cells must be inheritable.

- Hair type and colour differs from one individual to another and from one racial group to another. Cultural traditions mean that many of us colour our hair, perm it or shave it off altogether. None of these acquired characteristics can be passed on to our children. However, characteristics like the straight blond hair of northern Europeans, the dark tightly curled hair of many Africans and male pattern baldness are clearly inherited.

Congenital conditions

It is important to distinguish between inherited conditions and **congenital** conditions. After conception but before birth, embryos can be influenced or damaged by factors like poor maternal nutrition, physical injury and many drugs and chemicals. This can happen even if the embryo inherits a completely normal set of genes. Congenital conditions are conditions acquired before birth.

On the other hand, some infants are unfortunately born with inherited diseases and disorders, even if they are not subjected to damaging influences in the womb. These are inherited conditions, determined at conception.

Germ cells and body cells

Cell division has to be the mechanism for growth, repair and reproduction. All this can be explained if there are two fundamentally different kinds of eukaryotic cell and two kinds of cell division.

Sex cells are also called **germ cells** or **gametes**. We describe every other kind of cell as a **body cell** (see Figure 5.11).

Figure 5.11   Germ and body cells

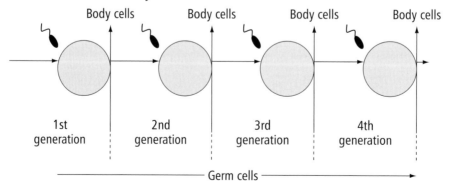

The germ cells of the previous generation must supply the chromosomes for the germ cells and the body cells of the next. The germ cells are passed from parent to offspring but the body cells are moved into a siding or cul-de-sac.

They can divide to give growth and make repairs, they can be altered or destroyed, but they never return to influence the germ line.

Evolution alters the germ line gradually over thousands of generations, because the genes of individuals that have not survived to reproduce die with them and are not transmitted further. Alterations in germ cell genes produce changes in body cells, but it never happens the other way around.

Chromosome number

It has been found that all eukaryotic species have a characteristic number of chromosomes in their body cells. This number varies considerably from one species to another, but males and females of the same species nearly always have identical numbers. The fruit fly is widely used in genetic research – it has 8 chromosomes; humans have 46. Chromosome number does not depend on the size or complexity of the species – many plants have more chromosomes than we do; chimpanzees have 48.

It is important to remember that the number of chromosomes does not alter across the generations in spite of the fact that two individuals are contributing DNA in sexual reproduction. Occasionally, infants are born with one or two extra or fewer chromosomes, but the vast majority of humans have 46 chromosomes.

Chromosome number is maintained because sex cells have only half the chromosomes of body cells. Human sperm and egg cells have 23 chromosomes. All other human body cells contain 46. Figure 5.12 gives the detail for a human germ line.

Figure 5.12   A human germ line

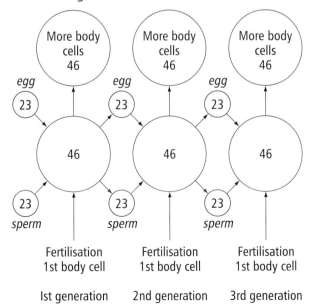

The female and male germ cells combine to produce a body cell with the normal 46 chromosomes. The cell division that produces the next set of germ cells is a reduction division – it gives eggs or sperm with 23 chromosomes.

Growth and repair of body cells involves a nuclear division called mitosis. The parent and daughter cells have the same chromosome number.

The production of sex cells is called meiosis. The daughter cell has half the chromosome number of the parent cell. Mitosis and meiosis are shown in Figure 5.13.

Figure 5.13   Mitosis versus meiosis

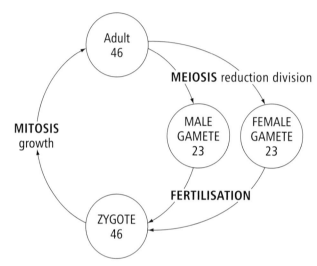

A **zygote** is the single cell formed at fertilisation. Repeated divisions, starting with the zygote, eventually produce the adult organism.

A gamete is another name for a sex cell or germ cell.

We now need to look at mitosis and meiosis in more detail.

6 Mitosis

We have outlined the need for two kinds of cell division. The formation of new cells from one original is the last of three stages.

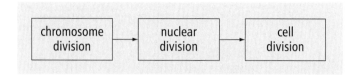

Some of the vocabulary used to describe nuclear division can be difficult and confusing at first. Most of the words are derived from Greek and occasionally Latin. It is worth looking at their English meanings:

Mitosis   *mitos* means 'a thread' and *-osis* means 'to split or separate'.
Meiosis   *meion* means 'to lessen or reduce'. Meiosis is also called reduction division.

We will describe mitosis in animals using humans as an example.

Nuclear division in plants, fungi and most protoctista is similar in principle but different in detail. By definition, prokaryotes do not have a nucleus and they nearly always multiply asexually using a simplified kind of mitosis. In this way, huge colonies of bacteria can grow from a single individual in hours or a few days. This is why food spoils rapidly and some diseases show symptoms within a few hours of first infection.

Diploid and haploid

Body cells with the full chromosome number, 46 in our case, are called **diploid**. Sex cells with half this number, 23 in humans, are **haploid**. In Greek, *di* means 'double', *hap* means 'single' and *–oid* comes from the word *eidos*, meaning 'form'. Therefore:

diploid   double form
haploid   single form

As previously discussed, chromosomes are thread-like structures contained in the nucleus, and they are easily visible under a light microscope during nuclear division.

All your body cells contain an identical set of chromosomes. All were made by the repeated division of the single cell, the zygote, formed when you were conceived.

Body cells are diploid – each has 46 chromosomes. These exist as matching pairs, called **homologous pairs**. You inherited one set of 23 from your mother and one set of 23 from your father.

A mature chromosome

In a simplified form, Figure 5.14 shows what a mature chromosome, one of 46 in our case, looks like.

Figure 5.14 A mature chromosome

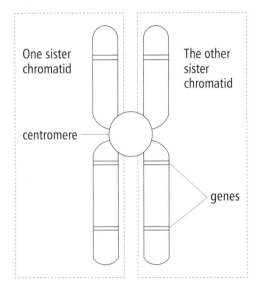

The chromosome at this stage is a double structure. Two identical units are joined together by a narrow waist.

The identical units are **chromatids**, often called sister chromatids. The central structure is a **centromere**. Each chromatid contains, amongst other things, a single DNA molecule.

Staining chromatids reveals a number of bands arranged along their length. These are genes. Each gene is a set of instructions to build a protein – different genes make different proteins. The simplified diagram shows just three pairs.

The only humans with completely identical sets of genes are identical twins. These are monozygotic twins, because unusually both originate from a single zygote. Conjoined twins result if the very early division of the zygote is imperfect so that some tissues and organs are shared.

The individuals of a species differ because they inherit slightly different sets of genes. If you look like your relatives, it is because you have many genes in common.

Medicine, chromosomes and genes

Every species and every individual, other than identical twins, has a different genome – this is the name for a complete set of genes. The 'human genome project' is an attempt to discover which genes are carried on which chromosome, their location on that chromosome and the protein that each gene manufactures.

We know much about the DNA and chromosome structure of hundreds of species, but three have been studied in enormous detail – man, fruit flies and the bacterium *E. coli*. Fruit flies have 8 chromosomes, that is 4 homologous pairs. Very unusually, the salivary glands of the larvae of some species of fruit fly contain giant chromosomes arranged as simple uncoiled strands. These can be studied in detail without the need for very high-power microscopes.

E. coli is a simple prokaryotic species with a very short generation span. The behaviour of its DNA can be observed easily.

During the 19th and 20th centuries, we discovered drugs and treatments to cure or control most of the worst infections or contagious diseases. Bacteria and viruses are constantly altering, and we are engaged in a continuing struggle to keep one or two steps ahead of the evolution of the organisms that damage or kill us. Provided we carry on winning this war, the medicine of the 21st century will focus increasingly on the treatment of inherited disorders.

It follows that modern medical research is increasingly becoming the study of genes and chromosomes.

Previously, we showed a simplified diagram of one of the 46 human chromosomes. Our chromosome number of 46 was first confirmed in 1956. Subsequent research has shown that each pair of chromosomes looks different. Some are larger than others, the centromere is not always in the middle of the strands and some chromosomes have structures called satellites. Table 5.7 gives examples, again in simplified form.

Table 5.7   23 pairs of chromosomes

Classification number	Description	Simplified diagram
Chromosome pair number 1	large, centromeres near the middle	
Chromosome pair number 6	medium-sized, offset centromeres	
Chromosome pair number 13	medium-sized, highly offset centromeres, satellites	
Chromosome pair number 22	very small, highly offset centromeres, satellites	

Our body cells have 23 pairs of chromosomes and 22 of these pairs are identical, as shown above.

Males and females – the 23rd pair

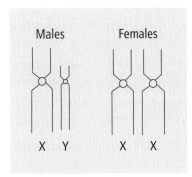

Males Females

X Y   X X

The 23rd pair of chromosomes, the **sex chro-mosomes**, is different. The X chromosome is medium-sized and closely resembles chromosome 6. The Y chromosome is very much smaller and looks like chromosome 22. In humans, females have two identical X chromosomes and males have an unmatched pair, one X and one Y.

This system is not universal. In most birds, the female is XY and the male is XX. Male grasshoppers are X and the females are XX – this means that female grasshoppers have one more chromosome than males, breaking the general rule that the sexes have an even and identical number of chromosomes.

Because all human body cells have 46 chromosomes, sex can be determined from the examination of any body tissue like skin, sweat, blood, tears and so on. Only male body cells have a Y chromosome.

The sex of a child is decided at conception. You get one of your mother's two X chromosomes and you have a 50:50 chance of inheriting an X or a Y from your father. Men determine their children's sex – it works the other way around for chickens.

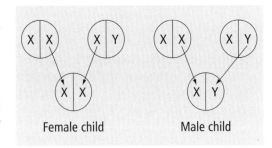

Female child   Male child

The cell cycle

We can now look at mitosis in detail. Figure 5.15 shows a typical cycle for an animal cell. Three distinct phases or stages are observed. Working clockwise around the diagrams:

- For more than three-quarters of the cycle, the nucleus appears to be resting. Little change or activity can be seen, even at high magnification.

- During mitosis, a cell nucleus shows many rapid and dramatic changes.

- Two new nuclei emerge from the final stage of mitosis. Cytoplasm and organelles collect around the nuclei, new cell membranes are formed and two new complete cells are produced. This final stage, cytokinesis, is cell division rather than nuclear division. *Kinesis* means 'movement or separation' – in this case of the cytoplasm.

Figure 5.15   An animal body cell cycle

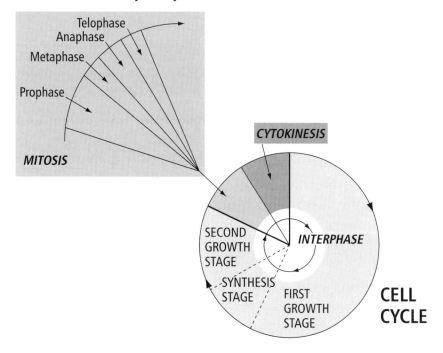

Chromatin and chromosomes

The apparent lack of action during interphase is an illusion. High magnification and techniques that track the movement of individual atoms and molecules show that interphase is the most active part of the cell cycle, not a resting period.

It is essential to realise that the double structures we have so far described are mature chromosomes – often called metaphase chromosomes – because this is when their compact double structure is easiest to see. The genetic code for each species and individual is carried by the DNA molecule. This exists in three different forms at different stages in the cell cycle: Chromatin, a single chromosome, and a mature or metaphase double chromosome.

Chromatin
A single strand of DNA with associated proteins. It is impossible to see its beginning, its end or much of its detailed structure.

A single chromosome
The single, very long DNA molecule is coiled, packed and folded in a very precise way. Only about half the weight of a chromosome is accounted for by the DNA molecule, the rest is protein.

A mature or metaphase double chromosome
This is made of two sister chromatids. Each chromatid carries an identical copy of the DNA molecule contained in the single chromosome.

Interphase

Interphase has three stages:

- First growth stage. Some organelles divide, and the cell makes the proteins and other molecules that are intermediates and essential components of a new cell.

- In the synthesis stage, the DNA content of the nucleus doubles. The cell makes its DNA molecule, and then combines this with protein to make a chromosome. Finally, it divides to make the double chromosome.

- In the second growth stage, the double chromosome begins to compress in preparation for mitosis and further organelle division takes place.

Accuracy and precision

Mitosis has four stages. A double chromosome enters the first stage and two identical single chromosomes emerge from the fourth stage.

Mitosis is almost unbelievably accurate and precise. An adult human has about 60,000 billion cells, every one of which is produced by repeated mitosis, starting with the single zygote cell formed at conception. It takes between 12 and 20 years to produce an adult human from a single zygote, but most cells have a limited life. Mitosis is the mechanism for healing and repair as well as growth. The number of individual nuclear divisions in a typical human lifespan of, say, 75 years is unimaginably large.

Mitosis eventually becomes inaccurate, slows down or ceases altogether. These processes lead to ageing and inevitably death for all organisms. Many cancers are uncontrolled or defective mitosis.

Mitosis is a continuing uninterrupted process. The diagrams and description that follow are best seen as representative frames or still shots taken from a moving film.

Prophase

Prophase is the first and longest part of mitosis. The centriole duplicates before prophase and during prophase the nuclear membrane breaks down. At late prophase, the chromosomes appear as condensed double structures with two sister chromatids and a centromere.

Figure 5.16   Prophase

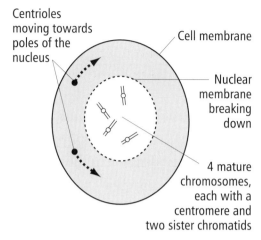

At the end of prophase, the centrioles have moved to positions equivalent to the North and South poles. Remember the cell and the nucleus are roughly spherical.

A structure called a spindle then forms. This consists of very fine tubes, microtubules, radiating from the centriole down towards the equator of the cell.

Figure 5.17   Spindle formation

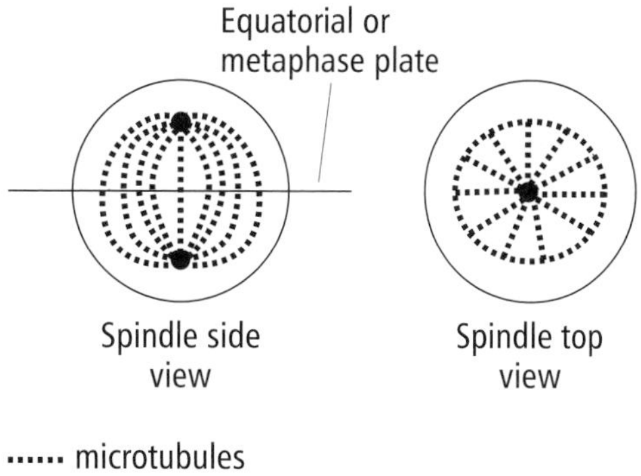

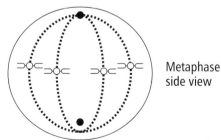

Metaphase

At **metaphase**, the chromosomes line up around the equatorial plate. Their centromeres become attached to the spindle.

Figure 5.18   Metaphase

Anaphase

At **anaphase**, the centomeres divide and this is followed by the separation of the double chromosome into two sister chromatids. As anaphase proceeds, the microtubules shorten and one set of chromatids is 'reeled in' towards the 'North Pole' and the other moves towards the 'South Pole'.

Figure 5.19 Anaphase

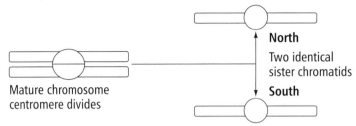

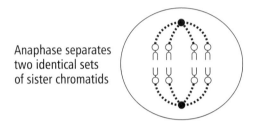

Through evolution, anaphase has become a virtually perfect process. The set of chromatids that travel north is identical to those that travel south.

Anaphase separates two identical sets of sister chromatids

Telophase and cytokinesis

Telophase is the fourth and final stage of mitosis. The nuclear envelope reforms and organelles collect around the southern and northern nuclei.

The chromatids begin to uncoil and decompress as they reach the poles of the spindle. This loosely coiled structure is chromatin. In each new cell, the chromatin enters interphase and the whole cycle repeats again.

Cytokinesis follows telophase:

Figure 5.20 Cytokinesis

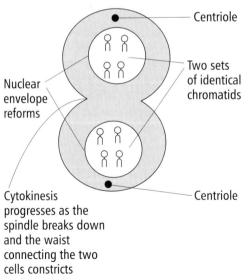

7 Meiosis and human variety

Meiosis can have eight stages and the process gets quite complicated. You will not be assessed on a point-by-point detailed understanding of these stages. However, you are expected to be comfortable with the principles. In particular, you must appreciate the differences between meiosis and mitosis.

The diagram below outlines mitosis and meiosis using humans as an example animal species. Remember, our body cells are diploid, they have 46 chromosomes in total.

The whole point of mitosis is to copy body cells precisely and accurately. If a daughter body cell differs from the parent body cell, then mitosis has failed. Failed or imperfect mitosis may mean that an organism will not grow or develop or that it will not be able to repair its tissues and organs.

Mitosis produces diploid cells from diploid cells or haploid cells from haploid cells.

Mitosis versus meiosis

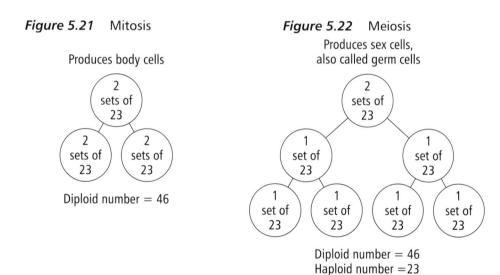

Figure 5.21 Mitosis

Produces body cells

2 sets of 23

2 sets of 23   2 sets of 23

Diploid number = 46

Figure 5.22 Meiosis

Produces sex cells, also called germ cells

2 sets of 23

1 set of 23   1 set of 23

1 set of 23   1 set of 23   1 set of 23   1 set of 23

Diploid number = 46
Haploid number = 23

Meiosis involves two consecutive divisions, so one parent nucleus produces four daughter nuclei.

Meiosis is **reduction division**. Each of the four daughter nuclei are haploid – they contain just one set of 23 chromosomes.

Meiosis was an evolutionary advance

Most importantly of all, the four daughter nuclei produced by meiosis end up with different DNA. Mitosis ensures that parent and daughters are identical. Meiosis is designed to make sure that parent and daughters are different.

Meiosis is concerned with nuclear division, not necessarily the production of four functional cells from one parent. The eventual result of meiosis depends on species.

Meiosis is an evolutionary advance over mitosis. Prokaryotes reproduce asexually. They do not have nuclei but one cell divides into two, using a process virtually identical to animal mitosis.

From time to time, bacteria evolve by one cell donating some of its DNA to another. This procedure is not fully understood, but it seems to be infrequent and haphazard.

If all the individuals of a species are identical, or very nearly so, then a change in the environment has the potential of destroying all of them – that is, the whole species.

Meiosis, and therefore sexual reproduction, gives evolution much more material to work with. Because the individuals of a sexually reproducing species vary, some of them are likely to survive even quite drastic environmental change. The survivors multiply and evolution continues.

Homologous pairs

Figure 5.23 shows human chromosome pair number 1 – the chromosomes in this pair are the largest of the 23 pairs, and they have centromeres near the middle of the chromosome. You inherit one of the pair from your father and the other one from your mother.

Figure 5.23 A homologous pair – chromosome 1

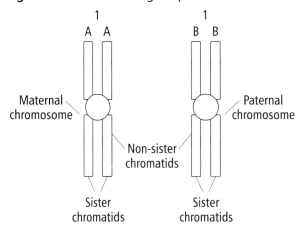

Each chromosome, at this point, is a double structure, the two sister chromatids marked A and A are identical, so are the two marked B and B. This has to be so, because the sister chromatids were formed by the simple replication of a single structure during interphase. The non-sister chromatids A and B are different.

With the exception of the X and Y chromosomes, all the other 22 homologous pairs have the following in common:

- They are the same length. In our example, the length of chromatid A equals the length of chromatid B.

- The centromeres are in the same place.

- Each chromatid has the same number of genes.

- The genes are in the same order or linear sequence along the chromatids. Each gene can therefore be found at the same place on the chromatid. This is the gene **locus**.

To understand how and why non-sister chromatids can differ, you need to know what a gene is and what it does.

Genes make proteins

A gene is a short section of a DNA molecule. Each gene carries the instructions for making one protein. Proteins are the working parts of all organisms. Cells are assemblies of proteins. Cells make tissues, tissues make organs and organs combine to make the individuals of a species. Each human chromatid has between a few hundred and a few thousand gene loci. Loci is the plural of locus.

Genes can alter. Unusually this results from copying errors when DNA replicates. Sometimes it happens because chemical agents or radiation break some of the bonds that hold the DNA molecule together. This change is called **mutation**.

Mutation is a chance event. The change in a gene's structure can vary from a trivial alteration through to a major change or even a deletion, where the gene is not copied at all.

Gross mutations nearly always produce an organism that cannot survive. The major cause of early miscarriage, properly called spontaneous abortion, is probably gross mutation in essential genes or sometimes in whole chromosomes.

Favourable mutations

Most minor mutations have little influence. They produce a different kind of body but the difference does not alter the individual's ability to survive, prosper and reproduce. From time to time, however, a mutation makes an improved body. 'Improved' means better able to survive in the existing environment – it does not mean better in any absolute sense.

Most of the obvious differences between humans are determined by groups of genes acting together, so they are not inherited in a simple fashion. Height, body build, skin colour and hair type are the most familiar examples.

We can use eye colour to illustrate gene mutation in the most general terms:

- The eye is a complex structure put together by combining the instructions contained in very many genes. A gross mutation in any one of these might cause blindness or defective eyesight. In primitive communities, any child inheriting this kind of mutation would have very poor life chances.

- The iris is a ring of muscle tissue that automatically increases or decreases the amount of light entering the eye. This muscle is a combination of proteins whose production is controlled by groups of genes at fixed loci on particular chromosomes.

- Our eyes differ in colour because the iris can contain different pigments. The combination of genes you inherit determines your eye colour. Again, in general terms, human eyes come in two different 'colour cards' – a brown series ranging from hazel through to almost black, and a blue series including many shades of blue, green and grey.

- Originally, all humans had brown eyes, because we originated in East Africa. A darkly pigmented iris gave better vision in tropical sunshine and prevented cataracts, a condition where too much sunlight eventually causes blindness.

- In this environment, a minor pigment gene mutation that produced blue eyes would have been a disadvantage.

- It is thought that the mutation which produced 'blue series' eyes first became established about 40,000 years ago in what is now modern-day Poland, in an area around the Baltic Sea.

- The blue pigment mutations in the changed North European environment became advantageous. In reduced sunlight, blue eyes can be more efficient and the cataract risk is greatly reduced. The 'blue' genes gradually spread in Northern European populations.

- Another rarer mutation prevents the production of eye and body pigment altogether. Albinos seem to have pink eyes because the blood vessels at the back of the eye are visible through a transparent iris.

- Today the great majority of humans still have the brown series or original genes. Only about 5% of the world's population show the 'blue series' mutations – all these are Northern Europeans or people like Americans and Australians of mostly Northern European descent.

The study of genes and chromosomes shows the absurdity of racism. We are not all just the same species, we are all the same subspecies. The differences between the typical appearances of, for example, a Nigerian, a Norwegian, a Bangladeshi, a Navajo Indian and an Australian aborigine are determined by just a tiny fraction of the total human genome.

Single gene mutations

Some differences amongst people are controlled by the mutation of just one gene. With several examples, we can illustrate the differences between non-sister chromatids that result from single gene mutation.

Red blood cells contain haemoglobin, a protein that transports oxygen around the body. Normal red blood cells are roughly spherical. A mutation of a single gene involved in making haemoglobin produces irregularly shaped red blood cells – these are sickle cells and they are less efficient carriers of oxygen.

Figure 5.24 shows the three possibilities for the homologous pairs of chromosomes that may carry this particular haemoglobin gene.

Figure 5.24 Homologous pairs

Homologous pairs

☐ normal gene

■ sickle gene

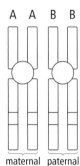

A A B B

maternal paternal

Homozygotes
A normal individual.
Sister chromatids and non-sister chromatids all carry the normal gene.

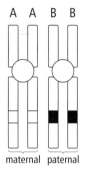

A A B B

maternal paternal

Heterozygotes
One pair of chromatids carries the normal gene.
The other pair carries the sickle gene.
Sister chromatids are identical, as always.
Non-sister chromatids are different.

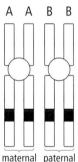

A A B B

maternal paternal

Homozygotes
Each homologous pair carries the sickle gene.
Sister chromatids and non-sister chromatids all carry the sickle gene.

The mutation that changes the normal gene to a sickle gene must have happened many times. In most places, carriers of one normal and one sickle gene, the heterozygotes, do not have any particular advantage or disadvantage over those with two normal genes.

In modern developed societies, the biggest killers are cancer, heart disease and strokes. This pattern is very recent and utterly different from most of human history. The majority of the humans that have ever lived died from malnutrition or infectious disease.

It has been estimated that malaria has caused between 15% and 35% of all human deaths since we became a separate species.

One type of mosquito is the carrier for malaria. The salivary glands of the female *Anopheles* mosquito become infected with a tiny **protoctista** called *Plasmodium*. When a mosquito bites a subject, this organism enters the bloodstream, where it rapidly multiplies. The *Plasmodium* needs iron to grow and reproduce – it gets this by attacking our red blood cells, as haemoglobin contains the iron it needs. By feeding on our blood cells, the parasite destroys them. The very high fevers typical of malaria are caused by an explosive release of *Plasmodium* into the bloodstream.

There are many species of *Plasmodium*. One of them, *Plasmodium falciparum*, causes a very severe malaria which is usually fatal unless treated.

Heterozygotes for the sickle gene – those individuals with one normal gene and one sickle gene – are resistant to *Plasmodium falciparum*.

This chance mutation gives a huge evolutionary advantage to the heterozygotes. Many more heterozygote children survive in malarial regions than those with two copies of the normal gene. In some parts of West Africa, more than a quarter of the population are heterozygotes.

Mutations usually give very minor advantage, if any at all, so the sickle mutation is exceptional. It normally takes tens of thousands of years for a mutated gene to become common in a population or region. Research suggests that the sickle gene has reached high frequencies in less than 1,000 years.

Marker genes

A significant proportion of modern day Brazilians, Americans and Caribbeans are descendants of African slaves. The sickle gene is still common in these populations, even though malaria has been eradicated where they now live. The sickle gene is a marker of African descent – if you carry this gene it is exceedingly likely that at least one of your ancestors was African.

Protection from malaria in this way comes at a price. As the percentage of heterozygotes increases, it becomes increasingly likely that a male and female heterozygote will meet and reproduce. A proportion of their children will then inherit two copies of the sickle gene – they will be homozygotes, but for the mutated gene rather than the normal one. From birth, these children suffer from sickle cell anaemia. If you have two sickle cell genes, most of your red blood cells are abnormal and inefficient transporters of oxygen. Worse still, these red cells decay to give products that block the smaller blood vessels. Homozygotes for the sickle cell gene cannot survive infancy without specialist help.

This reduced fitness explains why the sickle cell gene frequency does not increase beyond a certain level. Every time a child with sickle cell anaemia dies, two copies of the mutated gene are removed from the gene pool. This balances the increased fitness of the heterozygotes.

We think of malaria as a tropical disease, but this has not always been so. The word itself comes from the Italian for 'bad air'. Until quite recently, malaria was a problem in Southern Europe, the Eastern Mediterranean and large parts of Asia.

Many genes combine to form normal haemoglobin. Other mutations alter red blood cells in a way that gives resistance to different types of malaria. Several of these are inherited in a similar fashion to the sickle cell gene.

Cystic fibrosis

The sickle cell mutation is just one of many conditions known to be caused by a change in a single gene. The sickle mutation is widespread in Africa; cystic fibrosis is mainly a disorder of Northern Europe. It is most common in Denmark.

Cystic fibrosis involves the mutation of a gene that helps make the protein involved in the production of mucus. Mucus protects the surfaces of many organs, in particular the lungs. Normal mucus keeps the lungs moist and allows efficient breathing.

In principle, the inheritance pattern of cystic fibrosis is identical to that of sickle cell anaemia.

Figure 5.25 summarises the three possible combinations for the 'mucus' gene. It is carried on the homologous pair of chromosomes number 7.

Figure 5.25   The 'mucus' gene in cystic fibrosis

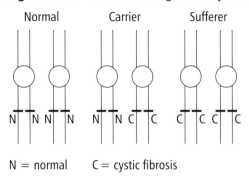

Normal   Carrier   Sufferer

N = normal   C = cystic fibrosis

The 'mucus' gene always occupies the same position or locus.

The first possibility is that both chromosomes carry the normal gene – it is present on all four chromatids.

The second alternative is that one of the homologous pair carries the normal gene and the other carries the mutated gene. Again, sister chromatids are identical but non-sister chromatids are different. These people are carriers – they do not suffer from cystic fibrosis but they can pass it on to their children.

The third option is that both homologous pairs carry the mutated gene. These are **homozygotes**. At the relevant gene locus, all four chromatids are the same. These people produce abnormally large quantities of very thick mucus leading to the serious disorder of cystic fibrosis.

In European populations, the frequency of the mutated cystic fibrosis gene is quite high. This must mean that the carriers or **heterozygotes** have some kind of evolutionary advantage, but this is not obvious in the way it is for the sickle cell mutation.

Research now suggests that heterozygote babies – those with one normal and one cystic fibrosis gene – are resistant to salt loss during bouts of diarrhoea, which, like malaria used to be a major cause of death.

The ABO blood group system

As a final example of how non-sister chromatids can differ, we briefly summarise how the ABO blood group system works.

Organ transplants are commonplace in modern medicine. These advances had to overcome two major obstacles – the difficult surgery involved and the risks of rejection. Rejection happens when the recipient's body recognises the donor organ as foreign material. In very general terms, the more the DNA of the recipient and donor differ, the greater the chances of rejection.

Blood is a liquid organ and blood transfusions are organ donations. The first recorded transfusions were tried more than two hundred years ago, usually as an emergency treatment for major haemorrhage. The surgery involved is straightforward but, on an apparently random basis, sometimes the patient recovered but sometimes death followed very rapidly after transfusion. Put differently, the organ donation was rejected.

The ABO blood groups were first discovered in the early years of the 20th century. In 1910, it was found that blood groups are inherited. The first practical application of genetics to human medicine came with the development of safe transfusion.

The surfaces of red blood cells are covered with many proteins and other biological molecules. At a particular locus, there are three possible gene variants – these are called **alleles**.

Allele	Description
A	Produces protein A
B	Produces protein B
O	Does not produce protein A or protein B

The O allele probably came first, but as most mammals also have different blood groups, the O allele may have originated in one of our ancestor species.

The ABO system is a bit more complicated than that for sickle cell anaemia or cystic fibrosis because there are three alleles involved, not two. A pair of homologous chromosomes can only carry one or two alleles – never three. Figure 5.26 shows the six possibilities.

Safe blood transfusions

Table 5.8 distinguishes safe blood transfusions from dangerous ones.

Table 5.8   Blood transfusions

		Donor blood group			
		A	B	AB	O
Recipient blood group	A	✓	✗	✗	✓
	B	✗	✓	✗	✓
	AB	✓	✓	✓	✓
	O	✗	✗	✗	✓

✓ = safe   ✗ = dangerous

A recipient with an AB blood group recognises both the A and B proteins as friendly, not foreign. It follows that a blood transfusion from an A, B, AB or O donor will be safe because none of these red cells introduce proteins that will be rejected.

A recipient with the O blood group will see both the A protein and the B protein as foreign. Therefore, blood of A, B or AB groups will be rejected. This rejection involves agglutination or clumping together of the red cells. In the worst cases, this causes catastrophic damage to tissues and organs. The only safe donor for an O group recipient is another O group individual.

Table 5.8 shows the other safe and dangerous combinations of donor and recipient.

There are about 30 different blood group systems – ABO was just the first to be recognised. ABO itself is not quite as simple as we have shown. The A gene, for example, has further mutated to give two alleles, A1 and A2.

Figure 5.26 ABO – six possibilities

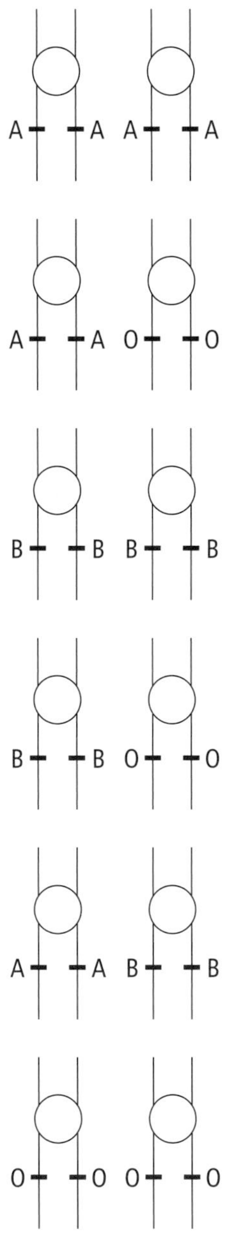

Homologous pairs	Chromatid description	Blood group
A A A A	Homozygote for gene A. Sister and non-sister chromatids identical.	Tests as blood group A.
A A O O	Heterozygote for genes A and O. Sister chromatids different from non-sister chromatids.	
B B B B	Homozygote for gene B. Sister and non-sister chromatids identical.	Tests as blood group B.
B B O O	Heterozygote for genes B and O. Sister chromatids different from non-sister chromatids.	
A A B B	Heterozygote for genes A and B. Sister chromatids different from non-sister chromatids.	Tests as blood group AB.
O O O O	Homozygote for gene O. Sister and non-sister chromatids identical.	Tests as blood group O.

Sickle cell anaemia, cystic fibrosis and the ABO system are just three examples of gene variation. There are many, many thousands of genes spread across the human chromosomes and a significant proportion of these have two, three or more alleles.

It becomes clear that the chances of non-sister chromatids on the same pair of homologous chromosomes carrying an identical gene sequence are very small indeed. These inevitable differences form the basis of 'DNA fingerprinting', now increasingly used in criminal investigation.

8 Meiosis – the mechanisms

Now we can look at the mechanisms of meiosis. Mitosis produces two daughter cells from one parent cell – it has four stages, resulting from one division. Meiosis produces four daughters from one parent after two consecutive divisions. Meiosis can have eight stages – Figure 5.27 overleaf shows the sequence.

In some organisms, one or more stages of meiosis are omitted or very much shortened.

Nuclear division is not always followed by cytokinesis – the separation of the cytoplasm – to form functional cells.

You should not be daunted or dismayed by this complication or the unfamiliar vocabulary – you just need to focus on the parts of meiosis that ensure genetic diversity.

Maternal and paternal contributions

Everybody understands what meiosis does. Children inherit characteristics from both of their parents. How many times have you heard someone say something like "She has her father's nose but her mother's eyes."? Similarly, two or more children with the same parents can be very different from one another.

Identical twins are an exception to these general rules because both have the same DNA, gene for gene and chromosome for chromosome. We know that non-physical characteristics like intelligence, aggression and extroversion can be inherited. However, there is continuing debate over how much of the personality is due to inheritance and how much to upbringing. Is a child aggressive because he or she has 'aggressive genes' or because he or she has learned to be that way?

Twin studies are used to investigate the balance between inheritance and environment in personality formation. The most valuable information comes from identical twins separated soon after birth and reared in different families. Differences in adulthood between separately reared identical twins must be entirely due to environment.

Figure 5.27 Meiosis

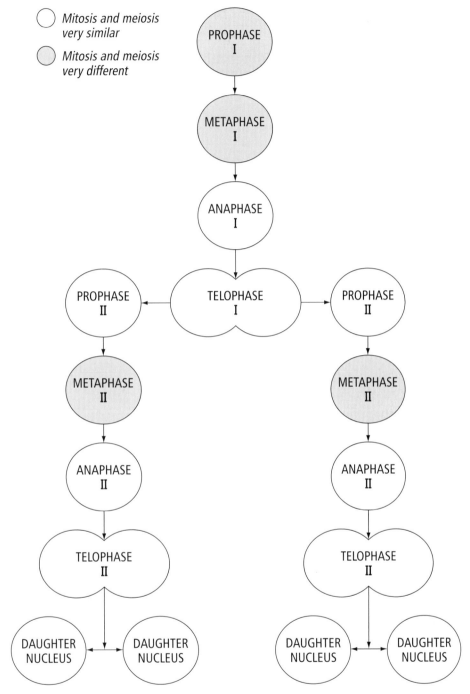

Crossing over

Figure 5.28 shows the events that produce two haploid cells from one diploid parent. During first prophase, the homologous pairs of chromosomes line up side by side. This alignment is very precise, because each of the homologous pairs has chromatids of exactly the same length with centromeres at the same position and genes in the same sequence.

During first prophase, which can last several days, non-sister chromatids fuse together at equivalent gene locations. Parts of the non-sister chromatids then cross over and finally separate as shown on the diagram. This mechanism produces new combinations made partly of maternal and partly of paternal genes.

The 'scrambled' homologous pair are then separated to produce two haploid cells. Figure 5.28 shows that the haploid cells are different from each other and from their parent.

Figure 5.28 Crossing over

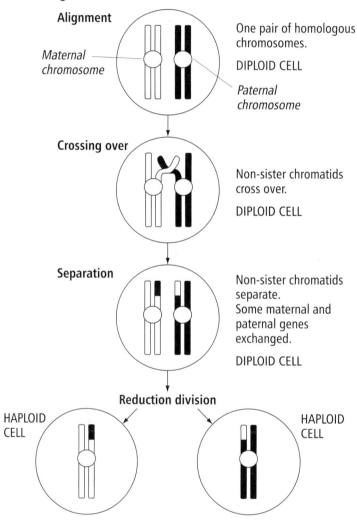

Four different daughters

Figure 5.29   Four different daughters

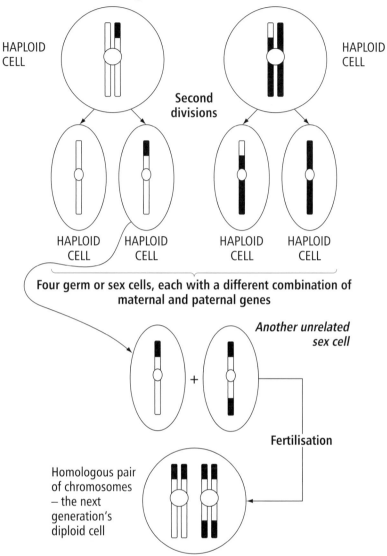

HAPLOID
CELL

HAPLOID
CELL

Second
divisions

HAPLOID
CELL

HAPLOID
CELL

HAPLOID
CELL

HAPLOID
CELL

Four germ or sex cells, each with a different combination of maternal and paternal genes

Another unrelated sex cell

+

Fertilisation

Homologous pair
of chromosomes
– the next
generation's
diploid cell

Figure 5.29 summarises the second part of meiosis – this results in four sex or germ cells, each with different DNA.

It is easy to see that crossing over gives recombination and therefore genetic diversity. In reality, non-sister chromatids cross over at many locations, not just at a single site as shown in Figure 5.28.

Meiosis shuffles genes in another way that is harder to visualise. In the first division, an homologous pair of chromosomes separates; in the second division, one homologous pair separates into two chromatids (Figure 5.29).

Figure 5.29   Two separations

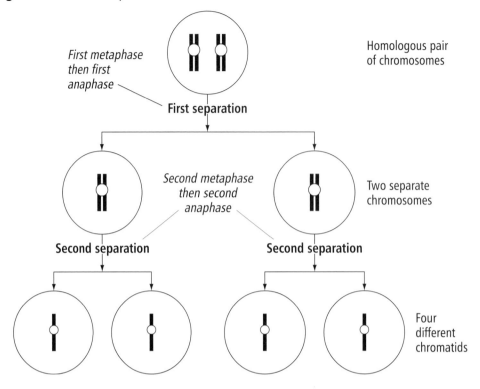

Independent assortment

Separation happens in metaphase and anaphase. During metaphase, the chromosomes line up around the equator of the cell. Spindles form, which connect the chromosome centromeres to the North and South poles of the cell. The spindles shorten, the chromosomes separate and one half of each structure travels north with the other half travelling south.

Figure 5.30 shows five chromosomes at metaphase. Purely by chance, the maternal chromatid can end up facing north or south. The greater the number of chromosomes the more random combinations of North and South are possible. The northern chromatids make the nucleus of one cell; the southern chromatids form the nucleus of the other.

Independent assortment happens twice, once at first metaphase and again at second metaphase. You do not have to be a brilliant mathematician to realise that crossing over followed by two rounds of independent assortment produces a huge number of equally possible sex cells.

Figure 5.30   Independent assortment

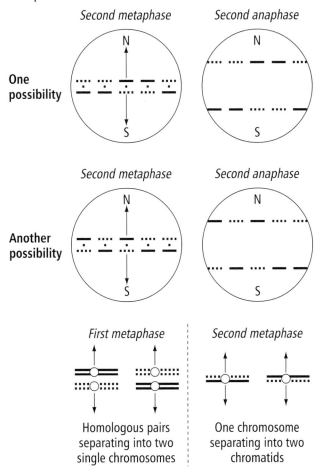

9 Genetics

Genetics is the branch of biology concerned with how characteristics are passed from one generation to the next in sexually reproducing organisms. It could be described as the study of meiosis and its consequences.

All eukaryotic organisms have the potential for sexual reproduction, and all use meiosis in one way or another. The details vary, but the principles are universal.

The genetics of one species can closely resemble that of another – many different kinds of laboratory animal have given valuable clues to human genetics, for example.

Gregor Mendel

Few researchers can claim to have founded an important branch of science single-handedly. Gregor Mendel, an Austrian monk and botanist, is a rare exception. His experiments with pea plants came years before the discovery of genes and chromosomes, but despite this, he discovered the basic laws that still underpin modern genetics. Mendel died in 1884. It was not until 1900 that the importance of his research was first recognised.

Before Mendel, inheritance was thought to involve the blending or dilution of parental characteristics into the next generation. Earlier investigators used paint or dye mixtures as a model. Combining a pot of black paint and a pot of white paint gives a shade of grey. The original colours can never be recovered, and as the generations proceed, the grey becomes more and more uniform.

Mendel disproved the blending theories. He realised that inheritance is the transmission of some kind of particle or object across the generations. He called these 'factors' – we now know they are chromosomes and genes.

Mendel's particulate model explains many observations that the blending theory cannot. For instance, a characteristic can skip one or more generations. In other words, the black or the white paint can, after all, be recovered from what looks like a pot of grey.

Mendel's choice of the pea plant was a happy accident, as other plants have reproductive cycles that would have produced confusing results not applicable to other eukaryotic species. Mendel kept meticulous records of many generations, covering thousands of breeding trials and hybrid crosses.

Genetic predictions are made in terms of probabilities. These probabilities can only be accurately confirmed by experiments with large samples.

Polygenic inheritance

The blending theory was an error, but an understandable one. Breeders of domesticated animals would have noticed that mating a large dog and a small one usually produced a litter of medium-sized puppies, for instance. Most of the obvious differences between animals are controlled by groups of genes rather than a single one.

Body size in humans is an excellent example of polygenic, or 'many gene' inheritance. The heights of adult men vary continuously between around 4 ft 10 in and, say, 6 ft 6 in. The particulate theory of genetics applies to height – but in a complex way that gives continuous variation. No single gene has a large effect and it is difficult to disentangle genetic and environmental influences. Because of a low protein diet in childhood, a man with the genetic potential to become 6 ft 1 in might never grow taller than 5 ft 7 in.

Over the last hundred years, the average adult height in developed countries has increased by several inches. A century is four or five human generations, and far too short a period for measurable genetic change to have occurred. People are getting bigger because of better nutrition and healthcare. In the most developed societies, the rate of increase in height has slowed significantly.

Single gene inheritance

Inheritance is easier to explain and understand if we start with conditions caused by the behaviour of a single gene rather than many. Previously we looked at cystic fibrosis as an example of single gene mutation. This also serves as an illustration of single gene inheritance. First, we need to revise some definitions previously discussed and introduce several new ideas.

Genes occupy given locations, or loci, on a particular chromosome. Some genes have two or more variations, produced by mutation. These are alleles.

An homologous pair of chromosomes with two identical alleles is a homozygote for the particular gene involved, an homologous pair with two different alleles is a heterozygote.

Reduction division during meiosis makes sure that only one of the two alleles ends up as part of a sex cell. This selection is random – each allele has an equal or 50% chance of being passed on to the next generation.

Each allele produces a different kind of protein and therefore a different body characteristic. However, some alleles can suppress the influence of others. A dominant allele inhibits the protein production of a **recessive** one.

Dominance does not imply superiority, and a recessive allele does not necessarily produce inferior offspring. Some very serious human genetic diseases are caused by dominant alleles.

The relative frequencies of different alleles usually stabilise in a gene pool, unless the environment alters rapidly. A dominant allele does not necessarily replace a recessive one – it mostly depends on the relative fitness of the homozygotes compared with the heterozygote.

If dominance is total, then it is impossible to tell the difference between a homozygote for the dominant allele and a heterozygote which carries one dominant and one recessive allele. What an organism looks like is called its **phenotype**. The genetic information it carries is its **genotype**.

Punnett squares

The inheritance pattern for cystic fibrosis is about as straightforward as human genetics gets. There are two alleles and the normal one is dominant to the cystic fibrosis mutation.

A **Punnett square**, named after its first user, is a simple and effective way of describing single gene inheritance. The square shows the alleles carried by each parent and the possible combinations of these alleles that their offspring might inherit. Remember, each parent contributes just one allele to the next generation and meiosis ensures that each of the two alleles has a 50% chance of being selected.

The first Punnett square shows what might happen when a heterozygote for the cystic fibrosis allele and a homozygote for the normal allele have children. By convention, the dominant allele is shown with an upper case letter and the recessive one with lower case.

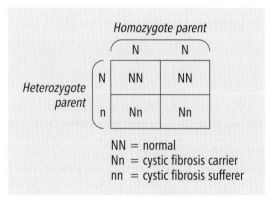

No child of these parents will suffer from cystic fibrosis, but half of them will be carriers like one of their parents. For any particular couple, there is no way of predicting which, if any, of their children will be carriers. However, in a sample of say 1,000 children of homozygote and heterozygote parents, close to 500 will be carriers.

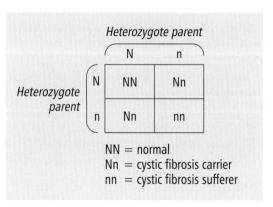

The next Punnett square shows the possible outcomes if both parents are carriers:

Here, the outcome is different. There is a 25% chance that their children will be normal, a 50% chance they will be carriers and a 25% chance they will inherit cystic fibrosis disease.

Fortunately, totally dominant alleles are very rare and may not exist at all. For obvious reasons, medical researchers have tried hard to find a test to distinguish normal individuals from cystic fibrosis carriers. There are small differences in the blood composition of homozygotes and heterozygotes, and in most cases a test now exists to tell one from the other.

Three alleles

ABO blood group inheritance is different again. There are three alleles, A, B and O. The A allele and the B allele are co-dominant and the O allele is recessive to both A and B. Blood tests can easily show if A proteins are present, if B proteins are present, or if a sample contains both or neither. The possible genotypes and phenotypes are shown here:

Six genotypes	Four phenotypes
AA, AO	A
BB, BO	B
AB	AB
OO	O

Who is the father?

Before DNA analysis was developed, ABO blood testing was sometimes used in cases of contested paternity. Blood groups can prove that a man cannot be the father of a child. However, they cannot prove that any particular man is the father of a child. Three Punnett squares illustrate the point.

An AB blood group father cannot produce an AB or O blood group child with an O group mother.

An A blood group father cannot produce an AB or B blood group child with an O group mother.

Paternity and other close biological relationships can now be proved beyond reasonable doubt by techniques that identify DNA gene sequences. Meiosis produces so many possible combinations that it is almost impossible for similar sequences to occur by chance. Blood relatives have relatively long sections of DNA in common.

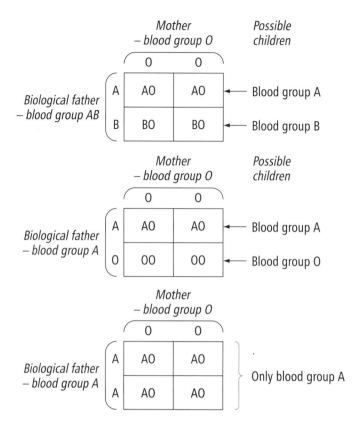

Monohybrid inheritance

The genetics of single genes that occur as two or more alleles is called monohybrid inheritance. The various combinations of homozygote and heterozygote matings are monohybrid crosses. Both terms were first used by Mendel.

A monohybrid cross of two heterozygotes for a gene with two alleles produces different offspring in the ratio 1:2:1 or 25% : 50% : 25%. The Punnett square gives a general example for a single gene with two alleles A and a.

	A	a	Genotype	%	Ratio
A	AA 25%	Aa 25%	AA	25	1
a	Aa 25%	aa 25%	Aa	50	2
			aa	25	1
				100%	

If allele A is totally dominant to allele a, then there will be two phenotypes appearing in the ratio of 3:1 or 75% to 25%.

Genotype	Phenotypes	Ratio
AA plus Aa	75%	3
aa	25%	1
	100%	

Percentages and probabilities

It is important to understand what these percentages really mean and how they are used in real-life situations.

For organisms that have few offspring, like us, the percentages show the chance of any one individual inheriting a particular combination of alleles. A couple who are both heterozygotes for the cystic fibrosis allele have a 25% chance of producing a child with the disease itself.

The selection of alleles entering the sex cells is governed purely by chance and each conception is an independent event that cannot be influenced by previous conceptions. It follows that no firm predictions can be given for any one child. Similarly, the chances of inheriting the disease are 25% for every conception. A couple who are both carriers with two unaffected children still have a one in four chance of their third child being born with the disease.

For ethical and practical reasons, genetic experiments with people are impossible. Families at risk from inherited diseases and disorders are always asked to provide all the information they can about their close relatives for as many generations as possible. Sometimes, for instance, a cousin's, an uncle's or a grandparent's medical history provides valuable information to help the counselling of a couple who are considering having a family.

The ideal genetic experimental animal is small, easy to keep, with a short life-cycle and the capability of producing many offspring. The fruit fly is ideal – it reaches sexual maturity in a few weeks and one pair can have thousands of offspring in a year.

In these cases, the percentages relate to actual numbers not probabilities. As we have shown, a three to one ratio of two phenotypes is strong evidence for monohybrid inheritance. For example:

	Number of fruit flies examined	Actual percentage	Monohybrid predicted percentage
First phenotype	3,121	74.08	75.00
Second phenotype	1,092	25.92	25.00
Total	**4,213**	**100.00**	**100.00**

Statistical analysis is used to compare observed experimental and theoretically predicted phenotype percentages.

Dihybrid inheritance

Dihybrid inheritance is concerned with the variety of offspring produced when two genes, each with two or more alleles, are passed onto second and subsequent generations. The principles of monohybrid and dihybrid crosses are the same, but their results are different.

For thousands of years, mankind has selectively bred animals to produce varieties that we find more useful, more manageable, or more attractive than their wild ancestors. The first animal to be domesticated was the goat, or perhaps the dog, followed closely by sheep, horses, cattle, camels, llamas, pigs and poultry. Animal breeding used to be a hit and miss affair but now we understand the genetics of a huge range of mammals, birds, fish, amphibians and reptiles.

Dihybrid inheritance determines coat type and colour for many mammals – we will use guinea pigs as an example.

Coat appearance is controlled by many genes, but for guinea pigs we know the gene for coat length has two alleles. That for short fur is dominant to the allele for long fur. Another gene has two alleles – the one for black fur is dominant over the allele that gives white or albino fur.

The Punnett squares show two possible crosses for each gene taken in isolation:

Fur length

	F	f
F	FF	Ff
f	Ff	ff

F = dominant allele
  – short fur
f = recessive allele
  – long fur

Fur colour

	B	b
B	BB	Bb
b	Bb	bb

B = dominant allele
  – black fur
b = recessive allele
  – white fur

Three genotypes	Two phenotypes	Three genotypes	Two phenotypes
FF	short fur	BB	black fur
Ff	short fur	Bb	black fur
ff	long fur	bb	white fur

Pure breeding strains

Pure breeding lines or strains of animals can be produced by selective matings over many generations. The first guinea pig mating is as follows:

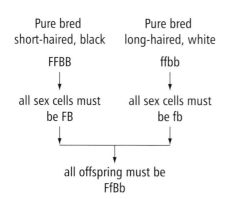

Each parent passes one fur length allele and one fur colour allele to their babies. All the offspring will have the same genotype and all will have short, black coats because F is dominant over f and B is dominant over b.

The next generation

The offspring of this first mating are then allowed to breed with each other.

Again, only one allele enters a sex cell because of reduction division at meiosis. Each allele has a fifty per cent chance of fertilising the next generation. Therefore, there are four equally likely but different sex cells:

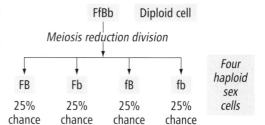

A 16 box Punnett square

The Punnett square for a monohybrid cross has four boxes, whereas that for a dihybrid cross has 16. The boxes show the genotypes and phenotypes for all the possible offspring of the second matings:

		Sex cells or gametes of one parent			
		FB	Fb	fB	fb
Sex cells or gametes of the other parent	FB	FBFB short, black	FBFb short, black	FBfB short, black	FBfb short, black
	Fb	FbFB short, black	FbFb short, white	FbfB short, black	Fbfb short, white
	fB	fBFB short, black	fBFb short, black	fBfB long, black	fBfb long, black
	fb	fbFB short, black	fbFb short, white	fbfB long, black	fbfb long, white

The dihybrid Punnett square can be summarised to show what the second generation guinea pigs look like – that is their phenotype:

Genotype	Fur phenotype	Phenotype proportion	Phenotype %
9 possibilities	Short, black	9 of 16	56
3 possibilities	Short, white	3 of 16	19
3 possibilities	Long, black	3 of 16	19
1 possibility	Long, white	1 of 16	6
16 possibilities	4 possibilities	16 of 16	100

This ratio of 9:3:3:1 is characteristic of dihybrid crosses, just as the 1:2:1 ratio is evidence of monohybrid inheritance.

We could draw Punnett squares for a variety of third generation matings. For example, two white, long-haired guinea pigs would only have white, long-haired babies, but mating two second generation short, black-haired guinea pigs would produce varied litters.

New kinds of animal

The dihybrid Punnett square shows that only two of the 16 possible 'grand-children' are genetically the same as one of their 'grandparents'. There is one potentially pure breeding short, black-haired guinea pig and one pure breeding long-haired white.

Selective breeding gives combinations of characteristics that may not have existed previously – for instance a long-haired, black or a short-haired, white guinea pig. This is how we have bred chihuahuas and spaniels from their original ancestors, which were wolves.

Mendel's laws

To finish, we can summarise Mendel's two laws of genetics, first made public in 1865. There is no better example of the scientific method than the experiments with pea plants which Mendel conducted and recorded about 140 years ago. He did not know that DNA, genes or chromosomes existed, but even so, his extraordinary experimental skills founded a science that has improved and will continue to improve the lives of most people.

- Mendel's law of segregation says that the pairs of alleles possessed by an individual separate into sex cells and then into different offspring. No blending of alleles takes place. An allele may have no observable influence in any one generation but it persists, and may influence the appearance or characteristics of future generations.

- Mendel's law of independent assortment says that alleles are distributed into the next generation by chance and therefore with equal probabilities. This law was proved by the 1:2:1 ratio for monohybrid crosses and the 9:3:3:1 ratio for dihybrid inheritance.

Mendel did not know that meiosis includes a stage where non-sister chromatids of an homologous pair of chromosomes cross over and exchange genes. Genes that are on the same chromosome may not move independently of each other. The closer two genes are, on any particular chromosome, the less likely it becomes that they will be separated by crossover during meiosis. This general idea is called gene linkage.

Appendix

Units of measurement

A quantity is a numerical value combined with a unit of measurement – for instance, 17 seconds, 28.4 grams or £12.45. With very few exceptions, we all use the same number systems but units of measurement vary, and have varied, from time to time and from place to place. In the UK, we use a mixture of units – petrol is sold in litres but road signs show distances in miles, and so on.

Scientists throughout the world use metric systems of measurement. All these work with multiples and sub-divisions of 10 rather than more awkward numbers. For instance:

metric – 1 metre = 100 centimetres;

but

imperial – 1 yard = 36 inches

SI base units

SI stands for *Système International d'Unités* – in English, 'the international unit system'. This recognises the seven basic quantities that all scientists may have to measure:

Physical quantity	Base SI unit	Abbreviation
Length	metre	m
Mass	kilogram	kg
Time	second	s
Electric current	ampere	A
Temperature	Kelvin	K
Amount of substance	mole	mol
Luminous intensity	candela	cd

As an Access student, you will be most concerned with measurements of length and mass, but in chemistry, you will also come across moles and kelvins.

SI derived units

All quantities can be measured in base SI units or in combinations of base units called derived units. Many of these are familiar, others are only used in some of the more specialist sciences:

Physical quantity	Derived SI unit	Abbreviation
Area	metre × metre (square metres)	m^2
Volume	metre × metre × metre (cubic metres)	m^3
Speed or velocity	metres/second (metres per second)	m/s
Density	kilograms/cubic metres (kilograms per cubic metre)	kg/m^3

Mass and weight

The terms mass and weight are often used interchangeably, as if they mean exactly the same thing. To be absolutely precise and correct, however, mass describes the amount of substance a body contains and weight is the force a body exerts in a gravitational field. An astronaut standing on the surface of the Earth and then on the surface of the Moon would have the same mass but two different weights. Mountain climbers 'lose weight' as they ascend, but not mass.

Mass is the preferred term. However, you will not be criticised at all for using expressions like 'the weight of the beaker was 125 grams'.

Temperature

The SI base unit for temperature is the Kelvin.

There is no theoretical maximum temperature. The centres of some stars reach millions of degrees. There is, however, a minimum temperature – absolute zero – and no place in the universe can be colder. Absolute zero is −273.16 °C. The correct name for °C is degree Celsius, although degree Centigrade is commonly and interchangeably used by many scientists. A temperature change of one Celsius degree is identical to a temperature change of one Kelvin, but the two scales have different starting points. For example, using rounded figures:

	degrees Celsius °C	kelvins K
Absolute zero	−273	0
Freezing point of water	0	273
Room temperature	25	298
Boiling point of water	100	373

A temperature shown in kelvins can never be a negative number.

Kelvins are used in physics and in some kinds of chemistry, but in most sciences, temperatures are quoted in degrees Celsius, °C. The Fahrenheit scale is not used.

SI unit prefixes

A useful scientific measuring system must be able to cope with very small quantities like the mass or diameter of an atom – and very large ones like the distances between galaxies. Any length could be expressed in metres but describing an atom in this way would involve many zeros to the right of the decimal point, and for interstellar distances dozens of zeros to the left of the decimal point.

The SI system uses a set of universally agreed prefixes – they always have the same meanings:

Multiples of SI units			Subdivisions of SI units		
Multiply by	Prefix	Symbol	Divide by	Prefix	Symbol
			100	centi	c
1,000	kilo	k	1,000	milli	m
1,000,000	mega	M	1,000,000	micro	μ
1,000,000,000	giga	G	1,000,000,000	nano	n
			1,000,000,000,000	pico	p

As an Access student you will not have much need for the two largest prefixes – mega and giga – although megabyte and gigabyte are used to describe computer memory capacity.

You will, however, be expected to learn the meanings of the other prefixes – in particular as they apply to length and mass.

The SI unit of mass is the kilogram, but the prefixes work with grams. The tables below explain.

Mass

Prefix	Prefixed unit	Symbol	Equivalence
kilo	kilogram	kg	1,000 grams
–	gram	g	–
milli	milligram	mg	$\dfrac{1}{1,000}$ grams
micro	microgram	μg	$\dfrac{1}{1,000,000}$ grams

And also

$$1,000 \text{ milligrams} \quad = \quad 1 \text{ gram}$$
$$1,000,000 \text{ micrograms} \quad = \quad 1 \text{ gram}$$

The symbol μ is the Greek letter m, pronounced 'mew'.

Many drugs and medicines are administered in very small quantities. It is obviously important that you understand the differences between grams, milligrams and micrograms.

The word 'kilo' used alone means a kilogram, never a kilometre.

Length

Prefix	Prefixed unit	Symbol	Equivalence
kilo	kilometre	km	1,000 metres
–	metre	m	–
centi	centimetre	cm	$\dfrac{1}{100}$ metres
milli	millimetre	mm	$\dfrac{1}{1,000}$ metres
micro	micrometre	μm	$\dfrac{1}{1,000,000}$ metres

And also

$$100 \text{ centimetres} \quad = \quad 1 \text{ metre}$$
$$1,000 \text{ millimetres} \quad = \quad 1 \text{ metre}$$
$$1,000,000 \text{ micrometres} \quad = \quad 1 \text{ metre}$$

Cell structures, for example, are described in millimetres and micrometres. A micrometer is occasionally called a micron.

Measuring volumes

The derived SI unit of volume is a cubic metre. This is a large volume and unsuitable for measuring dosages of medicine, for example.

There are other units for measuring smaller volumes:

$$1 \text{ metre} \quad = \quad 100 \text{ centimetres}$$

therefore

$$1 \text{ cubic metre} = 1,000,000 \text{ cubic centimetres}$$

A cubic centimetre is the commonest unit for small volumes. It has two abbreviations – cc or cm^3. You may also find cu.cm. used occasionally.

Litres and millilitres

Litres and millilitres are not SI units, but they are used in science, medicine and increasingly in everyday life:

$$1 \text{ cubic centimetre} = 1 \text{ millilitre}$$
$$1 \text{ cc} \quad = \quad 1 \text{ ml}$$

And also

$$1,000 \text{ cubic centimetre} = 1 \text{ litre}$$
$$1,000 \text{ cc} \quad = \quad 1 \text{ l}$$

and therefore

$$1,000 \text{ millilitres} = 1 \text{ litre}$$
$$1,000 \text{ ml} \quad = \quad 1 \text{ l}$$

You have to remember these. Most medicines are given as solutions in water. They are administered by volume, not by weight.

Calories and joules

The calorie is familiar as a description of the energy content of food and drink – it is not an SI unit.

Energy is a central concept in science. The derived SI unit for all forms of energy – mechanical, thermal and electrical – is the joule. Calories and joules have a precise relationship.

$$1 \text{ calorie} = 4.1868 \text{ joules}$$

therefore

$$1 \text{ kilocalorie, kcal} = 4.1868 \text{ kilojoules, kJ}$$

In the UK, food labels have to show energy contents in kilocalories and kilojoules.

Generally, food scientists, dieticians and health professionals in the UK talk and think in calories – knowing that what they really mean is kilocalories.

Other units

The SI unit of time is the second. No higher multiples are commonly used and scientists think in days, weeks, months and years with their usual meanings.

The SI supplementary unit for angle is the radian, but this is only applicable in some branches of maths and physics. Degrees are not SI units and they are not metric – there are 360° in a circle – however, nearly all scientists work with the traditional unit.

A metric tonne is 1,000 kilograms. The French spelling distinguishes this from the British long ton or the US short ton. Confusingly, the three are similar but not identical.

	Pounds, lbs
US short ton	2000
Metric tonne	2204
British long ton	2240

Scientists use metric tonnes to describe large masses or weights.

Singular and plural

It is wrong to add an 's' to an SI unit symbol to indicate the plural. For example:

$$1 \text{ metre} = 1\,\text{m}$$
$$12 \text{ metres} = 12\,\text{m}$$

but
$$12\,\text{ms} = 12 \text{ milliseconds}$$

SI prefixes are not separated or hyphenated, so, for example:

Correct	Incorrect
43 kilograms	43 kilo grams
	43 kilo-grams

Where do the names come from?

Two of the base SI units and many of the derived ones are named after famous scientists. To give just a few examples:

Lord William Kelvin	British	1824–1907
André Ampère	French	1775–1836
Anders Celsius	Swedish	1701–1744
James Joule	British	1818–1889
Georg Ohm	German	1787–1854
Allessandro Volta	Italian	1745–1827
James Watt	British	1736–1819

Glossary

How to use the glossary

This glossary is a series of brief summary explanations of the more important terms and concepts introduced in the Access natural science units. Inevitably, it cannot be a complete or comprehensive list of everything you need to know to succeed in exams and assessments.

You will find a glossary most useful as a help in private study and in revision planning. It is usually not a good idea to consult a glossary before you have studied the material in class.

The contents pages for each chapter show major topics. The index gives detailed page references in the usual way.

Acid, amino

One of the basic building blocks or monomers that are assembled to make proteins. There are 20 biological, or naturally occurring, amino acids.

Acid, ascorbic

An alternative name for vitamin C.

Acid, carboxylic

A family or homologous series of organic compounds, all of which contain the functional group:

Acid, essential amino (EAA)

One of eight naturally occurring amino acids that cannot be synthesised from simpler molecules by adult humans. Essential amino acids have to form part of the diet.

Acid, essential fatty

A fatty acid that cannot be synthesised from simple molecules by humans and must therefore form part of the diet.

Acid, fatty

Long-chain carboxylic acid, typically having 16 or more carbon atoms. A component of lipids.

Acid, nicotinic

One of the B complex vitamins.

Acid, nucleic

The collective term for DNA and RNA.

Alcohols

In chemistry, a homologous series of organic compounds, all of which contain one –OH group. Commonly used to describe ethanol produced by fermentation.

Allele

One of two or more alternative forms of a single gene produced by mutation.

Alpha-tocopherol, α-tocopherol

An alternative name for vitamin E.

Amylopectin

A polysaccharide made of highly branched chains of glucose units. One of the two major components of starch.

Amylose

A polysaccharide made of long straight chains of glucose units. One of the two main components of starch.

Anaphase

A stage in mitosis or meiosis.

Anion

A negatively charged particle produced from an atom, or group of atoms, by the addition of one or more electrons.

Anorexia

Properly anorexia nervosa. A psychological disorder where sufferers refuse or severely limit food intake.

Arithmetic mean

The proper term for the simple average of a set of numbers.

Assertion

A statement of opinion, unsupported or poorly supported by experimental evidence.

Assortment, independent

The process that ensures offspring receive a random selection of maternal and paternal chromosomes. A consequence of meiosis.

Assumption

A statement based on limited, unreliable or incomplete evidence.

Atom

The smallest unit of an element capable of independent existence and of taking part in a chemical reaction.

Atomic mass

Originally the mass of an atom as a multiple of the mass of one atom of hydrogen – the lightest element. Now defined as the mass of an atom as a multiple of 1/12 of the mass of one atom of carbon-12. Atomic mass, atomic weight, relative atomic weight and relative atomic mass are virtually identical terms.

Atomic number

The number of protons or the number of electrons in a neutral atom. Sometimes also called proton number.

Benzene

C_6H_6, an especially important and stable ring structure of six carbon atoms with the symbol:

Beta-carotene, β-carotene

A principal source of vitamin A.

Biotin

One of the B complex vitamins.

BMR

Base or basal metabolic rate. The body's minimum or resting energy need. Usually expressed as kcals/day.

Bond, covalent

A chemical bond formed when two atoms share a pair of electrons.
See also double bond and triple bond.

Bond, double

A covalent bond formed when two atoms share two pairs of electrons.

Bond, ionic

A chemical bond formed when one atom swaps one or more electrons with another atom, neutral atoms then becoming ions.

Bond, triple

A covalent bond formed when two atoms share three pairs of electrons.

Bonding, hydrogen

A weak bond formed by the attraction of a hydrogen atom with a small positive charge and another atom, usually oxygen, with a small negative charge. Commonly found in compounds with –OH groups.

Buffer solution

A solution that maintains its pH despite the addition of small amounts of acids or alkali.

Bulimia

A psychological disorder where, typically, 'binge eating' is followed by self-induced vomiting and/or the abuse of laxatives.

Calorie

Historically a unit used to measure all forms of energy. The term is now restricted to food energy content. Used in this way a calorie is a kilocalorie, kcal.

Carbohydrate

One of a major group of organic compounds. All contain carbon, hydrogen and oxygen only, with hydrogen and oxygen present in the ratio of 2:1, as in water.

Carbonyl group

A carbon atom joined to an oxygen atom with a double covalent bond:

Carnivore

An animal whose major or only source of food is other animals.

Catalyst

A substance that alters the rate of a chemical reaction without being used up in the reaction.

Catenation

The special ability of carbon atoms to bond to each other to form complex chains and rings.

Cation

A positively charged particle derived from an atom, or group of atoms, when one or more electrons are removed.

Cell cycle

A period of time or a sequence of events that take place between the start of one mitosis and the next.

Cell membrane

A partially permeable membrane that encloses the contents of all cells.

Cell theory

All living organisms are composed of one or more cells and new cells are formed by the division of older ones.

Cell wall

A rigid non-living structure that encloses plant cells and often also the cells of fungi, prokaryotes and protoctista.

Cell, body

In animals, a cell produced by mitosis, containing the diploid number of chromosomes – 46 in humans.

Cell, eukaryotic

The more evolutionarily advanced of the two fundamental cell types. All have a nucleus and a variety of other organelles.

Cell, germ

A cell containing the haploid number of chromosomes – 23 in humans – produced during meiosis.
Also called sex cell or gamete.

Cell, prokaryotic

The earliest evolving and more primitive of the two cell types. Lacking a nucleus and without complex organelles.

Cellulase

The enzyme needed to break down cellulose into its component glucose units.

Cellulose

The most abundant polysaccharide and the major structural material of plants.
A long straight-chain polymer of glucose.

Centriole

Small organelles found in animal cells.

Centromere

A region of the chromosome that holds sister chromatids together during some stages of nuclear division.

Charged particle

A proton or a cation with a positive charge or an electron or an anion with a negative charge.

Chlorophyll

Green pigment found in all plants and in cyanobacteria. Captures light energy during photosynthesis.

Chloroplast

An organelle containing chlorophyll found in most plant cells. The site of photosynthesis.

Cholecalciferol

Another name for vitamin D.

Chromatid

One of two identical parts of a chromosome formed during interphase by DNA replication.

Chromatin

A single DNA molecule and associated proteins.

Chromosome

A structure of DNA and proteins found in the nucleus of eukaryotic cells. Mature chromosomes visible at metaphase are double structures made of two identical or sister chromatids.

Compound

Two or more atoms joined together by chemical bonds.

Congenital

Used to describe a disease or disorder acquired after conception but before birth – not an inherited condition.

Copolymer

A polymer made from two or more different monomers.

Crossing over

The exchange of sections of non-sister chromatids that occurs during meiosis.

Cyanobacteria

Used to be called blue-green algae. Prokaryotic organisms with the ability to photosynthesise.

Cyclic compounds

An organic compound containing one or more rings of carbon atoms.

Cytokinesis

The final stage in cell division when two new cells are formed by the constriction and then the separation of the cytoplasm.

Cytoplasm

A complex aqueous solution in which cell organelles and other structures are suspended.

Denaturing

The partial destruction of a protein usually resulting from heating or extremes of pH.

Dietary reference value

A general term used to describe recommended minimum, average, maximum or safe levels of nutrient intake.

Diol

An organic compound containing two –OH groups.

Diploid cell

A body cell containing two full sets of chromosomes – 46 in humans.

Disaccharide

A carbohydrate made of two monosaccharide units. Disaccharides are sugars.

Discipline

The name given to a defined subject or area of study – for example, biology, physics, law or psychology.

Dissociation

The breakdown of a neutral molecule to give cations and anions.
Also called ionisation.

DNA

Deoxyribonucleic acid.

Dominance, dominant

A dominant allele prevents or suppresses the characteristics produced by a recessive allele.

Electromagnetic spectrum

Broadly, a term used to describe how the properties of radiation vary with wavelength. Visible light is just a small part of the electromagnetic spectrum.

Electron

A subatomic particle with one unit of negative charge; 1,836 electrons, usually rounded to 1,840, have the same mass as one proton.

Electron arrangement

The location of electrons in atoms. Also called electron configuration.

Electron microscope

A microscope that uses beams of high energy electrons rather than visible light.

Element

A substance that cannot be further subdivided by chemical methods. A constituent of the periodic table.

Element, trace

Elements that are an essential part of the diet, but only in very small amounts. Also called trace minerals.

Emulsion

A suspension of small droplets of oil or any other insoluble substance in water – not a true solution. Milk, cream and mayonnaise are emulsions.

Energy density

The number of calories in 100 g of a particular food. Manufactured high fat, high sugar foods have high energy densities.

Enzyme

A specialised protein that acts as a catalyst to increase the rate of a biochemical reaction.

ER

The usual abbreviation for endoplasmic reticulum, an organelle or structure found in all eukaryotic cells.

Error

In an experiment, the difference between the true value of a quantity and the value measured, observed or estimated.

Error, gross

A major mistake made in a measurement, the recording of a measurement or a calculation.

Error, random

A series of errors that tend in the long run to be self-cancelling. Usually a mix of underestimates and overestimates.

Error, systematic

A series of errors that tend in the long run not to be self-cancelling. Usually consistent underestimates or consistent overestimates.

Estimated average requirement

The amount of energy or nutrient that meets or exceeds the needs of about half of a group of individuals.

Fat

A lipid that is solid at room temperature. Usually of animal origin.

Fibre

The commonly used term for the indigestible polysaccharides found in many plant foods. Should be called NSP or non-starch polysaccharides.

Formula, display

A detailed representation showing the atoms, structure and bonds of a compound. Most often used in organic chemistry.

Formula, molecular

A system that uses element symbols, subscript numbers and sometimes brackets to show the composition of a compound.

Formula, structural

A summarised version of a display formula, used to describe organic compounds.

Gamete

A germ cell or sex cell containing the haploid number of chromosomes – 23 in humans.

Gas, noble

The gaseous elements of group 8, sometimes called group 0. They are inert, noble or unreactive because all have full outer shells of electrons.

Genotype

Genetic makeup of an individual. See phenotype.

Genus

A group of closely related species with a relatively recent common ancestor. Plural: genera.

Glucose

$C_6H_{12}O_6$, a simple monosaccharide produced by photosynthesis. The monomer for many polysaccharides and the starting point in the food chain for most living organisms.

Glycogen

A polysaccharide similar in structure to amylopectin, but produced as a short-term energy store by animals. Often called animal starch.

Golgi complex

An organelle of eukaryotic cells, also called the Golgi apparatus or the Golgi body.

Group

In chemistry, a vertical column in the periodic table.

Haploid

A nucleus or cell with a single set of chromosomes – 23 in humans.

Herbivore

An animal whose main or only food source is plants and/or fungi.

Heterozygote

An individual with different alleles of a particular gene on the maternal and paternal chromosomes of an homologous pair.

Homologous pairs

Two chromosomes of identical size and shape but with different alleles at one or more gene loci. One of the pair is of maternal origin, the other paternal. See sex chromosomes.

Homologous series

In chemistry, a family of similar organic compounds, different only in the length or arrangement of the carbon skeleton.

Homozygote

An individual with identical alleles of a particular gene on the maternal and paternal chromosomes of an homologous pair.

Hydrocarbon

An organic compound containing hydrogen and carbon only. Mainly sourced or manufactured from crude oil and natural gas.

Hypothesis

A proposition to be tested, or further tested, by experiment or observation.

Indicator

A compound or mixture that changes colour according to pH.

Infrared

Radiation whose wavelength is longer than the red end of the visible spectrum but shorter than radio waves. Invisible to the human eye but often detectable as heat.

Inheritance, polygenic

A pattern of inheritance involving many genes, each with a limited effect, and causing continuous variation in an organism's characteristics.

Inhibition

In chemistry, the reverse of catalysis. An inhibitor reduces the rate of a chemical reaction or stops it altogether.

Interphase

In cell division, the interval between the end of cytokinesis and the beginning of mitosis or meiosis.

Ion

An anion or a cation.

Ion, complex

An ion composed of two or more different atoms. For example, the nitrate anion NO_3^- and the ammonium cation NH_4^+.

Ion, hydrogen

The cation produced when a hydrogen atom loses its electron: H^+.

Ion, hydroxyl

A complex anion with a single negative charge and one hydrogen atom bonded to one oxygen atom: OH^-.

Ionic compounds

Compounds held together by one or more ionic bonds.

Ionisation

See dissociation.

Isomers

Compounds with the same molecular formula but different structural formulae. A central concept in organic chemistry.

Isotope

Different atoms of the same element. Isotopes have the same number of protons but different numbers of neutrons. The chemical properties of isotopes are identical.

Joule

A unit of energy.

Kilocalorie

See calorie.

Kilojoule

1,000 joules. Symbol kJ.

Kinetic theory

The particles, atoms or molecules that make up all substances are constantly moving. Their velocity increases with increasing temperature. At any given temperature, some particles will be moving more rapidly than others.

Kingdom

All living organisms can be placed into one of five fundamentally different kingdoms – prokaryotes, protoctista, plants, fungi or animals. Protoctista used to be called protista.

Kwashiorkor

A disease or disorder resulting from a diet with very little or no protein. See marasmus.

Lactose

A disaccharide component of milk, sometimes called milk sugar.

Law

A term loosely used in science to mean a long established theory or set of theories.

Link, peptide

The group of atoms that link amino acids together to make proteins:

Link, polymer

The bonds, atoms or groups of atoms that link monomers together to form polymers.

Lipids

The collective term for fats, oils and waxes. Also called triglycerides.

Locus

The position on a chromosome occupied by a gene or one of its alleles. Plural: loci.

Logarithmic scale

A number scale where a change of one unit represents an increase of 10 times or a reduction to 1/10. The pH scale is logarithmic.

Lysosome

An organelle found in all animal cells and rarely in plant cells.

Macromolecule

A large molecule, usually but not always a polymer.

Macronutrient

Proteins, lipids and carbohydrates – the nutrients required in relatively large amounts.

Magnification

For a microscope, the ratio of image size to object size. See resolution.

Malnutrition

Any major and prolonged departure from a balanced diet. Includes excess consumption as well as deficiency.

Marasmus

A disease or disorder resulting from a lack of proteins, carbohydrates, lipids and micronutrients. See kwashiorkor.

Mass number

For an atom, the total of the number of protons and neutrons it contains. Always an integer or whole number.

Metal, coinage

Usually describes gold, silver, platinum and copper – the least reactive metals that occur naturally as elements rather than compounds. Also called precious or noble metals.

Metaphase

A stage of mitosis and meiosis.

Micronutrient

A vitamin or mineral. An essential part of a balanced diet but needed only in very small quantities.

Mineral

Literally a substance produced by mining. In diet, it means a micronutrient that is not a vitamin.

Mitochondria

An organelle found in all eukaryotic cells.

Mixture

A loose assembly of elements and/or compounds. The proportions of a mixture are infinitely variable and there are no chemical bonds between its components.

Mole

Generally, the atomic mass, formula mass or molecular mass of an element or compound expressed as grams. One mole of water, for example, is 18 grams.

Molecule

The smallest unit of a compound capable of independent existence and of taking part in a chemical reaction.

Molecule, biological

A general description of any compound involved in the chemical reactions that sustain life.

Monosaccharide

Simple sugars made of a single ring structure. Glucose and fructose are the commonest monosaccharides.

Mutation

An inheritable alteration in a DNA molecule caused by radiation, chemical reaction or errors in replication. Alleles are alternative forms of genes produced by mutation.

Neutralisation

The chemical reaction between an acid and an alkali, or more generally between a hydrogen cation and a hydroxyl anion to produce water.

Neutron

A subatomic particle with unit mass the same as that of a proton, but with no electrical charge.

Niacin

One of the B complex vitamins.

Normal distribution

Continuous variables, like height in humans, usually follow a normal distribution. This allows statistical predictions of the numbers in a population who will differ from the average value for a given characteristic.

NSP

Non-starch polysaccharides – the correct term for dietary fibre or roughage.

Nucleolus

An organelle contained in the nucleus of cells.

Nucleus

In chemistry, the very small, very dense central part of an atom, which contains the protons and neutrons.
In biology, the central organelle in a eukaryotic cell, containing, amongst other things, DNA packaged into chromosomes.

Oil

A lipid that is liquid at room temperature. Usually of vegetable, fish or marine mammal origin.

Omnivore

An animal that has evolved to need a mixed diet of animals, plants and fungi. Humans are omnivorous.

Organelle

One of the many internal structures or compartments of a cell. Organelles are usually bounded by single or double membranes.

Organic

A word whose meaning has been altered and distorted by commercial advertising. In chemistry, a compound based on a skeleton or framework of carbon atoms.

Outer shell electrons

The number of electrons in the outermost electron shell or highest energy orbitals of an atom. These largely determine the chemical properties of an element. Sometimes called valence electrons.

PAL/PAR

An abbreviation for physical activity level or physical activity ratio. A number larger than 1 that, when multiplied by BMR, base metabolic rate, gives an estimate of the total energy needs for an individual. The more active the lifestyle, the greater the value of PAR/PAL.

Peer review

In scientific research, the constructive criticism or comment that follows the publication of the results of an experiment or trial. Peers are equals in a particular discipline.

Period

A horizontal row of elements in the periodic table.

Phenotype

The physical appearance of a living organism. Individuals who look the same may have a different genetic makeup or genotype.

Phospholipid

The main component of cell membranes. Lipids where one of the three fatty acids is replaced by a group of atoms that include phosphorus.

Photosynthesis

The most important chemical reaction of all. The manufacture of glucose in plant cells starting with water and carbon dioxide – using chlorophyll as a catalyst and sunlight as an energy source.

Plagiarism

Stealing or copying somebody else's work, ideas or research and presenting it as your own.

Plant

Any species that is a member of the plant kingdom.

Polymer

A large molecule formed by the combination of many smaller molecules or monomers.

Polymer, condensation

A polymer formed by the combination of two or more different monomers with the elimination of a smaller molecule, usually water. Biological polymers are made by condensation reactions.

Polymer, man-made or artificial

A polymer made in a factory or laboratory, rather than in the cells of living organisms. Plastics and artificial fibres are man-made polymers.

Polypeptide

Generally any polymer of amino acids joined together by peptide links. Broad distinctions are made between dipeptides, which contain two amino acids, tripeptides with three amino acids, and polypeptides and proteins, which are polymers of many amino acids.

Polyunsaturate

An organic compound containing two or more carbon-carbon double bonds. Usually describes lipids or fatty acids.

Précis

A condensed summary of a longer piece of writing, designed to retain the essential meaning of the original.

Principle

In science, and especially in physics, an ill-defined term used to describe a fundamental or long established theory or set of theories. See law.

Products

The elements or compounds produced by a chemical reaction.

Prokaryote

See prokaryotic cell.

Prophase

A stage in mitosis and meiosis.

Protein

A complex polymer of amino acids held together by peptide inks and with a defined and precise three-dimensional structure. The working parts of all living organisms.

Protein quality

High-quality protein foods have a high proportion of total protein and a mixture of proteins containing all the essential amino acids.

Protein, vegetable

Protein of vegetable origin, often deficient or lacking in one or more essential amino acids.

Protoctista

Species belonging to the protoctista kingdom, composed of one or many eukaryotic cells. Formerly called protista.

Proton

The subatomic particle with a unit mass of 1 and a single positive charge.

Punnett square

A diagram used in genetics to predict the outcomes of matings between parents with different combinations of dominant and recessive alleles of one or more genes.

Raw data

All the results or observations produced by an experiment or an investigation.
The raw material for further analysis or summary presentations.

Reactant

The elements or compounds present at the beginning of a chemical reaction.
See products.

Recessive

In genetics, an allele that produces physical characteristics that can be repressed or prevented from expression by the presence of a dominant alternative allele.

Reduction division

Another name for meiosis or the stages of meiosis that produce haploid cells or nuclei from diploid originals.

Reference nutrient intake (RNI)

The amount of energy or a nutrient that will meet or exceed the needs of about 97% of the individuals in a group.

Relative formula mass

See relative molecular mass.

Relative molecular mass

The mass of a molecule as a multiple of 1/12 of the mass of one atom of carbon-12. Relative formula mass is the preferred alternative term for ionic compounds.

Resolution

For a microscope, the ability to distinguish between two separate points.
See magnification.

Respiration

Generally, the release of energy from food, in particular from lipids and carbohydrates. In biology, respiration means more than just breathing.

Retinol

An alternative name for vitamin A.

Riboflavin

Another name for vitamin B_2.

Ribosome

Organelle found in all cells.

RNA

Ribonucleic acid.

Roughage

Common description for indigestible plant material, properly called NSP or non-starch polysaccharides.

Saturated

An organic compound without carbon–carbon double or triple bonds. Most often used to describe fats and fatty acids.

Scientific notation

A way of writing very large and very small numbers using powers. For instance, $10,000 = 10^4$ and $0.0001 = 10^{-4}$.

Sex chromosomes

In humans, the 23rd or X and Y pair of chromosomes. Unlike the other 22 pairs, the X and Y chromosomes are different in shape and size.

Site, active

The group of atoms in an enzyme molecule that form temporary chemical bonds with the substrate molecule.

Solution, aqueous

A gas, liquid or solid dissolved in water.

Species

A group of similar individuals who interbreed or have the potential to interbreed.

Standard deviation

A precisely calculable statistical measure of the spread or variation of a population about its average value. The more variable a population, the greater its standard deviation.

Starch

Polysaccharide food stores made by plants. Usually a mixture of amylose and amylopectin.

States of matter

Solid, liquid or gas – the three forms or states in which all substances exist.

Structure, primary

The sequence of amino acids in a protein or an enzyme.

Subatomic particles

Most often used as a collective term for protons, neutrons and electrons.

Substrate

A molecule, or group of similar molecules, that will react with the active site of an enzyme. Also called the enzyme's target molecule.

Sugars

Water-soluble monosaccharides and disaccharides. Nearly all have a sweet taste.

Sugars, extrinsic

Sugars not contained inside the cell walls of a food. Usually sucrose or common table sugar, often called 'added sugars'.

Sugars, intrinsic

Sugars found within plant cells, also called natural sugars.

Supplement

Nutrient preparation containing high concentrations of amino acids, vitamins and minerals – or any combination of these.

Sweetener, artificial

A manufactured product with an intensely sweet taste, contributing no, or very few, calories to the diet.

Telophase

A stage in mitosis or meiosis.

Theorem

In mathematics, a statement that can be proved to be correct in all circumstances.

Theory

In science, an explanation of events or phenomena not yet disproved by experiment and observation.

Thermogenesis

Literally, 'heat production'. The process that uses food energy to maintain body temperature.

Thiamin

Another name for vitamin B. Can be spelt thiamine.

Triglyceride

A compound formed from a triol and three fatty acids. Lipids are triglycerides.

Triol

An organic compound containing three –OH groups.

Ultraviolet

Radiation whose wavelength is shorter than the blue end of the visible spectrum but longer than X-rays. Invisible to the human eye.

Unsaturated

An organic compound with one or more carbon–carbon double bonds. Most often describes oils and fatty acids.

Vacuole

In plant cells, a central structure containing sap. Small vacuoles are also temporary features of some animal cells.

Variable

Any quantity that can vary.

Variable, continuous

A quantity that theoretically can have any value, determined only by the accuracy with which it is measured. For example, body weight in humans.

Variable, discrete

A quantity that is counted rather than measured. Discrete variables are nearly always positive whole numbers.

Virus

An organism with some of the characteristics of living things, but incapable of growth or reproduction outside the cells of one of the five kingdoms.

Water, metabolic

Water produced by biochemical reactions inside cells.

Zygote

A cell produced by fertilisation or the union of male and female sex cells.

Index

A indicates the Appendix; G indicates a Glossary entry